Union Jackboot

What Your Media and Professors Don't Tell You About British Foreign Policy

Union Jackboot

What Your Media and Professors Don't Tell You About British Foreign Policy

T.J. Coles and Matthew Alford

ATÉ Books

•

Cheltenham

First published by Até Books, 2018

ISBN-13: 978-1725924413
ISBN-10: 1725924412

Design: Jack Q. Boom

Printed and bound by Amazon CreateSpace

Contents

Contents...5

About the authors...7

Preface 8

Disclaimer 9

Introduction: Natural curiosity 11

Chapter 1: Britannia waives the rules 19

Chapter 2: Storm from a teacup: Britain and Russia 45

Chapter 3: Cream scones and genocide 69

Chapter 4: Little Britain, big world?.....................87

Chapter 5: Conspiracies, from reptilians to false-flags 107

Chapter 6: Brits abroad: Humanitarian intervention 131

Chapter 7: Rue Britannia: 'Using the big stick' 167

Chapter 8: Beware the eggheads 191

Conclusion: What can we do? 217

Endnotes 230

About the authors

Dr Matthew Alford teaches film, media, and politics at the University of Bath. In 2018, his first book *Reel Power: Hollywood Cinema and American Supremacy* (2010) was translated into French with a new introduction based on his latest research trip to Washington, DC.

Matthew produced and presented a documentary feature film, *The Writer with No Hands* (2014; 2017), which premiered at Hot Docs, Toronto, and won three prizes at festivals worldwide. He also writes and performs comedy.

T.J. Coles is a postdoctoral researcher at Plymouth University's Cognition Institute (UK) working on issues relating to blindness and visual impairment. His thesis *The Knotweed Factor* can be read online.

A columnist with AxisOfLogic.com, Coles has written about politics and human rights for a number of publications, including *CounterPunch*, *Newsweek*, the *New Statesman*, and *Truthout*. Books include *Human Wrongs*, *Real Fake News*, *Manufacturing Terrorism*, and *Privatized Planet*.

Preface

The idea for this book emerged from a series of phone calls made by the co-author, Matt Alford, to me. Matt seemed to like my answers to his questions and suggested recording them for upload to social media. Hating the sound of my own voice, I suggested transcribing them for a book instead. Matt agreed. I tweaked my answers via email and found sources for my claims. This is the result.

It was enjoyable being seriously challenged on sources, methodology, and logic. Although Matt and I agree on many issues, his playing devil's advocate makes (hopefully) for a much more interesting read than two academics engaged in a back-slapping exercise. Finally, I wanted to make the book 50% me and 50% Matt, but he seemed to be more comfortable asking the questions. Perhaps in a future volume, I'll get the chance to grill him?

T.J. Coles, October 2018.

Disclaimer

Jokes by Matt. Photos (but not graffiti) by Tim. Will Westaway captured the reptilian on the back cover. Finally, an earlier, uncorrected version of this book escaped onto the market. If you have it, retain it and watch it grow in value!

دمشق بغداد
BAGHDAD DAMASCUS

NO BOMBS

Introduction
Natural curiosity

Or: Why no one's talking about our national secrets...

Why are we listening to you?

Because you're asking me questions.

OK. But how do you know these terrible things about British foreign policy?

I've just taken the trouble to find out. It's amazing what's admitted in government documents and how the media don't usually report them. I have a natural curiosity about how the world works and a sense of trying to expose what's going on.

But why is it only you finding out these things?

It's not 'only' me.

Mark Curtis does really excellent work on British foreign policy. But much of it - except his current work on *jihadis*, as well as Britain's involvement in Papua, Nigeria, and a few other places, mainly focuses on the past.[1] His historical research is solid. It draws almost exclusively on declassified government documents. Any work on contemporary atrocities, which is what I tend to research, is more problematic because history gives you the sense of perspective that the present does not. Sources – like press reports – can be less reliable in the present and so you have to piece together limited information, which isn't the case when the official files are finally opened. However, the trouble with focusing on the past is that if you're interested in making the world a better place, you're not telling people about what's going on in the present, so you can't raise awareness about ongoing atrocities. I think Curtis strikes a decent balance between the past and the present.

To give some other examples: The website CrimesOfBritain.com has excellent historical and contemporary information. The mainstream journalist Aidan Hartley exposed what was going on in Somalia in late-2006, when Britain worked with the US and Kenya to impose a terrorist regime – the Transitional Federal Government – to rule that country. Hartley was writing for the right-wing newspaper, the *Daily Mail*, ironically.[2] Or perhaps not so ironically. This happened under New Labour, so the Tory-supporting *Daily Mail* presumably let the story run as a weapon against New Labour. To give another example: Phil Miller, who seems to really despise my work – professional jealousy, I suppose – also exposed what was going on in Sri Lanka, from the 1980s to the present, when the British trained forces engaging in ethnic cleansing.[3] Nafeez Ahmed has exposed Britain's links to *jihadis* in Syria,[4] but he's been reduced to crowd-funding his journalism because the mainstream won't touch his work. The *Guardian* terminated his environmental blog because he wrote about Israel's gas interests in Gaza in 2014.[5]

But people like that are few and far between. And I'm the only one who wrote a book – *Britain's Secret Wars* – about the more modern covert warfare. So I really don't know. I can only guess at several factors:

Number one, there's a general false assumption that Britain doesn't play much of a role in the world, except to follow the US into wars like Iraq and Afghanistan. So if that's the genuine belief of most people, few are going to question it. If you don't think to look outside the Afghanistan-Iraq box, you're not going find anything.

Number two is the culture. It doesn't seem to be culturally acceptable to question or even *think* to question what your own country is doing. This touches on the issue of nationalism as brainwashing. Many American intellectuals, for example, are happy to believe that Israel pulls the strings of its foreign policy[6] or that the British Empire is still secretly running the show.[7] Believing in these things absolve Americans of being responsible for the actions of their government. Tariq Ali – a revered figure of the left – is happy to publish things in his *New Left Review* about the USA, but the editors rejected articles I sent them about Britain's role in Sri Lanka and Somalia (too 'narrow' a focus, they said). I suggested they rename the journal *New Right Review*. In the end I published in the US – in

Peace Review and *Z Magazine* – because US editors are happy to publish things bashing the UK. You'd expect right-wing journals in Britain to reject my work, but not obscure left-wing publications. So this cultural denial is bipartisan.

Number three, when we do look at our own crimes, they are usually historical. So Tariq Ali's Verso Press, his book publishing outfit, is happy to publish important books about Empire,[8] but try getting it to publish something more topical about Britain's role in Sri Lanka or Somalia today.

Ian Cobain, the *Guardian* journalist, has written a couple of good books, too. *Cruel Britannia* is about Britain's post-WW2 record on torturing people all over the world, including in recent times, like helping the CIA's illegal kidnap and torture programme, known as 'rendition'. His latest book is about successive government efforts to destroy the official records. It's called *The History Thieves.*[9]

Number four, the few people like myself who do work on what you may call the 'hidden' aspects of contemporary British foreign policy put the fear of god into publishers. They are terrified of being sued for libel. The UK has some of the worst libel laws in the world, despite reforms.[10] An editor who has now left the publishing company, Oneworld, actually told me back in 2012 that, 'We love your *Britain's Secret Wars*, but we can't possibly publish it because it's a legal minefield'. That's an example of political censorship resulting from laws designed to protect the powerful.

Number five, groupthink. Academics tend to go with the flow. How can a radically independent researcher be taken seriously when they're destroying received wisdom? With the best evidence in the world, you can still be labelled a nutcase, or conspiracy theorist as they like to say these days. There's a saying in the sciences – which isn't literally true but it makes a good analogy – attributed, probably falsely, to the physicist Max Planck. It says: 'Science progresses one funeral at a time', when the older generation dies off and the new generation can make its own theories the norm. So maybe things will change in a few generations?

BOLLOCKS
TO BREXIT
IT'S NOT A DONE DEAL
#bollockstobrexit

I'm tough on immigration. I think we should **KICK QUITE A FEW FOREIGNERS OUT** of this country. Starting with MI6's terrorist assets. And then stop.

Chapter 1

Britannia waives the rules

Or: What's really going on with Brexit and Trump...

The people voted to Leave the EU. What's next for Britain?

In order to understand Brexit, I think we have to understand the nature of the British economy and what the Brexiteers hope to achieve. Britain or more accurately London is basically 'the money-laundering capital of the world'.[11] Political economists think they can boost Britain's GDP by inordinate reliance on the financial services sector,[12] which unlike manufacturing not only doesn't produce anything tangible – it produces dodgy financial products – its consumers are relatively privileged financial institutions, not ordinary citizens. We've long since moved from an agricultural and manufacturing base to an economic services base, hence the exclusion of 'services' from the Customs Union Bill. Britain's Brexiting elites think they can have an economy whose major export is financial services and whose major employment sector is general services.[13]

So Brexit is a battle between two factions of the mega-rich: the *status quo* neoliberals who support the EU and the *ultra*-neoliberals who want to make even more money outside Europe. Either way, ordinary people are screwed. If you're a Brexit supporter, ask yourself if multimillionaires pushing Brexit, like Jacob Rees-Mogg, have your interests at heart.

I should say first of all that neoliberalism is a propaganda term, but I don't know what else to call it. It's just a form of organised plunder. People confuse it with capitalism, which they see as simply maximising profit, which it is. But in order to maximise profit there have to be political conditions to allow that to happen. Neoliberalism sets those conditions. The main one is cutting back on social spending while putting public money into the pockets of big business. Some people call it socialism for the rich and capitalism for the poor. But it's not 'capitalism'. At the least you could call it an extreme form of capitalism.[14]

But we certainly don't have 'capitalism' as understood by the founders of the theory, like Adam Smith[15] and David Ricardo.[16] Capitalist corporations, according to this theory, would have to stand on their own two feet. What we have is state intervention in the economy, including subsidies and tariff protections – and the EU is part of this, but so are the politicians pushing to leave the EU. To make things more complicated, there's no definition of 'neoliberalism'. It's a portmanteau of new and liberal, but it's neither new nor liberal. It has its roots in 19th century British imperial economic policy, which caused a split at the time between the Tories and the Liberals, the so-called traditionalists and progressives. In reality, there wasn't much difference between them. Both factions agreed that Britain should rule the world by force – the Liberal Gladstone with his 'gunboat diplomacy' and the Tory Palmerston with his similar ideology, for instance.[17]

After WW2, there was a kind of state-capitalism – the Keynesian model. Since the '70s the Tories have been working hard to dismantle this. In fact, PM Edward Heath wrote in his memoirs that he put Britain into the EU's forerunner, the European Economic Community (EEC), as a way of undermining Labour's nationalisation projects. That's because the EEC started out as a kind of international-capitalist model. It was Labour PM Harold Wilson that allowed the public to have a say on whether or not continue membership of EEC.[18] At home, the Tories and New Labour – which were also the Tories in many ways – increasingly deregulated the economy. Manufacturing shrunk by more than half, contributing to record unemployment particularly in the North and in the Midlands,[19] which were the two main Brexit-voting regions. The public had to pick up the tab for the subsequent financial crises. Europe resisted this model somewhat until 1992 with the Treaty of Maastricht, which created the Eurozone and forced member states to meet economic targets.

It's important to note that a certain faction of the Tory government begrudgingly accepted the political and economic reality of Britain's membership of the EU but always harboured a desire to leave. Well, now they and their ideological predecessors are getting their way – it would appear. So in a nutshell, the EU gradually became more like the City of London – a deregulated financial economy that imposed crippling austerity on working people and relied on a large multicultural labour force to keep wages down. But Britain never really joined the EU. It didn't adopt the euro because it wanted sovereignty over the pound. It refused to join the Schengen Area of free movement because immigration is a big issue among the electorate. It has a record number of opt-outs from EU directives on everything from policing to immigration.[20]

On specifics like neoliberal EU legislation to privatise postal services, the government cited EU directives as reasons for privatisation. But that's a con. The massive privatisation bonanzas occurred under Thatcher, before we signed Maastricht. There are plenty of EU directives that the UK has refused to implement. So our successive governments have also picked and chosen which directives they want to follow. Britain really has its cake and eats it too when it comes to the EU. But the public don't get to hear about this because it's not a topic of discussion on the liberal BBC. In the right-wing print media – the *Daily Mail*, the *Express*, the *Telegraph*, and so on – the editorial policy on the EU is in line with the anti-EU faction of the Tory Party, that Britain spends too much on Europe, is flooded with immigrants, and so on.

One of the serious consequences of four decades of neoliberalism is the growth of the financial sector, which by now accounts for 6.5% of GDP but is the biggest export economy with a £70bn surplus.[21] It's also narrowly concentrated, meaning that just a few hundred corporations have a significant share of GDP. It's also a revolving door system politically. PM Theresa May came out of the finance world. More than 50% of hedge funds have donated to the Tories. After the financial crisis in 2008, the EU imposed a couple of directives – MiFID and MiFID II – which sought to constrain the actions of the financial services sector. The sector, which is mainly based in London – London being the least regulated European capital – balked at this and some of them signalled their intention to leave the EU. Being the main funders of the Tory Party, the Tories had to bow to the wishes of their real constituents – the financial sector in this case – and initiate the Brexit.

The Tories were moving away from Europe anyway. They began a series of studies into the feasibility of remaining in Europe and concluded that while it was better to stay, they should 'reform' the EU, meaning further deregulate.[22] The Tories' *Manifesto 2015* talks about 'turbo-charging free-trade'.[23] This coincided with the wishes of the hard-line, anti-EU faction, which consists of Nigel Lawson, Jacob Rees-Mogg, Boris Johnson, and people like that. So these are the political ultra-neoliberals. Elements of the financial sector are the business ultra-neoliberals. Call them the Lawson faction. Lawson had an article in the *Financial Times* saying that Brexit will enable us to 'finish Thatcher's revolution'.[24] Is that what the Brexit-voting working-class people want, more Thatcherism?

But what about the *status quo* neoliberals? In terms of corporations, they are companies like those represented by the Confederation of British Industry, the manufacturers and so on who enjoy a large, low-tariff market with the EU. Their political representatives are people like Michael Heseltine who support the EU politically. Call them the Heseltine faction. There's a tug of war between these two factions which has near-ly split the Party in half. Credit to them for being so bloody-minded and keeping it together for so long.

But one of the biggest Brexit tragedies has been the Labour leader Jeremy Corbyn's failure to capitalise on the mess. Corbyn is from a generation that saw – quite rightly – the EU's forerunner and thus the EU of today as an engine to destroy nationalisation. I don't think people of that generation on the left – and I'm talking about the left now – understand how far to the right the whole political spectrum has shifted. They're living the romantic delusion that if we could only get out of the EU, we could invest in domestic manufac-turing and industry. That's not what neoliberalism is about. Before you can talk about tackling domestic manufacturing, you have to get the neoliberals out of your political party, be it Tory or Labour.

The Tories are full of them. The Tory Party is nothing but neoliberals. This is why ex-Labour voters have migrated to UKIP. They're also under the delu-sion that UKIP represents working people. Its former leader and main ideologue, Nigel Farage, is not only from the financial sector, when he was leader he openly talked about 'free trade' and 'free markets'.[25] Plus he's buddies with Donald Trump who wants to do a 'trade deal' with the UK. This is exactly the same kind of neoliberalism we're getting from the EU – more migration, lower working standards, poor wages, and so on – but on steroids. Working-class UKIP vot-ers don't seem to get that. Corbyn has failed to win these people back to Labour by failing to make an explicit point about the nature of the global economy.

What do you make of the allegation that Corbyn is an anti-Semite?

There's a lot to say about that.

First of all, most British Jews are less liberal than American Jews. There's good polling data which show that American Jews tended to hate the Republican candidates from 2000–16: George Bush, John McCain, Mitt Romney, and of course Donald Trump. For better or worse, they voted almost entirely for Barack Obama and Hillary Clinton.[26] So American Jews are politically liberal. But most British Jews tend to be conservative. According to the *Jewish Chronicle*, a mainstream Jewish publication, nearly 7 in 10 British Jews were Tory supporters even *before* the allegations of anti-Semitism in Corbyn's Labour Party.[27] This was when Ed Miliband, who's also Jewish and a Blairite, was leading the Labour Party. By now it's nearly 8 out of 10.[28] So what can we infer from that? We can infer that British Jews are not neutral on the Corbyn issue. Even if some or all of the allegations are true, we should remember that those making the allegations and believing them have political motivations for doing so. That's not being discussed, 'Why are British Jews, nearly 70% of them Tory voters, attacking Corbyn?'.

Second, there's the issue of consistency. Most commentators agree that New Labour's Tony Blair was basically a Tory. He formally ended Labour's social contract – Clause IV, the commitment to socialism – and was widely regarded as 'Tory-lite'. So as most British Jews are Tory voters, they were quite happy with Blair.[29] When there were real anti-Semitic events taking place within the Labour Party, like then-Mayor of London Ken Livingstone – who is an anti-Semite – making jokes about the Holocaust to a Jewish journalist, that was tolerated. He was suspended but then all was forgotten.[30] Anti-Semitism wasn't used as a weapon against Tony Blair because most British Jews didn't care much. It was hardly an issue for them because the main priority was right-wing politics. So that's cynical hypocrisy.

Third, there's the bigger issue. The Tory government is currently allied to the Poroshenko regime in Ukraine. It's training the Ukrainian forces, which are in turn allied to the neo-Nazi Azov Battalion.[31] The Tories' biggest foreign ally outside the US is Saudi Arabia, where most of the world's oil lies. The Saudis didn't even let Jews visit the country until a few years ago when they granted work visas.[32] Then there's the Tory alliance at the EU with the Polish Law and Justice Party, which is notoriously anti-Semitic.[33] So considering the bigger picture, where the anti-Semitism is more blatant and on a bigger scale, we have to ask why British Jews and the media are ignoring this? Again, it's because they don't really care about anti-Semitism. They care about bringing Corbyn to his knees. If they did, they'd be more concerned with the things I've mentioned.

Fourth, what is anti-Semitism? Notice that the question is seldom asked. Even when the mainstream or people making allegations against Labour mention the International Holocaust Remembrance Alliance definition, they don't actually quote from it or analyse it. In order to determine if someone or an organisation is guilty of something, you have to define what it is. Anti-Semitism is a broad spectrum. At one end there are the old stereotypes, like Jews are tight with money. Then it broadens to not wanting a Jew in your family. Then it goes all the way to segregation and at the end of the spectrum that all Jews should be exterminated. Where is Labour on that spectrum? Certainly not at the Nazi extreme. But the Tories are allied, directly or indirectly, to those at the Nazi extreme, like the Azov Battalion I've just mentioned. Anti-Semitism is getting mixed into anti-Israelism and anti-Zionism. It's absolutely true that anti-Semites are disguising their hatred of Jews as anti-Zionist, but it's not true that every anti-Zionist is an anti-Semite. So how do you get to the truth of someone's views? The Chakrabarti report (2016) found no systemic anti-Semitism within the Labour Party.[34]

Fifth, who's making the claims within the Party? As the Chakrabarti report found no systemic anti-Semitism, where are the allegations coming from? They're coming from Blairites or centrists who hate Corbyn for political reasons, like John Mann[35] and Ruth Smeeth. Smeeth was exposed years ago by WikiLeaks for working as an informant against the Labour Party for the US State Department, then run by Hillary Clinton. She denies this but the cabals are there.[36] Why the hell hasn't she been banned from the Party? Outside the Party, it's the media, including the so-called liberal media, like the *Guardian*. There are good studies on extreme anti-Corbyn bias in the media, which have accused him of everything from being a spy for Czechoslovakia to having a grandfather who owned a workhouse.[37] It's been quite extraordinary and it seems to have had an effect in alienating working people from their own interests, i.e., putting people off Labour. You can find cases here and there of anti-Semitic or borderline anti-Semitic statements coming from Labour councillors and MPs, so the media have finally found something real to inflate and bring the Party to its knees.

The weaponisation of anti-Semitism – which is a term Corbyn rejects – became really obvious, if it wasn't already, when PM Theresa May faced mass resignations in June and July 2018 over her Brexit strategy. As this was going on, the headlines returned to, 'Corbyn is an anti-Semite'. It was pathetic.

Sixth, is it even true? Is Labour more anti-Semitic than other Parties? We don't know because no one's held an inquiry into anti-Semitism in the Tory Party. We do know from YouGov polling data that Labour and Tory supporters come out about equal when it comes to holding anti-Semitic views, like being unhappy about a Jew marrying into the family. In the aggregate, Tory-UKIP-voters are more anti-Semitic than Labour-Scottish National Party voters.[38] Another survey taken a year or two later found that Labour supporters are *less* anti-Semitic than Tory supporters.[39] How's that for a headline, *Tory voters more anti-Semitic than Labour voters*? So why isn't there an inquiry into anti-Semitism among Tory supporters? That's because it's not in the political interests of the nearly 80% of British Tory-voting Jews to demand such an inquiry.

Seventh, what about racism and prejudice in general? According to YouGov, of the major ethnic and religious minorities, Jews are by far the safest people in Britain when it comes to people holding prejudicial views. That wasn't true in the '30s or '40s, however, so we should be aware that times might change. But at the moment, YouGov data indicate that of Gypsy-Roma, black people, homosexuals, Bangladeshi, Pakistani, and/or Muslims, Jews are least hated. The racism and prejudice against Gypsy-Roma and Asian Muslims is astonishing.[40] If we care about human rights, the rights of those people should – at this point in history – be of greater concern that the rights of Jews at this moment in history. If this was the 1930–40s again, then we would be primarily concerned about Jews because they were being exterminated in Europe. But nothing like that is happening now. So why aren't we focusing on the far more prevalent prejudice against these other ethnic and religious groups? Again, it's politically motivated. So back in 2016, UNITE the Union published a dossier on racism in the Tory Party.[41] It reveals that every few weeks a councillor or even MP makes some xenophobic or racist remark, including the PM (then Cameron). Was anything done about it? Nothing. It barely got any coverage. Baroness Warsi, a Tory, twice called for an inquiry in 2018 into Islamophobia in the Party.[42] At the time of this conversion, nothing's been done. Then there's the Windrush Scandal – many of the tens of thousands of Afro-Caribbean peoples who came to the UK after WW2 suddenly found themselves being told to leave, having lived and most of them worked here for decades. That's the Tories. Apart from the resignation of Amber Rudd, the Home Secretary who took the heat for PM May, was much said about that? It was a scandal for about a week and nothing happened. The anti-Semitism row has gone on for years. Literally years.

So it's total hypocrisy to be focusing on alleged anti-Semitism in the Labour Party while ignoring the much greater levels of both anti-Semitism and prejudice in general emanating from the Tories.

One final thought on this: It's pretty astonishing that on the one hand the most progressive political movements in the US and Britain at the moment are being led by Jews: Corbyn, leader of the Labour Party, and Jon Lansman and James Schneider, who lead Momentum, the grassroots organisation behind Corbyn; and in the US Jill Stein leader of the Green Party and Bernie Sanders, leader of the Our Revolution movement within the Democratic Party. And on the other hand, some of these organisations, Corbyn's Labour Party, are smeared as anti-Semitic. It's an impressive achievement of both propaganda and doublethink. To his shame, Corbyn has not capitalised on this. He's not stood up to the media and said, 'I'm not going to allow you to accuse me and my Party of anti-Semitism while you give a free pass to much clearer cases of racism and xenophobia in the Tory Party'. He's conceded there's a problem – probably he cracked under pressure – and mumbles on about not tolerating any form of racism. Corbyn has also failed to back Remain in the aftermath of the Brexit referendum, even though 70% of Labour-voters voted Remain.

Wasn't Brexit 'the will of the British people?'

No. There is no 'the people'. There's an amorphous mixture of conflicting interests and concerns, even among the elites, as I've mentioned. You can't solve something as complex as Britain's membership of the EU with a simple in-out, Leave-Remain referendum. And that's not what the elite wanted. They want to make it up as they go along and have their cake and eat it. You could argue that a series of referenda on specific Brexit issues, like free movement or the rights of EU citizens, would have been more sensible.

There's plenty of empirical evidence, but let me give you a personal example. My father would have voted Leave, if he'd bothered to vote. That's because he's from a generation who saw all the industry leaving the UK as he was growing up, and he suffered as a result. The quality of his beloved railway services went more and more downhill. He thinks we should have never joined the EEC in the first place – and on that he's probably right. That's because at the time, the UK still had state-controls over the economy and as I mentioned Heath's agenda was to destroy Keynesian state economics. So in that way, my father is social-democratic. But he's also extremely racist. He's always going on about how foreigners should be shot and so on. So he would have voted Leave for two reasons: on the delusion that we're leaving because the government wants to bring back industry and on the immoral grounds of xenophobia. That's complicated enough but then there's the familial element. My partner is French, so my father would have voted Remain as a favour to me, so that her right to stay would be guaranteed, which now it's not. But that would have only been due to personal not political influence.

Well, I mention this because it generalises across the whole country. Everyone has a story like that. Brexit has really divided the country. If it's not a partner, it's a friend or work colleague. It's a case of weighing their interests with your own. Divide and rule is an old tactic of social and imperial control.

There's also the issue of what Leave and Remain mean. These terms are so vague that it was a blank slate issue. Write on the slate whatever you want to believe. If you want to Leave and never allow a European to come to Britain again, that was your Brexit. If you want a humanitarian Brexit that guarantees the rights of EU citizens, that too was your Brexit. Public relations firms which political parties use all the time are very good at making things as vague as possible – like the 'will of the people' slogan. This way, you can just read into it whatever you want. In the real world, as people are engaged in mental masturbation, the government gets on with implementing what its real constituents – the financial sector – want. Theresa May's advisors had all the Brexit plans laid out. Apparently, they never even showed them to the hardline Brexiteers like David Davis who was responsible for negotiating. This gave us the impression that May was sticking it to the EU. In reality, her advisors had softer Brexit plans which they were secretly showing to the European negotiators about which Davis and Johnson didn't even know.

Then there's the factual question about what constitutes 'the people'. What does 'the people' mean? In this case it means a plurality. There were over 46m eligible voters at the time of the Referendum in 2016. Of those 72% actually came out to vote. Of that 72%, nearly 52% voted Leave and just over 48% voted Remain. That means of all the Britons eligible to vote, only about 37% voted Leave.[43] Hardly 'the will of the people'.

Then there's the issue of what they voted for. Those who voted Leave are furious with the way it's being handled. It would appear that most Leavers voted for a hard Brexit. Their main concern was immigration. Nobody wants to admit to themselves that they're racist and xenophobic, and I doubt that they even believe they're racist. They say things, like, 'I'm not against immigrants, but ... They take our jobs, scrounge, exploit the NHS', and so on. And to give these people their dues, most think that EU citizens should be allowed to stay if they've already settled, though not claim benefits.[44] But many of the people who voted Leave also need to look in the mirror an ask seriously, 'Do I believe they take our jobs because that's what I believe, or do I believe it because I can't be bothered or don't know how to really understand the economy and I've found an easy target?'.

The Lord Ashcroft polls – an early analysis of who voted which way and why – reveals that the older the voter gets, the more likely they are to vote on the basis of immigration. It's quite striking to see the demographics. Young people tended to vote Remain, as we know, but young people who became parents between 2004-08, when the poorest eastern European countries were admitted to the EU and Poles and Romanians started moving here, suddenly this generation became Brexiteers. In fact, the older they get the more bizarre their world view becomes. The polls suggest that significant numbers of elderly people blame environmentalists and feminists for the changes in the culture that have upset the older generation. It's quite a sad state of affairs and really serious comment on how divided the society is and how effective the propaganda system is, where everyone is portrayed as the enemy – especially the very people who are making the world a better place.[45]

So you're saying that Brexit was plotted years ago. But how do you square that with the fact that the government at the time of the Referendum – Cameron's – was Remain?

Ask yourself why, after 40 years of refusing to hold a referendum, did the government suddenly decide to hold one now? And if they really were Remain, as admittedly many of them were, why did they hold it at a time of heightened Euroscepticism, when the outcome was bound to be Leave? They're not idiots. Cameron tried to 'reform' the EU from within, which means persuade it to further deregulate financial services so that London corporations could benefit. Back in 2015, the right-wing, pro-business *Telegraph* had headlines like, 'Cameron's four key demands to remain in the EU...'.[46] When it became clear that Britain simply doesn't have the power to do that, they orchestrated a referendum.

They knew that the public wrongly blamed Brussels – which had its own crippling, brutal austerity programme against Greeks and others – for the austerity here in the UK. That shows a lack of understanding of how the internal economy works. There are no good polling data, but based on anecdotal evidence, many British people seem to believe that the Bank of England is controlled by the European Central Bank. The government also understood the levels of racism in the country. People like Farage saw an opportunity to promote further anti-EU scepticism and outright hostility. Of course, the way this was sold to the public was that Cameron's advisors had a plan to beat UKIP by securing Remain. That's ridiculous because UKIP was never a threat to the Tories – it had won a single seat in the 2015 general election. The Labour Party under the Blairite Ed Miliband was a joke. It won just 232 seats. So the so-called Remain Tories were safe. There's no logic to the theory that they called the Referendum to secure more power. It was too much of a risk. The evidence is there for all to see: a gradual shift away from the EU and a willingness among a growing number of increasingly powerful Tory internationalists to seize the chance to revive the British Empire in the so-called 'emerging economies' and the already powerful US.

This was a tricky propaganda task because the majority of people who voted Brexit wanted less of what we call 'globalisation' – which really means corporate hegemony over foreign markets. In their minds, the culture has changed, there are too many immigrants, and in reality their standard of living has declined. This is what 'liberal internationalism' means to them. Under the delusion that the neoliberal Tory government is actually going to invest in local economies and rebuild the country, they voted for this vague thing called sovereignty. Also it was a probable case of reverse psychology. Everyone hated the incumbent Tory government, which won because they hated Labour even more. So when the government came out on a fake Remain platform – only a core like the Heseltine faction were true Remain ideologues – the public voted Leave just to piss off the government. So the reverse psychology worked. But the fact is that under the so-called Global Britain initiative dreamed up by Theresa May's advisors to sell Brexit, we're going to get more globalisation – only this time 'free trade' deals with the US, Australia, Japan, and so on, and all the wage decline, migration flows, automation, etc., that goes with it.

How the government could simultaneously sell Brexit as regaining sovereignty while plugging a global 'free trade' agenda – the very opposite – is quite an astonishing propaganda coup.

Yeah, but they say free trade deals will be made on our terms.

First of all the government doesn't represent public interests. That should be obvious by now. Representatives of the 'public interest' – whatever that means – usually include the trade unions, which are generally hostile to so-called 'free trade' deals.[47] Secondly, the UK plays second fiddle to the US. So whatever 'trade deals' the US wants, Britain will likely end up with. So if 'our terms' means the public, no they won't. If 'our terms' means in the 'national interest', that means in the interests of corporations who profit from US- and other markets.

It's also worth examining what we mean by 'free trade'. After WW2, the US and Britain – mainly the US – sought to shape the global trade and investment order in ways favourable to their corporations. But they also sought to create easy-to-manage political institutions like the General Agreement on Tariffs and Trade (GATT). This was part of the Bretton Woods system of regulated capital. The US also established via the World Bank, which it practically owns and runs, the Inter-state Dispute Settlements (ISDS) courts in the '60s. This means that if a country adopts some socialistic policy, like tightening environmental regulations or legislating to raise wages, corporations, mainly US ones, can sue. Canada, for instance, is the most sued developed nation under ISDS rules because it adopts environmental regulations which hinder US profits.[48] The Office of the US Trade Representative describes ISDS as a legal form of 'gunboat diplomacy' to privilege the US.[49] The GATT system was all about keeping tariffs, which are basically border taxes, low, so that the US can sell and, crucially, assemble its consumer products abroad and reimport them for domestic, US markets.[50] It's cheaper for Nike, say, to pay an Indonesian girl working in a sweatshop to make a pair of shoes destined for US markets, than it is to pay a US worker. So under GATT, Nike – just as an example – would export materials to Indonesia at next to nothing, thanks to tariff reductions, get it made at next to nothing prices paying sweatshop wages, reimport it to the US with virtually no border tax, and then sell it at a high price – a few hundred dollars – to wealthier US consumers. This model generalises across all consumer goods. That's 'free trade'.

Since the late-1990s, with the hi-tech boom, corporations have been much more concerned with intellectual property and copyright, so the World Trade Organization was formed, which China joined in 2001. Apple maintains its intellectual property for every iPhone produced. It gets the materials, like coltan, from genocidal conditions from slave labourers in Congo.[51] It benefits from technology, like touchscreen, developed in the military sector at taxpayers' expense. The materials are exported to China for assembly into iPhones and then reimported to the US for consumption at high prices. So the Chinese get little for it and US consumers pay twice. The only people who benefit are Apple and Foxconn, which owns the sweatshops that make the iPhones.[52] Again, that's 'free trade'. And again it generalises. So after Brexit, we'll end up with unregulated financial services that pay few taxes.

But whatever happens, we'll be able to trade with big economies like the US and China – and we've got the Commonwealth.

Trade implies something good. But what good did trade with the EEC do? Arguably, it helped to hollow out what was left of British industry by making us compete in a formal market with German, French, and Italian automakers.[53] What do you think more trade deals with the US etc. are doing to do? They're going to destroy even more jobs and drive wages down making British farmers compete with Brazilian beef. They're going to make British software designers compete with superior Indian designers – hence the early talk of visa relaxations for Indians. All the protections against US genetically-modified crops offered by the EU will lead to Frankenfoods. In the absence of Polish and Romanian agricultural labourers, fruit farmers are going to use machines and/or captive labour, like prisoners.[54] This is the nature of what we erroneously call 'capitalism'. If unions and a genuinely socialistic government were setting policy, we might have had a different Brexit outcome – real investment in the North, guaranteed rights for settled EU citizens, a globalization adjustment fund for communities already affected by migration, investment in British software engineers instead of reliance on Indians, and so on. But that's not what's happening because big business sets policy.

But isn't Trump contradicting that model? Isn't he bringing US businesses home?

That's just more propaganda. Trump was riding the wave of changes in the structure of globalisation that were already underway when Obama was in power. But neither Obama nor Trump are dictating these changes. Until about the 2010s, you had the model I described above. Then, as automation in software-writing became more sophisticated, companies like IBM no longer had to offshore to India because using robots (algorithms) was even cheaper than using poor Indian labour. In addition to this, US corporations like Ford Motors were furious that the big multilateral 'free trade' deals like TPP and TTIP didn't address hidden taxes, like VAT. So they lobbied Senators like Orrin Hatch and Mitch McConnell to push for bilateral deals, or one-on-one deals. In a multilateral deal, countries have strength in numbers. But in a bilateral deal, it's country *x* vs. the USA. And guess who's going to win?[55]

So by accident, this new form of globalization appears to benefit US labourers by bringing jobs back to America. Trump was able to ride this wave and take credit for it. This leads to further political divisions because the left-liberal types hate Trump so fanatically that they can't think critically and admit, yes, he is bringing jobs back, but why? He obviously doesn't care about people, so how does that work? It turns out to be a happy coincidence for Trump. But if you look at the actual data on jobs and labour, yes they've gone up but wages and job security are way down in most sectors – that's why I qualified with 'apparently'.[56] In fact, when CNN reviewed Michael Wolff's book on Trump – which is mostly trashy gossip about Trump's alleged mental state – they concluded with a statement like, 'Oh, well, Trump may be a lunatic but the economy's booming so that's what really counts' (paraphrase). So if the booming economy – and 'economy' means profit for big business – is booming, why is CNN wasting time attacking Trump, other than to feed this divisive dialectic?

I was listening to Trump's NATO summit speech and his press conference with Russian President, Vladimir Putin. He said some interesting that I agree with: That NATO members should be paying more; that he'd rather risk politics in pursuit of peace than lose peace

chasing politics; and that US-Russian relations have never been worse, so it's time to turn that around.

Pretty words, but what's the reality? NATO is an extremely dangerous organisation that arguably should have never existed, let alone exist after the collapse of the Soviet Union in the early-1990s. Is Trump reducing NATO's capabilities and thus de-escalating with Russia? No. He's simply saying that other countries should pay more, which will mean an increase in NATO capability. All the while, behind the scenes, the US works closely to pull NATO's strings. Trump let something interesting slip, that he was friends with the Secretary-general Jens Stoltenberg and that it was under US auspices that Stoltenberg's tenure was extended.[57] Trump also mentioned rivalry with Russia's pipeline.[58] NATO is quite open about the fact that its real mandate is what they call energy 'security', meaning stealing oil and especially gas from Serbia and Libya, which we can come onto.

But this whole thing about the US taking a back seat in international affairs – letting NATO members pay their way, using Saudi Arabia as a proxy to fight Yemen, etc. – this was all initiated under Obama. Trump is just being more blatant about it. If you read the Parliamentary transcripts from 2011–12 into the British role in the bombing of Libya, the security experts make it clear that the US is only pretending to take a back seat there[59] – also in Mali and elsewhere – all the while it drops proportionally most of the bombs of any power during a particular war, has the main energy interests, and does the heavy lifting. This is designed to play up the idea that America's influence in global affairs is declining. It's a complete joke. US war planners do read Sun Tzu's *The Art of War* – they quote Sun often in strategic documents[60] – and Sun said something like, 'Looking weak can be your biggest strength'.

So where's the 'peace' Trump talks about? It's good that he's making rhetorical moves toward de-escalation with Russia, which as he points out, has nuclear weapons. But has he ordered an immediate withdrawal of US forces and missile systems from Russia's neighbour's Estonia, Poland, Romania, and Ukraine? No. As Putin says, the so-called missile 'defence' system being expanded around Russia is a serious threat. Again, these moves did not begin under Trump. It's part of the US Pentagon's plan to dominate the world by force, 'Full Spectrum Dominance'.

RESIST

In fairness, **PRESIDENT TRUMP** has done some **GOOD THINGS**. He did well with **PYONGYANG** – I don't mean the negotiations with the **NORTH KOREAN** government. I'm referring to **PEE ON YANG**, the highly entertaining urine-themed East Asian porn film that the **RUSSIANS** are blackmailing him with…

Chapter 2

Storm from a teacup:
Britain and Russia

Or: How we quietly poke the Bear and shout about its retaliations...

There seems to be a consensus that we need a strong military because Russia is on the rise. What do you think about that rationale?

There's no consensus, except among European and American elites. Europe and America are not the world.

There are a lot of issues to consider with regards to Russia. Is it a threat? If so to whom? What kind of threat is Russia? So let's consider these questions carefully. As far as the British establishment is concerned, Russia is an ideological threat because it is a major power with a substantial population. It's also self-reliant where oil and gas is concerned, unlike Britain. So there's lots of potential for Russian political ideology to undermine Britain's status. In fact, there are European Council on Foreign Relations papers saying that Putin's Russia presents an 'ideological alternative' to the EU.[61] And that's dangerous. Britain, or more accurately its policymaking elites, have considered Russia a significant enemy for over a century. Under the Tsar, the so-called Great Game was a battle for strategic resources, trading routes, and so on. The historian Lawrence James calls this period the first Cold War, which went 'hot' with the Crimean War (1853–56).[62] Britain had a mixed relationship with the Tsars because, on the one hand, theirs' were repressive regimes and Britain tended to favour repressive regimes, hence their brief alliance with Russia's enemy, the Ottomans. On the other hand, Russia was a strategic threat to Britain's imperial interests, and thus the Crimean War (1853–56).

When the Bolsheviks took over Russia, beginning 1917, the relationship became much less ambiguous – Russians, and especially Bolsheviks, were clearly the enemy. Their ideology posed a threat internally. So Winston Churchill, who began as a Liberal and became a Conservative, considered the Labour Party, which was formed in 1900, as basically a front for Bolsheviks.[63] That shows the level of paranoia among elites. The Labour Party, at least at the beginning, was a genuine, working man's political organisation – women couldn't vote then, remember. So by associating this progressive, grassroots party representing the working classes as an ideological ally or even puppet of the brutal Bolshevik regime, the Tories had an excuse to undermine the power of organised, working people. So you had the Zinoviev letter in 1924, which we now know was a literal conspiracy between the secret services and elements of the Tory party to fabricate a link between Labour and Moscow. And it famously cost Labour the general election, since the right-wing, privately-owned media ran with the story as though it was real. It's an early example of fake news.[64]

That's the ideological threat that Russia has posed, historically. But where there's a threat, there's an opportunity. The British elites exploited the 'threat' then and as they do today by associating organised labour with evil Bolshevism and, in doing so, alienate the lower classes from their own political interests. Suddenly, we've all got to be scared of Russia, just like in 1917. And let's not forget that Britain used chemical weapons – M-Devices, which induced vomiting – against the Bolsheviks. Chemical weapons were 'the right medicine for the Bolshevist', in Churchill's words. This was in 1919, as part of the Allied invasion of Russia in support of the White Army.[65] So if we're talking about the historical balance of forces and cause and effect, Britain not Russia initiated the use of chemical weapons against others. But this history is typically inverted to say that Russia poses a threat to the West, hence all the talk about Novichok, the Skripals, and Dawn Sturgess, the civilian who supposedly came into contact with Novichok and died in hospital a few days later.

The next question: What *sort* of threat is Russia? According to the US Army War College, since the collapse of the Soviet Union and since pro-US, pro-'free market' President Boris Yeltsin resigned in 1999, Russia has pursued so-called economic nationalism. And the US doesn't like this because markets suddenly get closed and taxes are raised against US corporations.[66] That's the real threat. But you can't tell the public that: that we hate Russia because they aren't doing what we say. If you look through the military documents, you can find almost nothing about security threats against the US in terms of Russian expansion, except in the sense that 'security' means operational freedom. You can find references to Russia's nuclear weapons, though, which are described as defensive, designed 'to counter US forces and weapons systems'.[67] Try finding that on the BBC. I should mention that even 'defensive' nukes can be launched accidentally.

The real goal with regards to Russia is maintaining US economic hegemony and culture of open 'free markets' that goes with it, while at the same time being protectionist in real life. (US protectionism didn't start under Trump, by the way.) Liberal media like the *New York Times* run sarcastic articles about Russian state oil and gas being a front for Putin and his cronies. And yes, that may be true. But what threat is Russia to the US if it has a corrupt government? The threat is closing its markets to the US. The US is committed to what its military calls Full Spectrum Dominance. So the world needs to be run in a US-led neoliberal order, in the words of the US military, 'to protect US interests and investment'.[68] But this cannot be done if you have 'economic nationalism', like China had until the 'reforms' of the '70s and '80s, and still has today to some extent. Russia and China aren't military threats. The global population on the whole knows this, even though the domestic US and British media say the opposite.

What about military threats?

The best sources you can get are the US military records. Straight from the horse's mouth. The military plans for war and defence. It has contingencies for when political situations change. So they know what they're talking about. There's a massive divide between reality, as understood from the military records, and media and political rhetoric. Assessments by the US Army War College, for instance, said years ago that any moves by NATO to support a Western-backed government in Ukraine would provoke Russia into annexing Crimea. They don't talk about Russia spontaneously invading Ukraine and annexing it, which is the image we get from the media. The documents talk about Russia *reacting* to NATO provocation.[69]

If you look at a map, you see Russia surrounded by hostile NATO forces. The media don't discuss this dangerous and provocative situation, except the occasional mention of, say, US-British-Polish war-gaming on the border with Russia. When they do mention it, they say it's for 'containment', the containment of Russia. But to contain something, the given thing has to be expanding. But the US military – like the annual threat assessments to Congress – say that Russia's not expanding, except when provoked. So at the moment as part of its NATO mission, the UK is training Polish and Ukrainian armed forces, has deployed troops in Poland and Estonia, and is conducting military exercises with them.[70] Imagine if Scotland ceded from the UK and the Russians were on our border conducting military exercises, supposedly to deter a British invasion of Scotland. That's what we're doing in Ukraine. Britain's moves are extremely dangerous. In the 1980s, the UK as part of NATO conducted the exercise, Operation Able Archer, which envisaged troop build-ups between NATO and the Warsaw Pact countries. Now-declassified records show that the Russians briefly mistook this exercise for a real-world scenario. That could have escalated into nuclear war. This is very serious.[71]

But the biggest player is the USA. It's using the threat of force and a global architecture of hi-tech militarism to shape a neoliberal order. Britain is slavishly following its lead. I doubt that Britain would position forces near Russia were it not for the USA. Successive US administrations have or are building a missile system in Europe and Turkey. They say it's to deter Iran from firing Scud missiles at Europe. But it's pointed at Russia. It's a radar system based in Romania and Turkey, with a battery of Patriot missiles based in Poland. The stationing of missiles there provoked Russia into moving its mobile nuclear weapons up to the border in its Kaliningrad exclave, as it warned it would do in 2008.[72] Try to find any coverage of that in the media, except for a few articles in the print media here or there. If Western media were interested in survival, there would be regular headlines: 'NATO provoking Russia'.

But the situation in Ukraine is really the tipping point. Consider the equivalent. Imagine if Russia was conducting military exercises with Canada or Mexico, and building bases there. How would the US react? It would be considered an extreme threat, a violation of the UN Charter, which prohibits threats against sovereign states.

So we've extended NATO to pretty much the Russian border? But there's a hard border there. Everyone knows we're never going to attack Russia, both for reasons of morality and self-preservation. So maybe this situation is safer than you imply.

There's no morality involved. States are abstract, amorphous entities comprised of dominant minorities and subjugated majorities who are conditioned to believe that they are relatively free and prosperous. The elites of those states act both in their self-interests – career, peer-pressure, kickbacks, and so on – and in the interests of their class, which is of course tied to international relations because their class thrives on profiting from resource exploitation. So you can't talk about morality in this context. Only individuals can behave morally. The state is made up of individuals, of course, but they're acting against the interests of the majority. As we speak, they are acting *immorally* – or at least amorally – but creating the geopolitical conditions that imperil each and every one of us.

As for invasion, we're not going to invade Russia. This isn't 1918. Russia has nuclear weapons and can deter an invasion. But that's not the point. Do we want to de-escalate an already tense geopolitical situation or make it worse to the point where an accident happens? So while it's not about invading Russia directly, the issue is about attacking what are called Russia's 'national interests'. Russia's 'national interests' are the same as the elites' of the UK. National interest doesn't mean the interests of the public. It means the interests of the policymaking establishment and the corporations. For example, the Theresa May government sacrificed its own credibility to ensure that its *Brexit White Paper* (2018) appeased both the interests of the food and manufacturing industries that want a soft Brexit – easy trade with the EU – and the financial services sector which wants a hard Brexit – freedom from EU regulation. Everyone else be damned. That's the 'national interest'.

So for its real 'national interest', Russia wants to keep Ukraine in its sphere of influence because its oil and gas to Europe pass through Ukraine. About 80% of Russia's export economy is in the oil and gas sector. It's already had serious political tensions with Ukraine, which on several occasions hasn't paid its energy bills, so Russia has cut supplies. If Europe can bump Ukraine into its own sphere of influence it has more leverage over Russia. This is practically admitted in Parliamentary discussions by Foreign Office ministers, and so forth.[73] Again, omitted by the media. Also, remember that plenty of ethnic Russians live in eastern Ukraine. In addition, Russia has a naval base in Crimea. That's not to excuse its illegal action in annexing Ukraine, it's to highlight the *realpolitik* missing in the media's coverage of the situation.

No one's going to start a war by invading Russia, but war could happen by accident. There's—

Why do we care, Tim? Our elites, the Russian elites – they're just the same old bunch of scumbags. This is just the old Great Game. But they won't have an actual, territorial fight so it's the same old thing to us, as the little people.

For a start, the weapons are infinitely more powerful. A hundred years ago, the most potent weapon we had was air power and chemical weapons. They killed a few people – the bombs and chemicals – but not many. We didn't have a weapon of mass destruction. But now we have tens of thousands of nuclear weapons. We could destroy the world and the biosphere several times over, even with accidental nuclear detonations. There have been dozens of cases of human and computer error since WW2, when nuclear wars were nearly started by mistake, where nuclear bombs were accidentally dropped and didn't detonated: and even cases where missiles have been launched.

In one case in the 1980s at Cheyenne Mountain, an ICBM was accidentally launched from a silo and the US military had to park a truck on top to stop the silo doors from opening. There was a case just a few years ago, where Trident was being tested and the missiles were supposed to hit island targets off the coast of Africa – because what else is Africa for, if not acting as a place to test-fire missiles? – and the weapon malfunctioned. It went towards Florida. Either it was shot down or self-destructed.[74] On that occasion, it was not armed. But suppose that happens one day with an armed missile? And suppose it heads toward Russia? It's unlikely, but the stakes are so high that you don't take any chances, assuming you want to live, of course. And these examples are just normal computer error. But when you're playing a strategic game and you're building up forces around Russia there could easily be a miscalculation or mistake and set off a nuclear war.

The Ministry of Defence knows this – they have at least a couple of documents. One talks about a possible 'doomsday scenario'.[75] Their words. The other mentions that, over the next couple of decades, the use of nuclear weapons by non-Western states, which could easily mean Western states, 'cannot be ruled out'.[76] Again, in their words.

Did you see the other day there was a study recently that said that the detonation of just 100 nuclear weapons would cause an unacceptable level of damage even to the aggressor?

I wonder what an 'acceptable' level of damage would be. There was also a peer-reviewed scientific study in *Earth's Future*. Their most optimistic scenario for the outcome of a small nuclear war between India and Pakistan was that there would be a nuclear winter for the whole planet and plunge millions into famine conditions.[77] So we should be doing all we can – if we want to survive, maybe we don't, maybe we don't care. But if we want a chance for decent survival, we should be working hard to de-escalate.

The one good thing that Donald Trump did during his campaign to become President was his rhetorical efforts to de-escalate tensions with Russia. The so-called liberal media went berserk over this: Trump is gullible, selling out to Putin, and so on. From their point of view, it's better to risk nuclear apocalypse than show any kind of weakness. It's pathological. Trump was presumably gesturing peace toward Russia for cynical reasons, because of business interests, I guess. But out of that self-interest, any such policy of normalisation could have de-escalated these tensions.

But pressure from other Republicans, Democrats, and the elite corporate media essentially pushed him back to accepting the same hostile agenda as his predecessors. That's US imperialism.

I was pleased Trump beat Hillary Clinton in 2016, though I was cautious. He's followed through on North Korea and I have the impression he wants to see the world as one horrible garish shopping mall. But at least that's better than it being a battle ground of irradiated tanks and dead bodies.

It's faulty logic. Consider the case of Iraq and the terrible choices. The choice the elites granted themselves in 2003 was: Do we let our governments leave Iraq's dictator Saddam Hussein in power and help him oppress the population, or do we remove him and kill a million people with Shock and Awe – the aerial bombing campaign – and divide and conquer? That's a false dichotomy. There's always a third option, a fourth, a fifth, and so on. One option was to let the people of Iraq overthrow Saddam. That option was denied them by our elites because they wanted to invade Iraq. The choice with Trump, if he de-escalates with Russia, is either a global neoliberal order, which might not even survive because of its own structures, or the potential for nuclear war. But as with Iraq or any foreign policy, there's a third and fourth option, etc. One option is for grassroots activists in the Democratic Party to mobilise in further support of Bernie Sanders, who is also a hawk on foreign policy, by the way. This has already been done to some extent with Our Revolution.

But more needs to be done. A mass, dedicated, grass-roots movement – like Our Revolution – could bring forward a candidate on a peace platform. Another option is to use that organisation, successful or not, to put pressure on both Trump and the Democrats. But that's not happening.

With Trump and Clinton it was very hard to judge who would be worse on foreign policy. On domestic issues Clinton wanted to maintain the status quo and maintain some structures to help America's poorest, via social security, for example. Trump, under the cover of nationalism, is dismantling the social safety-nets. Take the issue of global warming. Clinton wanted to put some limits on coal production, but she was notorious for supporting fracking, for pushing it on eastern European countries. Trump is much worse on this issue. He's committed to burning everything: coal, oil, gas, and pursuing fracking. But that's not a problem for most Trump supporters because they think that climate change is a hoax. So with Trump, we've potentially limited the risk of nuclear war with North Korea and Russia by avoiding the super-hawkish Clinton administration, but we've increased climate change. But it's not even clear that Trump is less hawkish in totality than Clinton. He's dropped a record number of bombs on the Middle East and North Africa in proportion to the time he's been in office.[78]

We should also remember that what military planners call the 'iron fist' of militarism is needed to support the 'velvet glove' of economics and diplomacy. Yes the world would be as horrible as a giant shopping mall, but for that to happen it must also be encircled with nuclear weapons to make sure nationalist movements don't come to power in other countries and change the direction of that country away from the shopping centre model.

Trump aside, Britain is now getting so hostile with Russia that the May government is putting us all at risk. Why? I assume that if Brexit goes ahead and Britain becomes a so-called independent power, it will probably still want to have so-called security interests in Europe. There's some evidence for this, with the RAND Corporation, for instance.[79] With Trump appearing to wind down support for Europe's military and supposedly making it support itself more, the UK can at least pretend to be Europe's security guarantor. Britain's elite like to boast that ours is one of the only countries meeting its NATO target to spend 2% of GDP on so-called defence.[80] So it's to the benefit of the government if Britain can inflate the Russia threat. Britain can sell itself and thus the arms industry as the defender of Europe in the supposed absence of full US commitment. In reality of course, this is nonsense. And the situation becomes much *less* stable because Russia is getting provoked.

We appeared on Russia Today (RT) together. But that's okay because it's independent, right? The people we saw had no editorial control imposed from Moscow.

There are two issues here. Number one: Is RT pure propaganda or does it have independence?

RT is about as independent as the BBC – which means it's not independent at all. The BBC has a charter. It's regulated by OFCOM, the agency which enforces the communications acts. The executive can and has censored the BBC. The queen has veto power over any domestic legislation. It's called the Royal Prerogative. We saw what happened when a single journalist – Andrew Gilligan – hinted, at 6am, on the radio, that according to his sources the Blair government might have exaggerated some claims about Saddam's non-existent weapons of mass destruction. His report happened *after* the invasion, so it wasn't as if it had much influence. But that minor act of defiance was enough to bring the BBC to its knees. The Director-general Greg Dyke was basically forced out after being criticised in the government's Hutton Inquiry (2004). Gilligan lost his job (resigned, technically). The organisation was threatened with privatisation. And the Neil Report (2004) recommended that a 'college of journalism' be established to teach journalists not to ask certain questions.[81]

If anyone questioned the state and the basic operations of British foreign policy and to a large extent domestic policy, the BBC would quickly get rid of them. But more importantly, that cannot happen. No state is going to allow a media to operate against its interests. Pick on politicians and expose their lies, that's fine. In fact, it's preferable to supporting them because the media then look like attack dogs and thus not propaganda outlets. The BBC is basically run by the Oxbridge set. They are not going to shape an organisation in ways that hurt their class interests. It's board of governors – now called Trustees – are often representatives of banks, water companies, supermarkets, and so on. They are not teachers, nurses, firefighters – the people who do the important work. Nor are they low-level cashiers at the banks or the checkout girls in supermarkets. I say 'girls' because women not men, overwhelmingly young and old, the more exploitable ones, work in supermarkets.

So in terms of state interests, it's the same with RT. It exists to promote the Kremlin. If anyone challenges Russian foreign policy in a sustained way on RT, they wouldn't get very far. So it's a propaganda outlet for the Kremlin. No question. But within that, you have a lot of room for manoeuvre, as you have with the BBC. For example, Dr Tara McCormack was invited on BBC radio to answer allegations that an academic group she was associated with were apologists for Putin and Assad of Syria. The BBC took her to task for claiming that the White Helmet civil volunteers – which are actually funded by the British and other governments[82] – were a front for 'al-Qaeda'. It's a ludicrous accusation. But McCormack did manage to turn it around and say that her source was the BBC itself – that their documentary series Panorama had exposed some *jihadists* working among the White Helmets (which is a stretch to call the organisation an al-Qaeda front).[83] Another example is a Newsnight episode exposing the fact that the British were sent to Brazil after the 1964 coup to help torture Brazilian socialists and political dissidents. The old torturers were too crude, using electricity and sodomy, and so on. Some victims ended up dead, which defeats the point of torture. So the British were called in to show them how to do it right: how to destroy people mentally, with sleep deprivation and so on. The BBC exposed that.[84] So within these rigid propaganda systems, there's still plenty of room to move.

RT won't impose any editorial control if we're criticising Western foreign policy. And they probably won't care if there's an occasional episode here or there which—

Yeah, they were able to tolerate a short 30-second burst of news anchor Abby Martin going off script and criticising Russia's annexation of Crimea. But not at a systematic level. Same as if someone went on the BBC and continually had a go at London.

That's just not going to happen. And Abby Martin left shortly afterwards for reasons still unclear, to work with teleSUR, which is a propaganda outlet funded by Venezuela, for which I've also written. Rather comically, RT responded to Martin's monologue as follows: '[She] noted that she does not possess a deep knowledge of reality of the situation in Crimea ... As such we'll be sending her to Crimea to give her an opportunity to make up her own mind from the epicenter of the story'.[85] That's like the BBC saying they'll send Gilligan to Porton Down laboratories to let him make up his own mind about WMD. If that's not propaganda, what is? But propaganda is so deeply ingrained on all sides that I doubt that the people who wrote that get the comedy of it. As a supporter of Jeremy Corbyn, even I cringed when Labour released a funky, hip-hop style video of the man meeting constituents and delivering his speeches bombastically, like he's Jesus. They didn't seem to realise they were mimicking the worst days of the crudest Soviet propaganda.

Just to conclude with Martin: Even more hilarious, she apparently didn't know anything about the planned Crimea 'educational' trip!

Earlier, I said there are two points to consider about Russia as a threat. Turning to point number two: Are we propagandists for Russia because we went on the show? Well, I don't know about you but I'd be happy to be invited onto the BBC. But that's never going to happen. By that logic, I would be a propagandist for the British state by my virtue of my appearing there. So because we were knocking UK foreign policy on RT, we *are* indirectly helping Russian propaganda. We know that. We're not idiots. Again, I can't speak for you, but I appeared on RT UK not because I want to talk to Russians about how bad the UK is, but because it's an opportunity to talk to British people about British foreign policy. To tell them things they won't hear on the BBC or ITV, or any of the channels.

I've noticed with RT that as soon as the US starts to be more conciliatory with Russia, the severity of their attacks on the US lessens. So when Trump came to power, initially on a promise to de-escalate tensions with Russia, *Crosstalk* presenter Peter Lavelle and pundits like Lionel were suddenly saying the alt-right – the neo-fascist movement that supported Trump – isn't so bad, they're demonised by the liberal media, what about the alt-left? (which doesn't even exist),[86] and so on. But there's no ideology there. If you had a liberal president come to power, one who also wanted peace with Russia, you'd get RT saying that the ultra-right Republicans are terrible.

To give another example. The US backs Israel over the Palestinians, so RT's coverage of Israel was relentlessly negative. They broadcast documentaries about Gaza being a prison and people having to smuggle livestock into Gaza under tunnels – the kind of thing that CNN and the BBC should be showing. It was all true, but it was obviously being broadcast by RT as a weapon against the US, to say, 'Look at how awful America's close ally Israel is'. But I noticed a few years ago under Obama, when Israeli ambassadors left the US during rare US-Israeli tensions, RT's coverage of Israel-Palestine changed literally overnight. They suddenly had a little news item from the point of view of the illegal Israeli colonisers living in Palestine, saying how difficult it was there. The context was that the colonisers – or settlers as the US calls them – were pawns of their evil government, but the coverage was uncharacteristically sympathetic to the colonisers. It even described the colonies as 'controversial', instead of illegal, which they are under international law.[87] Then, as soon as US-Israeli relations were back to normal, so too was the anti-Israeli RT coverage.

It's the same with the BBC. You shouldn't take your own state-media seriously. During the Cold War, most Russians didn't seriously read *Pravda* because they knew it was ridiculous propaganda. Many listened to the BBC and Voice of America.[88] They knew it was propaganda for Britain and America, but they also knew that they were getting some truth about Russia itself, which they weren't reading in *Pravda*. It's the same with RT. I listen to it because it tells the truth about the UK. Things that we don't get from the BBC. But I don't listen to RT to get information about Russia because obviously it's going to be pro-Russian propaganda. So afterthe Russians attacked Grozny in 1999, RT did a show over a decade later. They said that, yes, Grozny was bad, but it was a necessary war to defeat terrorists and now it's been rebuilt as a great town – they showed pictures of shiny new buildings and called it 'the Dubai of the Caucasus' – whereas Fallujah is still a wreck.[89] Well, that was true about rebuilding Grozny, but that's not how you evaluate morality. The Russians committed horrendous war crimes in Grozny, so it's pathological to justify that by highlighting a single positive outcome, especially when you're only using it as a weapon against your enemy, not remembering the dead of Grozny.

How many people did Russia kill in Grozny?

At least a couple of thousand.

Is that a case where you have to make an omelette, so break some eggs?

That was what we said about Fallujah, Iraq. But look at the context – illegal occupation, and so on. Fallujah was a city that resisted the occupation. It was an outright lie concocted by the US military that, 'al Qaeda' was operating there.[90] There are counterinsurgency documents released WikiLeaks[91] that say, 'We'll just call the resistance group operating there "al-Qaeda," so we'll have just cause to bomb the city and weaken the will of the population to resist' (paraphrase). It's worth remembering also that Fallujans started out protesting peacefully in 2003 and a dozen were shot dead by US forces.[92]

So twice in 2004, the US and Britain attacked the city. A private contractor – American, of course – had been awarded a contract to 'repair' Fallujah's water system, which had been destroyed by the US-British sanctions in the 1990s.[93] One day, some Blackwater mercenaries also known as private contractors were taken from their jeep, killed by Iraqis, burned and strung up from a bridge, the same one that had been bombed by the US in the Gulf War. Well, these displays of resistance can't be tolerated. So the US and Britain went crazy in Fallujah in two additional attacks. They prevented civilians leaving the city by blocking the city with wire and unleashed masses of artillery, the chemical weapon white phosphorous, and so on. At some point, they used a secret radiation- or even a nuclear weapon. Epidemiologists found higher levels of radiation in Fallujah in 2004 than in Hiroshima in 1945. And now you get ongoing intergenerational deformities.[94] At one point, Fallujans had to wear yellow arm bands, which evokes some memories, because the government didn't want them contaminating anyone else in the country.

So you can make any kind of case you want about omelettes and eggs, but that doesn't detract from the fact that we're committing war crimes. Same as the Russians did in Grozny.

What would have happened if Russia hadn't intervened in Grozny?

It's not in the interests of ordinary Russian people for their state to fight in Grozny, because it provokes violence from the Chechen independence movement, some of which is polluted by an Islamist ideology funded by Saudi Arabia. It's in their interests to de-escalate. But Russia's elite want the country as unified as possible, so they're preventing independence. It's rather like what we did in Northern Ireland.

DROP
PILLS
NOT
BOMBS

I can see a **BETTER WORLD**,
a more peaceful world, a happier
world... and I can see us
INVADING THAT WORLD
and stealing all of its best stuff.

Chapter 3

Cream scones and genocide

Or: Why we killed half a million Iraqi kids in the '90s...

Why do you have a problem with British foreign policy?

It's not just me. It's the victims, who are quite substantial in number, since Empire and even before. Mark Curtis reckons that British foreign policy has killed, both directly and indirectly, 10 million people between 1945 and 2004.[95]

But what is Britain and who are Britons? The UK itself has an interesting history. If you go back far enough you find various kingdoms and tribes, the early Britons, who were opposed to being conquered. Some of them fought the Roman conquest. Then you had other empires and nascent empires trying to take over Britain. The Norman invasion is regarded as the beginnings of modern England, at least in the popular culture.[96] A century later, the conquerors, who were by then 'Anglo-Norman', also took over Ireland. So both the early Britons and the Irish were victims of the Normans.

By the 17th century you have the idea of creating Englishness and finally Britishness in the modern sense with Cromwell,[97] to the point where we now think of British people as a homogenous group.[98] That made it easier for nearby peoples, like the Irish, to identify Britain and modern Britons, as opposed to 'Anglo-Normans', as the enemy and perpetrator of certain crimes, including genocide. Then, by the time you have the nation state, you have crimes of Empire in places like India - but take your pick - which can be clearly attributed to elites who call themselves British.

Beginning World War 1, but certainly by the end World War 2, the British Empire was finished and America achieved - partly by virtue of the UK's decline - unprecedented wealth and power. So Britain's role in most cases today, not all, is to follow America's lead and avoid falling out with America's elites. We continue to create great suffering, just as we did in the Age of Empire, admittedly on a smaller scale. We make enemies whenever the United States does.

One of the great tragedies of the modern era is what we've done to Iraq. It's difficult to get exact figures, of course, but the best empirical, epidemiological studies suggest that at a million Iraqis died in the decade following the invasion in 2003.[99] Physicians for Social Responsibility estimated 1,300,000 deaths if you include Pakistan and Afghanistan, with the overwhelming majority of deaths being in Iraq.[100]

But we don't usually directly kill them, though, do we? We may have helped create the conditions but it's not really the same as, say, executing six million Jews.

There's no comparison between the Holocaust and the invasion of Iraq. Every atrocity is unique in some respects and similar in others. Iraq wasn't a genocide because we never intended to wipe out every Iraqi, the way the Nazis tried to wipe out all Jews, and in fact all non-Aryans. But the invasion of Iraq caused such high levels of death that it reached genocidal levels. The Nazi genocide was the result of a particularly strange elite in Germany, which believed in a particular form of racial superiority – I mean, every nation believes in its own superiority, but the Nazis took this to a new extreme—

But isn't the point that these deaths weren't caused by our own bullets and bombs but really were mostly the result of fighting between Iraqi factions?

Just to finish up on the Nazi comparison. Iraq was not a systematic attempt to murder every Iraqi in the way that the Holocaust was a way to murder every non-Aryan. But there are similarities. For example, about 500,000 Gypsy-Roma are said to have perished in the Holocaust.[101] That's about the same number of Iraqi infants who were dead by 1996 because of the US-British sanctions.[102] The mass murder of Gypsy-Roma by Nazis was because they weren't Aryan. The mass murder of Iraqi infants was a side-effect of a policy to weaken Iraq. Both crimes are comparable in scale and both perpetrators guilty, but for different reasons and with different ends in mind. Does that mean we exonerate the Thatcher, Major, and Blair governments because they didn't *intend* to kill half a million babies?

And you've got both Holocaust deniers, like Nick Kollerstrom, and Iraq sanctions deniers – people who deny that the sanctions caused an increase in infant and child mortality – like the economist Michael Spagat at Royal Holloway. Kollerstrom says there was no systematic Nazi effort to exterminate non-Ayrans, especially Jews. Kollerstrom just ignores all the evidence contrary to his claim. Spagat just says – without evidence – that the 1995 mortality study was based on interviews with people chosen by Saddam Hussein, meaning they spouted Saddam's propaganda. Simple logic debunks that.[103] So what was the response? Kollerstrom was stripped of his honorary fellowship by University College London. Spagat is still employed as a respected economist, which also says something about our culture. It's like Congresspeople in the US today. Some are lobbied by the Turkish government so they openly deny the Armenian genocide, for which the Turks were responsible.[104] That's because Armenians have no lobby to defend their interests, unlike the Israelis. Can you imagine a member of Congress denying the Nazi Holocaust?

But to return to your question about Britain's direct role in mass murder:

The highest levels of death in pre-invasion Iraq directly caused by so-called sanctions, which was really a naval blockade. There's a book called *The Scourging of Iraq*,[105] which goes through the list of every physical item you can imagine banned from entering Iraq – medical gauzes, women's sanitary pads. Members of Voices in the Wilderness and the Teddy Bears for Iraq campaign were threatened with jail for breaking the blockade by trying to send a couple of thousand teddy bears to Iraq.[106]

The pretext for this was to punish Saddam Hussein for his invasion of Kuwait in 1990. The effect was to destroy the society almost completely. For example, prostitution was pretty much unheard of but it became common because of the embargo.[107] You had a complete restriction of medical supplies under the ludicrous pretext that Iraq could use these supplies in its weapons of mass destruction programme. All the while, UN weapons inspectors were there (UNSCOM 1991–1998, then UNMOVIC 1999–2007) to ensure the biological and chemical elements that America and Britain had sold Iraq were being dismantled.

So you had, by 1996, at least half a million children under five, who had died due to the embargo. And this was put to Madeleine Albright, President Clinton's Secretary of State, on *60 Minutes*. She was asked if the price was worth paying and she said, well, it's a tough choice, but yes, killing half a million babies is 'worth it'.

We learned from the government's Chilcot Inquiry that the living standard of Iraq dropped from that of Greece to Burundi, 'worse than the Democratic Republic of Congo',[108] one of the poorest and most devastated African countries. About a third of Iraqis didn't have clean drinking water. So this laid the foundations for absolute disaster when the 2003 escalation occurred. It wasn't so much a new attack as an escalation, since Iraq had already been under a blockade and was subject to airstrikes to enforce the No Fly Zones.

It was easy to blame the majority of killings on Iraqis between 2003 and 2008, the period of the greatest post-invasion violence, but even that was a deliberate US policy called 'the Salvador option', which involved sponsoring death squads.[109] The US air war was a blatant violation of the Geneva Conventions, which are supposed to protect civilians. If you read the air war strategy, *Shock and Awe: Achieving Rapid Dominance* (1996), it's amazing what is public, it's just that journalists don't seem interested to read it. It explicitly advocates targeting civilians on a massive scale to destroy morale, and then it's much easier to occupy the country. Well, it didn't quite work because the US didn't use as much air power as they did in, say, Vietnam.

The teddy bear thing seems insane. That's not about oil or economics – it's just not rational.

A lot of it is still secret, in terms of internal memos, but one of guys responsible for implementing the sanctions, Carne Ross, told John Pilger in *The War You Don't See* that the attitude in the Foreign Office was total indifference to suffering. He said that his colleagues said it was 'a bit wet' to talk about human rights in the context of Saddam Hussein, as if the innocent Iraqis hurt by the blockade were Saddam.

So that's some limited evidence as to why, following the US lead, the British planners would engage in such a vindictive policy. In the real world, this rationale was total madness. And it was about the oil, as well, contrary to what you said. The sanctions initially prevented Iraq from selling oil. Under the Oil-for-Food Programme (1995), Iraq could receive credits by manipulating oil production and sales on terms favourable to the US – they hoped.[110] The US wants to control oil prices and it doesn't want countries to over-produce or under-produce. So they had an arrangement and Saddam Hussein, who initially rejected the Programme was just exploiting this, as was entirely predictable. He was profiting from it while the whole country collapsed.

I think the US wanted to collapse Iraq with sanctions to make it easier to occupy long-term. There's a Colonel William J. Bender who told the US Army War College in 2002 that as a result of the sanctions Iraq's military was sufficiently weakened for the invasion. So there are indications like this, that there had been a longer-term intention to invade, among some policymakers.[111] The Project for the New American Century, for instance, in the year 2000 spoke of the need for a 'substantial American force presence in the Gulf', which 'transcends the issue of the regime of Saddam Hussein'. The regime 'provides the immediate justification', but longer-terms pretexts are needed.[112] So it seems that the US-British strategy was to destroy Iraq with sanctions so they could build their permanent military bases there.

Didn't we leave Iraq years ago?

That was just propaganda. It gives the impression that we can leave Iraq to become a sovereign democracy. The reality is that the US and Britain did withdraw the majority of forces, but we set up the architecture to mould Iraq as we wanted it: training the police, army, navy, selling them weapons, and so on.[113] We sent more forces there when Daesh (a.k.a., the Islamic State) started taking over. After the supposed withdrawal and before Daesh, there were at least several hundred US military personnel and private contractors operating in permanent bases – there was talk of dozens of bases but there are certainly two major ones, Camp al-Asad being perhaps the biggest. The bases had their own bus routes, ice cream parlours, and so on. So American military personnel were protected behind fortified blast-proof concrete barriers, while what's left of the country disintegrated.[114]

But hasn't there been some kind of democracy installed in Iraq and doesn't it have independence now? It's not a puppet state, is it?

It's difficult to say because it's a mixed picture. There are Shia elements, Sunni elements, Kurdish elements, and others. Even people within these groupings don't all agree on their support for the government. For example, a lot of Sunni supported Saddam Hussein because they were part of the whole security-state infrastructure. He was their employer and a lot of Shia resented it. Shia were often the ones getting sent to torture chambers.[115] At the same time, the regime was so awful that many Sunni – like Shia – were pleased when it was overthrown. But most Iraqis wanted the US and Britain, having gotten rid of Saddam, to immediately withdraw in mid-2003.[116] In that context, it's very difficult to impose any kind of democratic system, but that wasn't the objective anyway.

Democracy was a PR exercise in Iraq. In 2005 you had Cambridge Analytica's parent organisation, the SCL Group, operating in Iraq to swing elections in favour of Western candidates.[117] But it looked good for the British and American publics to see Iraqis going into polling booths with little ink dots on their fingers to show they'd voted. But if you look at the political situation, the picture was very different. You had the 'elected' government of Nouri al-Malaki (2006–14) essentially carrying out ISIS-style repression of the public. According to Amnesty International and Human Rights Watch, under our puppet al-Maliki, a thousand Iraqis were on death row, many of them union leaders and students. Journalists were killed. Everyone in Europe went into mourning when *Charlie Hebdo* journalists were attacked in 2015, but who knows about the journalists killed in Iraq by the US-British-imposed government? That was hardly reported. Perhaps you could find references to it at the margins, like in the *Guardian*. But it wasn't part of the public consciousness. The Iraqi police who were being trained and armed by Britain and America were drilling holes in prisoners' flesh.[118]

What did we see on the TV news? John Simpson walking around the streets of Baghdad in a market, saying that Iraq is returning to normal. By 2013, the war was in the past and everything was fine. That was the picture. Meanwhile, under the surface, you had a radical Islamic insurgency brewing – that turned out to be Daesh - and people working towards genuine, grassroots democracy were put on death-row or imprisoned and tortured by the government, as they had been under Saddam.

Is Iraqi society better now than under Saddam Hussein?

It's very hard to measure. Saddam's state was a torture and killing machine, which Britain and America enabled. Saddam fought a war with Iran, in which a million people on both sides died. So in the context of casualties, injuries and trauma from war, you could argue it was just as bad. However, for others it was worse under Saddam. For example, many Kurds felt that until Daesh came along, they were better off without him. Kurdistan was relatively untouched by the carnage wrought across the rest of the country after the 2003 invasion. In the 1980s, tens – maybe hundreds – of thousands of Kurds were wiped out in the *Anfal* genocide by Saddam, who was using British- and American-supplied weapons, including chemical weapons, for which we supplied the precursors.[119] So for Kurds, it was arguably better to live in a comparatively prosperous Kurdistan free from Saddam Hussein.

But then you compare Kurdistan to the rest of the country, and for most Iraqis the answer is no, though the polling data are mixed. Many Iraqis feel that at least under Saddam Hussein, they had clean water to drink. The sanctions and invasion in 2003 ruined that. At least under Saddam, you didn't have 4 million refugees, two million of whom were internally displaced. You didn't have intergenerational genetic mutations, as you have now in Fallujah, thanks to the US-British use of radiological warfare in 2004.[120] Though you did in Kurdistan, where he used US-British-supplied weapons, including chemical, to kill and deform Kurds in the '80s.

What kind of alternatives could we have taken over the past 15 years or so? What alternative was there for deposing Saddam? Smart sanctions? And wouldn't there have been consequences leaving him in power that would have been at least comparable?

We shouldn't have imposed sanctions at all. It's not for us or anybody to do anything, especially if it will harm civilians in that or any country. What we could have done is to sanction our own governments for selling arms and the chemical and biological weapons' precursors. There are laws against blanket sanctions, for example the Geneva Conventions, which prevent collective punishments. And there are democratic elements in Iraq like trade unions, which we crushed by supporting Saddam.

Even after the 1991 Gulf War, the options faced by the Western powers were a political vacuum that could have been filled by a grassroots, left-wing government, or keep Saddam in power while destroying the country with sanctions. The US chose to back Saddam rather than risk a political vacuum getting filled by a gov-

ernment antithetical to its interests. So the US authorised Saddam, even when he was still supposedly an
enemy after the Gulf War, to crush the joint Shia-
Kurdish uprising in 1991 that might have deposed
him.[121]

And would you want the Iraqis to have a left-wing government?

It's not up to me, it's up to Iraqis.

But if you could wave a magic wand...

I would just let Iraqis deal with their own affairs. If I
could wave a wand, Britain would not sell weapons to
any country and we would mind our own business.
And at a grassroots level, you could have associations
between Iraqi and British unions, say, and relatively
free movement of people, etc.

Wouldn't you just have Russia and China selling a lot more arms and filling that vacuum?

That's the reason often given by politicians who justify
the arms trade. But it makes no sense. If other countries are doing it anyway, why are we also doing it?
That question is never raised. From this point of view,
it follows that it makes no moral difference if we do it,
because everyone's doing it. But that also makes no
sense because criminals don't plead their defence by
saying, 'Other people are doing it'.

We're operating in an international context, so there's no reason why the British public couldn't push for an arms embargo, for example via the UN, in which we manufacture weapons for our own country, but it's made unlawful to sell them to another. But that's way off in the future – it's not the real world. We don't have magic wands.

If we do allow the Russians and Chinese to fill the arms vacuum, we've at least taken ourselves out of the moral equation, and we might then have more credibility when we talk about notions like humanitarian intervention.

I heard an interesting news report recently about Britain selling arms to Saudi Arabia while a government minister was saying, 'We're on the wrong side of this war. We need to live up to our moral obligations in the world...but we're still going to sell the arms'. Is that as bullshit as it sounds to me?

Politicians are all over the place. They're trying to serve multiple constituents. First of all, they get their statements written for them by Foreign Office bureaucrats, whom they regard as the experts, because they, the politicians, know little or nothing about foreign policy. Then they feel pressure from the Ministry of Defence, because not supporting our foreign policy is unpatriotic. Then they have pressure from the arms industry, the ones who help write foreign policy strategy documents.[122] There's pressure from constituents because they fear that if we stop selling arms and close down factories, they'll be out of a job and their local community that has an arms factory nearby will suffer. Politicians like the tax revenue that comes from arms sales.

In contrast to that, you've got organisations like Campaign Against the Arms Trade pointing out that it's illegal – despite what the High Court ruled[123] – to sell arms to brutal regimes committing war crimes, like Saudi Arabia. Other constituents, ordinary people, are asking why we're selling weapons at all in a brutal war.

So in that context, a politician's answers are going to be cognitively dissonant. You're going to get double-think and double-speak because it reflects the contradictory nature of the issue. That's why it's important to support politicians that oppose the arms trade and a violent foreign policy. Within this rigid system, we need to find political candidates who have a clear moral centre and who can also appease communities that rely on the arms industry by retraining workers to make renewable energy technologies, for example, instead of weapons. That way, advocating that the factory stays open, the arms company-cum-renewables firm profits, and everyone's happy, except the fanatical statist elites, of course.

If the world is really that bleak, isn't it all just hopeless? If we do something we'll kill a million people and if we don't a million people will die. Certain countries are just so screwed, maybe we should just blow it up?

Innocent people don't want to be blown up. As far as killing innocent people goes, we have to be specific. In the case of Iraq, we had non-violent choices for dealing with Saddam Hussein. When he killed the Kurds in the 1980s, for instance, we could have tried to stop him by not selling weapons and dual-use chemical components. It's also important to distinguish between people's grassroots actions and the actions of the government. The British government had every interest in supporting Saddam during his worst atrocities. But ordinary people could have put pressure on the British government to withdraw support, as could ordinary Americans with respect to their own governments. Solidarity movements could have been fostered, and so on.

How much suffering is British foreign policy actually causing?

It's like the question, 'Are Iraqis better off...?' It depends who we're talking about.

In the case of a small country like Papua, where the British are – or until recently were –training and arming the Indonesians, who are occupying half the country, Britain's role is relatively important.[124] Even if the UK's influence is small in the sense of just a few advisers training the Indonesian police, that training will have a disproportionate effect on Papuans, given how unbalanced the power dynamic is between the UK and Papua. Papua is nowhere near the size of the UK in terms of population, paramilitary skills or its economy. The Indonesians would go on repressing Papua anyway, without our help, but they would be less efficient without British training.

In the case of bigger countries, Britain's net influence is marginal, again because of the balance of power. When the British sell weapons to the US, for instance, that makes much less difference because the US is the world's biggest arms manufacturer and the sheer number of weapons it produces dwarfs the UK. However, if a child was killed, let's say, by an American bullet fired from a British-made gun, the parents would consider the UK's role in the microcosm of their lives very significant.

LESS
WAR
MORE
NHS

The threat from **TERRORISM IS OVERBLOWN**. Al Qaeda killed **THOUSANDS** on 9/11 but then just **HUNDREDS** in Bali, only **DOZENS** in London, and **NO ONE AT ALL** at Glasgow Airport. If we extrapolate based on existing data we find that within a few years Al Qaeda will have become a charity health organisation helping infertile American neoconservatives to make babies.

Chapter 4

Little Britain, big world?

Or: Why we're bigger than our leaders pretend...

Britain's just a faded power, a shadow of its former Empire. So who cares about our foreign policy?

People on the receiving end of it care – Afghans, Iraqis, and so on. And that's just the people most Britons know about. As I've documented elsewhere, Britain currently – or until recently has – trained death squads in Bangladesh, Colombia, Somalia, all over the place. We're the second biggest arms dealer in the world now,[125] though that changes every few years. And, from a selfish point of view, when we get so-called 'blowback' in the form of terrorism, which is largely a reaction to our foreign policy, the victims and their friends and families care. Part of the role of propaganda is to make it unthinkable that terrorism is caused in large measure by our foreign policy. You're not even supposed to *think* that, let alone raise the question. The media went ballistic – no pun intended – when the leader of the opposition, Jeremy Corbyn, timidly said that we should recognise the role our foreign policy plays in creating terrorists. The trouble is, the polls show that most people agree with him![126]

It's a fascinating appraisal of the achievements of propaganda that significant numbers of British people can simultaneously agree with Corbyn but also be convinced that he's a threat to our 'national security' – whatever that means – by being weak on foreign policy.[127] And who is levelling these accusations of danger at him, that he's a sympathiser with terrorists? Theresa May. Who is Theresa May? She was Home Secretary when the so-called security services – another propaganda term – had what experts call an 'open door' policy in the early-2010s. They were using *jihadis* from all over the world to fight proxy wars in Syria and Libya. The so-called 'moderate rebels' that we hear about are largely head-chopping, Daesh-style Islamists who were closely allied to the state.[128] Yet, it's Corbyn who's called a supporter of terrorists! After the Manchester Arena bombing in 2017, the May government should have collapsed. The alleged perpetrator, Salman Abedi, had been allowed to train with Daesh in Libya because of this 'open door policy'.[129] And his father, Ramadan, had been granted asylum because he was part of a terrorist group – the Libyan Islamic Fighting Group – which MI6 paid to depose Gaddafi in the '90s. Again, it's remarkable that the Tories can get away with almost nobody noticing this.

I think also, if British people knew that their tax money – about £500 per head, per annum – was going to the military to defend an economic order from which they don't personally benefit, they'd care very much.

But I don't agree with the premise of your question, anyway. Yes, compared to the days of Empire, when Britain alone controlled over 20% of global GDP, its power has faded. Today, it controls just under 4%. But compared to other countries – that's still enormous, considering it has about 0.8% of the world's population. Russia's share of global GDP is half that of Britain's, even though its population is more than double the size.[130]

After WW2, the British political establishment understood that if they wanted to continue playing a role in shaping the global order in the interests of British corporations, they'd have to play second fiddle to the USA. By then, the Soviets had built up quite an impressive military, though it was nothing compared to the might of America – despite all the Cold War propaganda. In fact, studies by the US establishment show that the Soviets were using US technology to build up their armed forces, and often with components sold to them by US corporations.[131] But that's just business as usual: help enemies for short-term profit. The French Empire never reached the heights – or lows, depending on how you look at it – of the British, but by the end of the Second World War, they were about equal to the UK in terms of the power they had to crush the so-called third world.

So until the rise of Asia, such as it is, in the 1980s and '90s, the main powers were the USA and the Soviets, and Britain, France, and eventually Germany.

Turning to Britain today, let's look at the facts about this so-called irrelevant nation. Britain is the fifth or sixth biggest economy in the world by GDP, depending on the year. About 20% of that is with the

City of London Corporation,[132] as are the foreign policy decisions. So 'Britain' really means London, and a particular class of London. What influence did the people in the Grenfell Tower have over British foreign policy? None – same as a guy sitting in Devon in a shed. We're talking about a tiny number of people, usually from the upper classes, making decisions about the future of the nation and its role in the affairs of others. We should also remember that, despite cuts to the armed forces, Britain retains its so-called 'global reach'. That means the power to deploy forces and beat enemies anywhere in the world – something even China doesn't have.[133] When Argentine generals authorised the invasion of the Falkland Islands – which don't even belong to Britain, legally speaking, the—

Wait, wait, wait! Hang on. Are you saying the Falkland Islands aren't British?!

The Argentines call them Malvinas. They were taken from Spain by Britain in 1765. The UN has since declared that Argentina, which is a former Spanish colony, and the UK should work peacefully together to decolonise them, which the UK refuses to do, despite Argentina's efforts.[134] Until oil was discovered there by UNESCO in the 1970s, the islands were becoming a liability and the government was looking for a way to hand them over without looking weak. Even now-declassified Foreign Office memos say that we could end up looking like 'international bandits'[135] by holding on to islands that aren't even ours. So Britain refuses to work with Argentina to resolve the issue. A few years back, when the Kirchner government raised the issue at the United Nations, Britain's Cameron government went berserk, sending a 'nuclear submarine' – it was implied that the sub was nuclear-armed – to 'defend' the islanders—

But shouldn't they be defended?

Against a possible effort by Argentina to kick them off? They should, but by the United Nations. Not by the British armed forces, which has no legal right to maintain a colonial territory, which is what the Falklands are.

But you just said they belong to Argentina, so how can the British people living there be defended if they have no right to—

No. I didn't say the islands belong to Argentina. I said they *don't* belong to Britain. There's a difference. It's not up to me to decide who they belong to. I'm just citing the historical facts, that they were taken from Spain and that Argentina is a former Spanish colony, now independent, and I'm citing international law—

So do they belong to Spain, since we took them from Spain?

Not according to any legal specialist I've read.[136] If Britain does what it's obliged to do and decolonises, the islands would likely go to Argentina under the principle of *uti possideti* (as you possess under law). But that's not for me to decide. Personally, I think the issue should go to the International Court of Justice, but Argentina is afraid of losing and Britain knows it doesn't have a leg to stand on, so it's in the interests of both parties not to say anything. As for the people there, I do *not* want to see them forcibly removed as an act of decolonisation. If the UK abandons them and they want to become an independent people, called Falklanders instead of British, then they can form an army and take their case for independence to the UN. But that's not going to happen. I also think that the UN should provide some military protection for them in case Argentina uses force to remove them. But this is all hypothetical—

So what about Gibraltar?

As far as I can tell, that does belong to us, legally speaking. But there are some unresolved issues about Spanish shipping rights.

But anyway, getting back to Britain's influence in the world. When the Falklands were invaded and PM Margaret Thatcher sent the armed forces to fight the Argentines. The mythology is that we nearly lost because Britain's power was diminished. In the real world, we had 20,000 troops still stationed in Germany—

Are you saying we were occupying Germany in the '80s?

We still are, last time I checked. They don't call it occupation, of course. And the Germans still have a lot of guilt about WW2, so they don't tell us to get out. The number of forces based in Germany – as a 'symbol of friendship', as the British government calls it[137] – was 20,000 in 2010. But now I think it's less. The Germans just accepted this. Unlike the US bases in Japan, where the Japanese public regularly hold protests, there were no Germans protesting the British presence, as far as I can tell.

Anyway, getting back to the Falklands and the point about 'global reach': The reason we struggled at first, before winning what historians call a 'decisive victory' – is that 1) it was mostly a naval operation, we didn't escalate, thankfully, by bombing targets in Buenos Aires and 2) that reliance – mainly, but not entirely – on a single arm of the military meant that ships that were in the Persian Gulf intimidating Iran and Iraq, had to suddenly be deployed thousands of miles away—

But wasn't that a good thing, kicking out the Argies?

There were no civilian casualties, but obvious war crimes were committed.

For one thing, we now know that Thatcher deployed a nuclear-armed submarine – nuclear armed. That could have escalated into a serious international situation. Threats are a violation of the UN Charter, which was adopted after World War 2, supposedly to prevent war, not legitimise bullying. Britain and Argentina both violated a UN Security Council resolution calling for an end to hostilities on both sides.[138]

Then you had specific war crimes, like the sinking of the retreating Argentine vessel, the *Belgrano* – which was sold to Argentina by the US, it was called the *USS Phoenix*, but it never rose again – where Britain killed 323 people – around half of all Argentine deaths in the war.

Then there's the psychological impact of war – the families on both sides who lost loved ones. There's the famous veteran Simon Weston, he was just a kid at the time, 19 or 20. He has permanent facial disfigurements. It's understandable that he calls people like me who challenge the narrative 'idiots'. There's a veteran of the special services who lives near me. He was obviously traumatised by the war. He's a very decent man, always asks how you are and offers to help. But he drinks a lot and any conversation you have with him eventually descends into surreal nonsense, and then about Jesus and salvation.

So that's what war does. And this was nearly repeated in 2012, when Kirchner complained to the UN about the UK's policy of refusal. Polls conducted at the time were shocking. They not only said that most Brits support a second Falklands War, they implied that most people in the UK would be willing to use nuclear weapons to defend the islands![139] That shows the incredible achievements of propaganda and the education system. First of all, that nobody seems to realise that we have no legal title to the islands. Second, that nobody seems to realise that UN Peacekeepers exist for these kind of situations. Third, that even from a purely self-interested view, we should not use nuclear weapons. Ever. That could cause serious environmental damage which, if escalated, could make life unliveable for everyone. I suppose the worst part of it is the fanatical nationalism. With issues like this, otherwise rational people are driven to madness, where they'd even potentially support nuclear war to defend islands that most Britons couldn't even point to on a map and don't even know that the islands don't belong to us. Here I think the media are very dangerous.

Because they make people do crazy things?

They set the framework of understanding – or misunderstanding. So if your frame of reference is incorrect, your conclusions are not only going to be wrong, but in this case potentially catastrophic.

But Britain is respected throughout the world. How do you explain that?

By who? Certainly not by Argentines, except perhaps some of the upper classes who are quite happy to have British investment pouring in. The US establishment doesn't respect us. The US establishment uses our expertise in counterinsurgency – which means keeping foreign masses oppressed – in its own wars. Europe now considers Britain a threat, given its arrogant position in the Brexit negotiations. Britain brazenly announced that it didn't need or want Europe. Its elites use the 'Global Britain', post-Brexit slogan. They appointed a racist, Boris Johnson, as Foreign Secretary, refusing to guarantee residency rights for EU citizens already living here, and so on. In fact, most Europeans have never considered Britain part of Europe, given how insular the culture is. When I go to France, for instance – my partner is French – you hear French, Spanish, and English music on the radio in taxis. It's more culturally diverse. Here, there's nothing but American and British music on the radio. That's just a small example of our comparative cultural insularity, which Europeans resent.

Then there's the Commonwealth, whose citizens people like former Foreign Secretary Boris Johnson insults by calling them 'piccaninnies' (young black children),[140] saying that they'd still be eating 'plantains'[141] were it not for the civilised colonists who taught them how to mass-produce monocultures, poison themselves with pesticides, and sacrifice their self-sufficient livelihoods to the whims of the international food market. It's true that plenty of people love the idea of monarchy. But they tend to be the class of Commonwealth citizens whose ancestors mostly benefited from the Empire. In any imperial situation, you've got two oppressed classes: the domestic majority, who have to fund the empire through taxation and go off and kill, and die in its wars. In addition, the elite class of the Empire at home does very well, getting fat off the 'spoils' – a word used even today by neo-imperialists, like the historian Niall Ferguson[142] – and so does the super-rich, corrupt, collaborator class.

You see it today in Palestine, for example. The Palestinian Authority – whose police forces are trained by Britain and US, incidentally[143] – is led by wealthy sell-outs who help keep the population of the West Bank oppressed on behalf of Israel, which in turn works on behalf of the USA. So in the British Commonwealth, this collaborator class loves Britain, because they've done very well out of the Empire. The Rwandan farmer whose land is being privatised by the Department for International Development doesn't feel so keen.

Does that happen?

It's happening. That's another scam that would outrage the public if they knew about it. There's a kleptocratic system in place, where the public hands tax money over to the Department for International Development under the cover of an international aid programme, and all that happens is that foreign resources are privatised – including land, water, electricity, and so on – and British companies make a mint from low-cost resources and international markets. So the invasion of Libya by NATO in 2011 – which acted as an air force for the anti-Gaddafi terrorists – was sold to the public as a humanitarian intervention by the Prime Minister who led it, David Cameron. He pointed out that Tony Blair had made a deal with Gaddafi – with BP, to explore Libya's energy, it turns out – and Cameron turned that to his advantage. He said, 'While Labour were doing those dodgy deals with dictators in the desert ... we – the people of this party', meaning the Tories, 'were out volunteering in Rwanda, building schools and teaching English, showing what real compassion means in practice'.[144] This is why nobody but elites takes Britain seriously:

The leader of Rwanda at the time, and today, was Paul Kagame, an ethnic Tutsi. Kagame makes Gaddafi look like a small-time thug by comparison. Kagame fled Rwanda and lived in Uganda, where many Rwandan Tutsi refugees were based in the 1980s. He joined the Rwandan Patriotic Front (RPF) with the intention of 'returning' to Rwanda, which meant invading and taking over. He was trained by the US at Fort Leavenworth[145] and armed by France. Kagame played a significant role in two – not one, but *two* – genocides. The first was Rwanda, when the RPF invaded and starting slaughtering 800,000 Hutu, men, women, and children – not just with machetes as the propaganda said, but mainly with assault rifles and rocket-launchers. And the other was the ongoing genocide in Congo, which is not targeting a specific group but is such a bloody civil war that it's reached the levels of genocide – about 4 million people killed. So here you have Cameron praising Britain's role in Rwanda by working with a double-genocidist, a dictator, and a guy opening the country to British land privatisation. Only an ignorant and well-indoctrinated public could hear that and not fall open-mouthed in astonishment. The BBC, for instance, has articles on its website with headlines like, 'Rwanda's Paul Kagame – visionary or tyrant?'.[146] Imagine the BBC praising Gaddafi for making Libya the best country in Africa in terms of human health indices and then asking, 'Gaddafi – visionary or tyrant?'.

While the Arab Spring was happening in Libya, Cameron praised it, saying that the people of Libya should rise up against oppression. That's because we wanted Gaddafi overthrown. At the very same time, Cameron was in Kuwait telling the Kuwaiti government – you can read the transcript on the government's website[147] – to do whatever is necessary to maintain order. This implied killing protestors if necessary. That's because we wanted the Kuwaiti government to stay in power.

But you just said that BP had a deal with Gaddafi. So wouldn't we want him there?

No, because part of the deal was to make reforms – meaning open the country to US, British, French and Italian oil and gas companies. Libya has the largest reserves of oil in North Africa. But Gaddafi wasn't making the 'reforms'. Technical publications, like oil journals, and investment brochures, like the European Union's Libya 2020 strategy, said the reforms were only 'cosmetic', so Gaddafi had to go.[148] In fact, the WikiLeaks emails reveal that Cameron and Sarkozy – the French President at the time – were in meetings with the anti-Gaddafi terrorists, who we call 'rebels', to ensure that oil and gas companies can still get their mitts on the only thing that matters.[149]

Some of your sources at least look a bit dodgy. In one book, you cite Lyndon LaRouche, the batshit crazy guy from the USA, and the sleazy British tabloid, the *Daily Star*. Should people take you seriously when you use some of this material?

You're talking about *Britain's Secret Wars*. First of all, 99% of the sources there are primary – the British Parliament, arms export documents, Chatham House studies (Chatham House being funded by arms and oil companies) – or mainstream, *Times*, the *Guardian* and so on. So the general question is, 'Do I take statements out of context or invent things that aren't there?'. No one's accused me of that. So the 'dodgy sources' as you say, are so few and far between we should examine them on a case-by-case basis:

In the case of the *Daily Star*, the journalist who wrote the piece from which I quoted was being fed propaganda by the Ministry of Defence. They quoted a security source who said that Britain's decision to send navy vessels to the Strait of Hormuz during a period of tension with Iran a few years ago, was 'all about petrol prices'. So it's the *Daily Star*. Does that mean they invented the quote? Does that mean we shouldn't listen to the MoD official, just because his statement was printed exclusively in that tabloid? The newspaper was saying (paraphrase), 'Our brave boys are off fighting for us in Iranian waters'. So it was propaganda for the Armed Forces, and in a circuitous way the oil companies. Often, the right-wing papers are more honest because they don't see anything wrong with gung-ho militarism. In fact, they love it.

In the case of Lyndon LaRouche, I wasn't quoting him or his associates. I was quoting a local Welsh newspaper which was quoted in an article published in a journal owned by LaRouche, *Executive Intelligence Review* (EIR). The journal, like any, is mixture of nonsense and facts. But that's beside the point. I was quoting the Welsh newspaper but I found the quote in EIR. So unless you're a plagiarist, you cite the source where you found the quote, not the original source. People like the journalist Phil Miller don't like the fact that I discovered Britain's involvement in the massacre in Sri Lanka that happened ten years ago, where 40,000 Tamil civilians were wiped out in 2 months. Miller wanted to get there first and expose that, but I suppose he feels like I stole his thunder. In private emails, he even accused me of plagiarising his work! This kind of competitive attitude is pathetic, when real lives are being destroyed. We should be working together, not nitpicking each other's sources.

That's been my biggest disappointment with the book, *Britain's Secret Wars*: the fact that the progressive, anti-war crowd didn't take to it. It was reviewed in *Peace News*, and all the reviewer Ian Sinclair could do was focus on a couple of the more questionable claims and ignore the 99% of solid evidence—

But shouldn't a serious book be 100% solid?

Name one book that doesn't have a flaw. Or one that you agree with 100%. I think the real reason that people on the so-called progressive left didn't like it is that the book forces us to take responsibility for the actions of our own government. People are happy to protest Iraq, for instance, because that was a US-led war. Or to criticise Israel because that's someone else committing atrocities. But what about our own involvement in Israel's oppression of Palestinians? There's a moral issue, 'What should we be doing about our own governments?'. But if you don't have the same moral ideas, there's also a tactical question, 'If we want to make the world a better place, do we waste time criticising foreign governments that we can't influence, or do we weaken the power of those governments by making our own governments withdraw support from them?'.

I was quite deeply involved in Palestine solidarity when I lived in Exeter. There's a group there and I did a lot of activities. They were generally happy with me suggesting vigils, helping to set up stalls, posting petitions, and so on. But as soon as I suggested that we target the British police for training the Israeli police, and being trained by them, they were much less enthusiastic. The funniest time was when a member of the group asked me if I knew who trained the Sri Lankan military during its ethnic cleansing of Tamils. Naively, I thought she was going to say Britain. She said, 'It was Israel!'.

And was it?

It was Israel as well, according to *Electronic Intifada*[150] – an admittedly anti-Israeli publication – yes. That's because the US, which was also involved, contracts Israel out to train other armies on its behalf. The power of the US is such that it's hard to grasp.

But anyway, the point is that when I told this person that Britain had trained the Sri Lankans, too, she went very quiet. As long as we can criticise others, it's fine. You see this all the time in the US – it's the Zionist lobby really controlling US foreign policy, it's 'globalists' trying to undermine America, it's the British Empire, which hasn't really died – that's the LaRouche line. Anything but take responsibility for ourselves. We see that in the UK, too. Take the ongoing outrage in the British media about Donald Trump's policy of separating refugee and migrant women from their children. Before we criticise that, why not first look at our own horrendous facilities? Like the Yarl's Wood refugee and migrant removal centre, which effectively holds women and children in captivity in sickening conditions.

You talk about 'responsibility', but what responsibility do I have for what David Cameron or Theresa May does?

If you don't accept the designation 'British', maybe you – and therefore none of us – has responsibility. Some people feel that if we pay taxes, we are responsible for what's done with our tax money. But tax is basically legalised theft. You go to prison if you don't pay. So you could just as well argue that no one has responsibility, except the people planning and executing the wars.

So let's not think of it as a matter of responsibility. Let's think of it as a matter of personal concern. Do you care that people are suffering? If so, do you care enough to dedicate some of your time to helping them, to making the world a better place? Maybe you don't. Maybe you do, but you've got too much going on in your life – work and family concerns, etc. But if you care enough and have enough motivation, you have to think tactically. Do we rant against others, like Israel, because expressing moral outrage – 'virtue signalling' as they call it now – makes us feel better? Or do we ask, 'What's the best way to help suffering people?'. As far as I can see, the best way is to look where the power lies. The power lies with the state. The state has the power to sell arms or not sell arms, train death squads or not train them. So if we agree that the state has power, we then ask, 'What's most practical?'. Is it more practical to get British people to protest against Israeli foreign policy in Palestine or Lebanon? Or to put pressure on our own governments and corporations not to sell weapons to Israel? Or pick whichever country you like.

The sense of paranoia and confusion running through the streets
of the down and gritty. The trapped corner of enjoyement ~~called hell~~
blessed from hell that people enjoy to suffer pretty.
The crazed disgraced that smacks the welcoming good
in the face, but the ruling wine cooler that locks you
up in a horrid place.

Pentagon satellites can read a newspaper **OVER YOUR SHOULDER** all the way from space. If they're that tight **WHY DON'T THEY JUST NICK ONE** from the first class carriages like the rest of us?

Chapter 5

Conspiracies, from reptilians
to false-flags

*Or: Why some people believe bullshit and others refuse
to face facts...*

Aren't you just a conspiracy theorist?

I think a definition of 'conspiracy theory' would be helpful, because it's such a blanket term. Conspiracy is also a broad spectrum. At one end there's a clear legal definition of conspiracy, for which people can go to prison. The legal definition is a plot, arranged in secret, to do something illegal for personal, political, or even financial gain. There's no question that conspiracies in that sense occur, otherwise laws against them wouldn't exist. And there are plenty of cases of people being sentenced on conspiracy charges – terrorists, for instance. So that's one end of the spectrum. It's clear and easy to prove.

Then, at the other extreme, you have absurd ideas about how the world works, such as the idea that reptilian creatures secretly rule the world. So on that wide and diverse spectrum we can look for evidence and ways to evaluate it. Take, say, the reptilian-lizard idea. The main proponent, David Icke, finds references to lizard-like beings in the mythology of various cultures throughout history. He collects testimonies from people today who believe they've seen shape-shifting lizards, and he concludes, on that basis, that the lizards are real and have been here for millennia.[151] There's a kind of logic to that, but the evidence connecting the dots is so tenuous as to be non-existent. And it's a good illustration of how an erroneous logical basis can lead to preposterous conclusions.

It's also worth remembering that people in power tend to be the biggest conspiracy theorists. They see conspiracies against them and their interests everywhere, hence the creation of a massive surveillance infrastructure. Elites of all stripes feel the need to retain their power, which makes them very paranoid. They have rivals in their own class, rivals in the form of the lower classes whom they suppress, rival governments, and so on. They constantly have to act in ways that maintain their power, which is no easy feat.

Take, for example, the Combination Acts (1799–1800). At the beginning of the 18th century, about 3% of English people had the right to vote – according to the National Archives, that's about 214,000 people.[152] They were mainly the aristocracy. Over the centuries, ordinary working-class people pushed for political representation and safety-in-numbers in the form of unions, or combinations as they were called then. The elites of the day, including business owners, were terrified about people plotting in secret to organise for better pay and working conditions. So laws were passed to make it illegal to form combinations. The elites were the original conspiracy theorists, only their target was the population. Parliament was secret for centuries. It was only with Hansard, the transcripts, that ordinary people got to read what was being said in Parliament. If you look at the digitalised debates of the early 19th century, you find politicians referring to each other as conspiracy theorists. So by the early-20th century, it had become a political term of abuse used by elites against members of their own class.[153]

So the term conspiracy theorist was used in the 19th century in England? We often hear that the term was popularised by the CIA in the 1960s as a way to deal with difficult questions about the JFK murder.

People who believe that conspiracies run the world – and they're right in some cases – get very defensive when that label is applied to them, understandably. So they cite a CIA memo and turn the accusation back on the accuser, that the accuser is inadvertently a CIA puppet because the CIA is promoting the term 'conspiracy theory' to discredit those who get too close to the truth. The trouble is, the memo they cite doesn't actually say much about conspiracies. It says that too many people are asking uncomfortable questions about JFK, which is a propaganda coup for the Soviets because it makes the US look bad. So in order to counter this, the CIA and its assets should present 'facts' about JFK to the public – that it really was Oswald who killed him.[154]

Obama's advisor, Cass Sunstein, had a similar idea. He wrote a paper advocating what he called 'cognitive infiltration', to help people gain trust in government by debunking conspiracy theories.[155] Then, coincidentally or not, you get websites like Metabunk.org popping up, self-styled conspiracy debunking sites. The CIA memo says the same thing, use information to counter conspiracy theorising, which hurts the US's credibility. It doesn't talk about slandering truth-seekers as conspiracy theorists. That CIA memo and the way it's been handled says a lot about the so-called conspiracy community in a nutshell: taking one tiny fragment of evidence, interpreting it incorrectly, and then running with it. So it might have been popularised in the 1960s, but the actual term 'conspiracy theorist' goes further back in time. You have books like John Robeson's *Proofs of a Conspiracy* (1797) – which made claims against Freemasons. Powerful people were seeing plots everywhere from the public.

Weren't they right about that, that people were moving against them?

Yes, but they took it to such a degree they were obviously paranoid. And the public pushed in a nonviolent way. The Chartists, for example, led the way for the right to vote. It was as late as 1884 with the Third Reform Act that working men over the age of 21, not women at that point, not even men of 18, got the right to vote. So these were very minimal rights they were demanding and, again, doing so non-violently.

And did the elites get wrongly paranoid that the Chartists and others were plotting violence? Were the elites literally thinking that the workers were reptiles or plotting to blow up Parliament?

Only in their own minds. You can always find aberrations, but objective history – if there is such a thing – shows that the examples of social revolution in the UK, unlike in France, were overwhelmingly nonviolent. In fact, the modern Conservative Party was founded largely in response to what was happening in France with the Revolution.[156] But in the UK, there was a mass movement that demanded pretty minimal rights and that came at the minimal expense of elites, who had to sacrifice absolute power. So in that regard, there was no threat to the existence of elites by the working classes. But in their minds, it was an extreme threat. They thought the working classes would destroy them by changing the power dynamic.

That's why I say elites are the ultimate conspiracy theorists. Nowadays, this has been inverted so anyone who questions power is a conspiracy theorist. The psychologist Michael J. Wood calls the conspiracy label a way of 'pathologizing dissent', though it doesn't appear to be very effective in changing people's minds, he says.[157] As for the question, 'Did the elite think the peasants were reptiles?', they certainly considered them vermin. If you read Christopher Hill's histories, the elite regularly refer to commoners as vermin.[158] MI5 had a file on Hill, by the way. They suspected him of being a 'communist' and were worried about

his corrupting influence on the minds of the young –
more evidence of elite paranoia.[159]

Why do so many people buy into the more irrational wing of conspiracy theorising?

We have to look at specific cases. After 9/11, for example, a famous Zogby poll suggested that 50% of New
Yorkers thought that 9/11 was either an inside-job or
was allowed to happen. Most people, if you present a
case, could agree that the Bush administration at least
allowed 9/11 to happen – and that's pretty clear now,
with headlines like '9/11 Bombshell: Bush Knew' (*New
York Post*) – because it served their interests. This is
indicated by the Project for the New American Century's *Rebuilding America's Defenses* document, which came
out a year before 9/11. PNAC was basically the Bush
administration in waiting. It had practically the same
members. In the document, they yearned for what
they called 'a catastrophic and catalyzing event' to justify a new century of US military domination: space
weapons, tearing up missile treaties to expand ICBMs,
drones to 'project US power' globally, permanent forces in the oil-rich Gulf, and so on.[160] So it's rational to
allow a major terrorist attack to occur if your goal is
world domination.

However, when you then claim that the Bush administration *engineered* 9/11, that it was an inside-job,
that's when things become less credible in the minds
of ordinary people. The Bush administration was a
group of self-interested neo-cons. They had connections to the intelligence services, like the President's

father being the former head of the CIA. The Vice President, Dick Cheney, was a former bigwig at Halliburton. Secretary of Defense Rumsfeld had a background in private business, and so on. But how can these civil servants have enough power and influence to orchestrate something like 9/11? That's the thinking of the average American or European. That's the perspective from which most people are coming at the problem—

I'm going to disagree with you, here, and it's a bugbear I have with those who disparage the 9/11 insidejob theory. Yes, the idea that the Bush administration planned 9/11 is totally ridiculous. They're not going to have sat around a cabinet meeting of 40 people and said, 'Any other business?' 'Oh yeah, we should destroy the World Trade Center next Tuesday'. That's a straw man argument. But there can still be a conspiracy if one person in the American state knew what was happening – it could have been the head of the CIA, a director of Halliburton, or just a bloke working at an insurance company in the Twin Towers. By definition, that would still be an American, elite-based conspiracy.

There's nothing to disagree about, because that's exactly what I was going to come on to—

It's frustrating listening to people like Noam Chomsky on this. He makes the obvious case that the Bush ad-

ministration didn't do it. But that's missing the point entirely. Of course the idea of the Bush administration doing it is just fucking ridiculous. But it could easily have been a nexus with the state-corporate apparatus. It could have been two people or ten people.

From the point of view of the general public, they see 9/11 conspiracy theorists as being people who think 'Bush did it'. And maybe, technically, permission had to come from the top, ultimately. But who knows?

So getting back to what I was saying: The public has one view, 'How can civil servants pull off something like that?'. But 9/11 was basically a military operation. The timing, execution, efficiency. So if it was an inside-job, the only people with the power and self-protection to do something like that would be either the US military or at least clandestine special operations units within the military. However, there was a general cultural understanding among top military brass and the political executive that the survival of the US as a great Empire was under threat and that excuses were needed to accelerate total US global domination. And you can see the power that the military has over the political class from the 9/11 Commission transcripts – not the nonsense that made it into the final report, but the archived testimonies. As soon as the politicians questioned the military, they got stone-walled.[161] So yes, the 'Bush did it' hypothesis is ridiculous, and so conspiracy theories about 9/11 seem ridiculous from that narrow perspective. But when you widen the perspective, you gain credibility. Consider the Pentagon, the CIA, other agencies. They are highly secretive and have ultimate protection from disclosure and prosecution under various national security legislation. They have black budgets, compartmentalised operations, and they have a track-record of carrying out false-flag attacks, at least in other countries. When you consider the military-intelligence element of the equation, the conspiracy becomes much more credible.

We do have an historical analogue to the issue of military units operating successfully in secret. During the Vietnam War there was a project called Operation Popeye (1967–72), a weather modification programme, which involved the US military dispersing silver iodide into the skies above Vietnam to flood out the Ho Chi Minh trail, and probably destroy food production through flooding.[162] This went on for years with only a few hundred individuals knowing about it: the top-level executive, the unit undertaking the programme, and not many others. It was later revealed in the Pentagon Papers and reported by Seymour Hersh and others. There was a Congressional hearing about it. We learn from the Congressional evidence that the Defense Secretary, Melvin Laird, had initially told Congress that they were not modifying the weather. Then, when the documents were leaked, 'Oh, yeah, we *have* been weaponising the weather' (paraphrase). Assuming he was being truthful, even Laird didn't know – and he was Defense Secretary![163]

So if a secret operations unit could manipulate the weather for years with literally a few dozen people in the know, it's not such a stretch of the imagination to think that a small black ops unit in the Pentagon could have carried out 9/11. Once the job is done, the media and most intellectuals fall into place like a herd of sheep, bleating without question the 'al-Qaeda' line.

And why do people believe all the crazy bits of conspiracies, like Bush or Obama are alien reptoids?

Remember that people call us crazy, too, simply because we believe – and have what we think is convincing evidence – that 9/11 was an inside-job. As if it's so outlandish that in the absence of real threats, elements within the most powerful organisation in human history, the US state, would attack members of its own population to justify a new century of global domination. Equally, we think people who can't see the evidence are crazy or at least in denial. That's why you need science in order to have some grounding. Science is flawed – seriously flawed – but it's the best we can do. So on that broad spectrum, where at one end you believe everything the authorities tell you, all the way across to the other end, where you believe that everyone in authority is a literal demonic entity, you have to have some sensible methods for evaluating evidence. And with conspiracies, where information is not only classified but probably not even written down anywhere, it's tough.

But it's a very interesting anthropological and sociological question. It's something that's interested me for years, 'Why do people believe absolute nonsense?'. We should remember that we're talking about a very small number of people – 4% of Americans believe in the reptiles.[164] The more outlandish stuff can become a cult. With organised religion, you can understand it. You're born into it, your family practises it, and your culture is tied to it. So to reject organised religion, even if believing it is a form of madness, is to reject everything in your culture. In doing so, you run the risk of making yourself a social pariah. From an evolutionary perspective, following the group makes some degree of sense. You ensure your survival by integrating into the group's customs. So that's a plausible answer for religion. But very few people are born into a conspiracy cult. So what attracts them to it?

Let's take two cases at opposite ends of the spectrum: David Icke and Alex Jones. They seem to be the most well-known conspiracy researchers, shall we say. They're both very different. Alex Jones started as a libertarian, which in America basically means getting rid of government and giant corporations but championing smaller corporations and entrepreneurs. It's very different from European libertarianism, which at least in theory is social-democratic, despite its being an elite, liberal concept.[165] American libertarians tend to want to dismantle social security and keep healthcare private, because they see taxation as tyranny, not in the social good. They're basically anarco-capitalists, as they ridiculously call it. That's the idea that if you eliminate government and let free enterprise reign, there can be prosperity for all.[166]

Incidentally, most conspiracy theorists have tended throughout history to be right-wing.[167] I think it dates back to the founding of the United States on European libertarian principles, at least in the minds of the founders. The reality for natives, black people, women, and the lower-classes was somewhat different. Those who came out of the counter-Enlightenment tradition criticised the Founding Fathers for being Freemasons.

They said the Masons were corrupting Christianity. So given that the Church has been traditionally right-wing, it's not surprising that the cultural foundations for right-wing conspiracy theorising were laid early on, in the US at least. Today, the doctrines of ultra-right neoliberalism, or 'anarcho-capitalism' have replaced the Church, hence the annual Anarchapulco conference organised by the kind of people who believe in a central, globalist conspiracy. I don't know if they're joking, but their slogan is 'Make anarchy great again!'. Keeping with the spirit of voluntary association, you can attend in sunny Mexico for just $395.[168]

Well, all this says something about the kind of people who'd listen to Alex Jones. They tend to be fairly well-off, but not mega-rich. Poor people – even many employed poor – rely on social security subsidies and government support, so they can't champion that form of libertarianism. It's only the upper-middle-classes, who rely on a dependent lower-class, that can support it. In the early days of his career, the mid-1990s, Jones was not necessarily supporting Republicans or Democrats. He appealed to a significant number of Americans by working on local radio and public access television. He was picked up by a major network, GCN – which is Christian, so we're back to the right-wing element. It's also possible that he has CIA connections. Not that anything he says can be believed *prima facie*, but he said once in an interview that his family used to take in Soviet dissidents living in the US.[169]

Jones's theme, even in the early days, was that a cabal of what he called 'globalists' were selling out America to the British, Chinese, whoever. That they were jealous of America's success. Before long he was spouting outright lies. One of the worst broadcasts was on the eve of the Millennium, when many of his volatile followers – militia-types[170] – were already paranoid about the 'new world order' coming to get them because of the supposed 'illuminati' significance of the year 2000. (Actually, in the mythology 2001 was the start of the Millennium, not 2000. So that itself was an inside-joke.) Jones was blaming every power failure, like a nuclear plant shutting down, on the Millennium Bug, saying that everything was spiralling out of control. He closed the show by saying that Russia had fired an ICBM with a nuclear warhead at the United States. Literally.[171]

Even back then, he was talking nonsense. But it was more realistic than the reptilian claims of David Icke—

Are you sure about that?

It was more realistic, but still far out. Some scientists were genuinely worried that the year 2000 would cause some technology to malfunction due to time-code resets, and so on. So it is vaguely credible that a nuclear plant may have problems because of that. (It wasn't true, though.) It is also vaguely credible that Russia might have experienced a missile malfunction and fired an ICBM to the US. There have been accidental near-launches. But to say that Putin is a lizard, the kind of thing that David Icke says (not that specifically), takes it to another level of insanity.

So to finish with Jones: He gained in popularity and his claims became more and more absurd, concluding with outright racism. He's claimed that the Black Lives Matter movement, perhaps the most important resistance movement of black Americans since the Civil Rights struggle, is really a communist plot to destroy America, funded by globalists like George Soros. But Jones was popular in part because he initially broke from the Republican-Democrat dialectic. He was apolitical in that sense. But as he became more politicised, he became a mouthpiece for Donald Trump, people—

Was YouTube's ban an infringement of Jones's freedom of speech?

I don't think so. YouTube is a private entity. Jones claims the opposite: that, as a social media platform, it's a public service. That may be true to a limited extent, but as a self-professed 'free market capitalist' – whatever that means – Jones has to abide by the rules of the private entities with which he works, YouTube in this case. Saying, 'I want to be a "free market" capitalist, but I also want private platforms to behave as if they're public services and protect freedom of speech', is called having your cake and eating it.

YouTube, by Jones's own admission, had repeatedly warned him about his 'offensive' content – again, whatever that's supposed to mean, upsetting Sandy Hook parents, for instance – and he violated YouTube's terms, the very terms to which he had agreed. That's a private contract between YouTube and Alex Jones. If you want to champion business, as he does, you have to abide by their rules.

The ban is more a reflection of the cynical nature of big corporations and their response to public activism than anything else. As long as no one complained to YouTube, Jones could denigrate whoever he liked: Muslims, Mexicans, immigrants in general, transgender people. As soon as public pressure mounted and YouTube, meaning its advertisers, were threatened with boycotts, they acted to make their platform more humane, meaning more profitable, by banning Jones's hate speech. More positively, it's also a reflection of how progressive society is gradually becoming. If a platform enables content to degrade certain peoples, it will not be financially viable in the long-term. The right-wing likes to twist that as a violation of freedom of speech. But very few are taking about shutting down Alex Jones completely.

I think that the more important question is, 'Should Jones be banned from the internet altogether?' I think not. I think he *should* be allowed to spout his offensive garbage, but on his own platform. Neither you nor I have a right to ban him or anyone else, any more than he has a right to ban us. If he upsets people, they can simply unsubscribe from his site or challenge his garbage, just as the right-wing can ignore or challenge us. So if the government banned him from every platform, *that* would be an infringement of his freedom of speech. That's wrong, in my view.

But kicking him off YouTube is only marginally an issue of freedom of speech. It's much more an issue of the rights of corporate power over individuals and private vs. public agreements. There's also the issue of money. Like it or not, the more money you have in our system, the more freedom you have. Jones is wealthy, as far as I can tell. He has plenty of funds to promote himself in the way that you and I don't. But no one's whining about our impaired freedom of speech caused by lack of funds. That's also a reflection of the culture.

You know what really fucks me off about Alex Jones? When people say, 'Yeah he doesn't always make sense but he knows a lot and he can talk for such a long time with amazing recall of information'. Well, yeah, but it's fucking garbage – disgusting, stupid, moronic, shouted, screaming horrible, vile garbage.

That's a good point about the style of presentation. There's a lot of anger in the United States. Not just in the USA, but everywhere. If you look at Quantcast and other data on who actually visits Alex Jones's website, it tends to be older, white men in the upper-middle-, but not highest, income brackets. These are the people who have seen the most obvious changes in their lives over the last 40 years – the same length of time as the neoliberal programmes. They've seen demographic changes, black people and Mexicans becoming more numerous. They've seen their wages stagnate or decline and they have no political representation.[172]

The Republicans mobilise them on issues that don't really matter, like social morality and Christian values. And the Democrats not only continue to undermine their socioeconomic status, they preach even more alien secular values, like abortion. So these people have a lot to be angry about. That's why Trump's biggest grassroots constituents were middle- and upper-middle-class white people, people earning over 50k a year, the same sort of people who listen to Alex Jones. Of course, you can always find exceptions.

If we turn to David Icke: Icke is generally more progressive than Alex Jones. Icke came out of the New Age meditation, New Age guru tradition. He has a similar audience to Alex Jones in terms of income and age. Not so much now, as younger people get interested, but when he started out, his audience was mostly older, middle-aged- to elderly people. The same kind of people who witness social changes and have no control over them. Even today, his audiences seem fairly well-off – it's not generally poor people that can afford £60 to listen to someone talk for ten hours.

So why do people believe in it? Icke comes across as spiritual. He talks about the nature of time, space, the meaning of life, and so on. These are universal themes which we all find interesting, and for which there are no real answers. He seems to be tapping into some kind of spirituality that's been lost, as we've become more secular and scientific. He's also tapping into people's creativity. Putting aside how silly it all is, it's quite creative, like a fun fantasy novel, to think that space-travelling lizards built the Moon and use it as a malign tool to influence our minds and bodies on an energetic level. Politics is so boring – and I wonder if that's deliberate, to make people disengage. But anyway, shape-shifting lizards makes politics more interesting.

I also wonder if listening to David Icke makes people feel better. We all have strange ideas about 'god' and the universe and how things work. With David Icke, you've got somebody who appears to be putting their neck on the line by saying, 'I believe in reptilians'. This provides a sense of relief that, 'Maybe I'm not so crazy after all, if this guy believes something so strange'. So maybe he's appealing to people's insecurities about their own helplessness? A friend of mine was very mentally disturbed. She grew up in an ultra-conservative Christian household. Her father abused her and her mother called priests in to exorcise her demons. She turned to drugs and prostitution and really saved herself through alternative health and meditation. But those 'demons' – figuratively – are still there. She's mad on David Icke. From what I could see, she related to Icke's omnipresent reptiles and compared them to her own demons. I suppose it was a way to forgive everyone who's done wrong by her, that they couldn't help abusing her because they're possessed by reptiles.

I went to Icke's Bristol 2018 talk and it went on for at least four hours. He talks about the 'hidden hand' but he never seems to reveal who these people are. At one point he says '…And the hidden hand is pissing itself'. And I'm like, what a garbled metaphor that is — how can a hand piss itself? And it's things like that which make me think Icke is a creative, poetic figure but he is astoundingly thick — he doesn't have an analytical part to his brain. He's just letting it all flood out of him, like a channel of diarrhoea going into the Heavens.

That's a nice image.

Flying into a portal of shit. That's David Icke's thought process. And we get splattered by it.

I don't want to resort to *ad hominem* by calling Icke stupid. It's fine for people to enjoy. His reptilian stories, I mean – not getting splattered. But, each to their own...

The numbers of people who follow David Icke and Alex Jones are relatively low, so it's statistically insignificant as far as enacting political change is concerned. But it does mean that people who regard themselves as serious researchers – and I'm sure David Icke regards himself as a serious researcher – get associated with the absurdities. So for example, it is a fact that explosive residue was found in the dust of the World Trade Center. *Bona fide* chemists thought this was significant and published their findings in a peer-reviewed journal.[173] It hasn't been retracted. That should set off alarm bells everywhere. But try raising the issue with journalists and academics and you're immediately associated with the lizards. When Icke was on the BBC talking to presenter Andrew Neil, it started well, talking about real conspiracies in the cabinet to undermine a hard Brexit. Then it moved onto 9/11. Soon 9/11 was conflated with the lizards. Neil says: 'I can see the point that you might question 9/11, but if you also think that Buckingham Palace is inhabited by lizards it kind of undermines you'.[174] And it undermines everyone else, like the chemists who found explosive residue in the dust of the WTC.

I agree, although actually I think the danger is a bit worse than you indicate. Two thousand people turned up to this ridiculous, long winded, flatulent talk in Bristol. How much of a good effect could those two thousand people have had if they're turned up to something more serious like a union meeting? It's a huge redirection of energy. I bet if you added a couple of thousand people to the Chartists, that'd surely have been significant. That alludes to another question about whether conspiracies are designed to distract.

I don't think so. As I say, the numbers of people that really follow conspiracies are politically insignificant. It's possible that Alex Jones mobilised enough people to tip the electoral balance to Trump in the 2016 election at the Electoral College, but there are deeper, underlying reasons that Trump won. As for Icke, people find union meetings boring, especially in comparison to theories about a holographic universe and a hollow Moon. If the kind of people who attend David Icke's presentations were that committed to social change they would see through him anyway, or maybe go to the union meeting and then get some entertainment with the reptiles. But why would they if my observation is correct, that most Icke followers are relatively privileged?

People who are getting hurt by long-term government policies have already taken action. They've joined the Labour Party – half a million of them – because the Party was finally led by a moderate, quasi-socialist, who is defamed as 'hard left' by the ultra-right media. In fact, the public's support for Corbyn's Labour Party via the grassroots Momentum movement is the first constructive public response to decades of neoliberalism. If the CIA, or whoever, wanted to use conspiracies as distraction or redirection of energy, they would promote groups that appear to be active, like the 9/11 Truth Movement, but actually go nowhere. But these kind of groups barely exist.

Wasn't there a memo that suggested the CIA sometimes used conspiracy theories to distract the public?

The importance of that has been inflated. It was a document published by a private contractor, Booz Allen & Hamilton, in the late-1990s.[175] They were working for the US government on ways to handle Freedom of Information requests. With the new FOIA laws and the internet becoming more accessible, government agencies were just flooded with FOIA requests – so many, they couldn't cope. So someone suggested strategically 'leaking' information, which was presumably going to be declassified anyway, or at least was low-level sensitivity, to lessen the number of FOIA requests. The logic was that if the public thinks the information is already out there in a leaked document, they won't have to bother filing for more information. There was one reference in it to what they called 'distraction material', where they reference JFK. I wonder if this is what WikiLeaks is about, in part at least...

DESTROY EVERYTHING

If you **DON'T LIKE** Jeremy Corbyn, I suggest you **REGISTER THAT DISGUST** by placing a dirty great **BIG CROSS** next to his name on the ballot at the next election.

Chapter 6

Brits abroad: Humanitarian intervention

Or: Killing people with bombs to save them from dictators

I was thinking recently about how many people have been killed directly by top-down Western structures. I roughly tallied up the figures and realised if you include wars, proxy wars – maybe even if you omit deaths by starvation – you're still looking at hundreds of millions of deaths. If you count the role of companies, even just cigarette companies, you might even be looking at Western civilisation being responsible for billions of deaths. Is that a fair estimate?

I don't think there's a sensible way of estimating a specific or even general toll. We're getting into vague moral questions about the limits of responsibility. On a wide spectrum from no-one's responsible for anything, to everyone's responsible for everything, you have to have some kind of way of evaluating these questions.

I would add that the underlying structures of the nation-state and colonialism laid the foundations centuries ago for today's poverty. Susan George has an interesting book called *Ill Fares the Land*.[176] She goes through the colonial records of the French, Italians, and British. She shows that settled, nomadic, and pastoralist societies with independent subsistence agricultural practises were immune to famines because they had sophisticated methods of storing seeds and grain in case of crop failure. The colonies destroyed this way of life and turned these complicated, self-reliant societies into systems of mass production for export. As a result, they overproduced, ruined acres of arable land, turned biodiversity into monocultures, and became acutely vulnerable to global economic shocks.

The British in India took it even further and by the late-19th century, were making money by speculating on food markets. So during the famines, Indian soldiers collaborating with the British, the *sepoys*, were under instruction to keep grain, rice, and wheat literally locked up under armed guard because that artificially inflated the prices for stock traders in London. Meanwhile, people starved to death. If they tried to storm the padlocked warehouses, they were shot on the streets. That's only a small example. Mike Davis[177] goes through the colonial record, much of it from the original documents of the time, and concludes that in the 2,000 years prior to British rule, Indians suffered few famines precisely for the reasons I mentioned earlier – sophisticated methods of grain storage. By the time the British were kicked out, India had suffered a dozen famines in just a couple of centuries, killing 29 million people in the last quarter of the 19th century alone. Indians lost their livelihoods when Britain imposed the gold standard – many Indians previously used silver. They lost arable land for crop production due to land privatisation. Water was privatised. The strength of monsoon winds increased because acres of forest were felled. And so on.

So the whole colonial system was set up centuries ago and contributes to today's crises just in food alone. So if you tally up the number of people starving today, history is one of the causes. Another cause is the International Monetary Fund, with its structural adjustment programmes. The IMF was set up by the US and Britain after WW2 as a way of ensuring that the creditors, mainly US corporations, get their money back from loans given often to dictators by the World Bank, which was also set up by the US. The poor of the third world are the guarantors of this debt.[178] The third world saw this as neocolonism, just a bit more sophisticated because it was hidden from the populations of the US and Britain. There's an article in *International Affairs* – the establishment journal of British foreign policy – describing America as an 'Empire by denial'.[179] Instruments like the IMF and World Bank are a way of maintaining this empire. The third world calls it 'neocolonial dependency'.[180]

Sub-Saharan Africa is one of the worst-affected regions on the planet. By abandoning the neoliberal programmes – the so-called Washington Consensus, which was imposed in part via the IMF – Latin American governments, under the so-called Pink Tide, lifted tens of millions of people out of poverty. There was a middle-class for the first time. The same happened in Asia. Countries like China, Singapore, and South Korea ignored the Washington Consensus, for a while at least, and their economies boomed – not just in terms of GDP, which is a poor measure of success because high GDP doesn't necessary mean equality, usually quite the reverse. This was until the mid-2000s or so.[181] Now there's a right-wing neoliberal government in power in Brazil. South Korea has pursued neoliberalism, and socioeconomic indicators start to stagnate.

Until then, these regions did well in terms of socioeconomic equalisation. But that didn't happen in Africa. If you look at Martin Meredith's book,[182] he shows that for a brief period in the 1970s and '80s – after decolonisation and just before the IMF came along with its new, US-led colonisation – Africa was actually improving in terms of life expectancy, child mortality, education, and so on. That proves that when you leave people alone, they're quite capable of organising their own affairs. As soon as the IMF got involved, the system collapsed again. Suddenly, governments were told to implement privatisation policies, cut back on social spending, hit growth targets, and so on. This is called 'fiscal responsibility' and 'sensible planning', etc. It should be called institutionalised theft – rob the poor of their resources and put the profits into the pockets of US multinationals. So you have 24,000 infants dying every day from starvation, lack of water, and from easily preventable and curable diseases.[183] The majority are Asian and African. Exactly what percentage of that is caused by Western policies is hard to measure, but many of these counties are or until recently were run by dictators: Kagame in

Rwanda; Obiang in Equatorial Guinea, who likes to boil opponents to death; the Transitional Federal government in Somalia; Mugabe in Zimbabwe, whose forces were trained by Britain in the '80s; and so on. If we didn't rely on Ethiopian slave labour, which benefits mining companies, or the ethnic cleansing of traditionalistic societies – 'bushmen' – in Tanzania, we could be helping to end Africa's oppression and, consequently, allow the continent to recover.

And it's not just in the so-called third world where underlying socioeconomic structures cause mass deaths. If you look at the UK, every year 40,000 British lives are cut short by pollution.[184] But the government doesn't impose emergency legislation to make sure that roads are cleaner. According to the BMJ, because of austerity, between the years 2010 and 2020, 120,000 people have died and will die – mostly elderly people in homes, who are even more vulnerable to shocks. One of the Cambridge professors involved in the study said, 'it's no exaggeration to call it economic murder'.[185] That's 12,000 people a year. The Islamic State can only dream of killing that many people.

If you generalise this 'excess deaths' model across the planet the death toll is going to be exponential. But we're trained not to think in these terms. We're trained to hate and fear more tangible but less powerful monsters, like the Islamic State.

Talking about India, wasn't Winston Churchill responsible for some of that?

Well, that was more towards the end of the Empire in India. Churchill's main contribution to Empire, arguably, was the creation of what became the Royal Air Force. He helped pioneer the massacre of civilians from on high by new death machines. Try finding any reference to that in the July 2018 RAF centenary celebrations.

Haven't conditions improved in Africa over the past couple of decades?

It depends on where you mean. If you're talking about North Africa, Tunisia, Egypt – what are conditions like? Egyptians have to rely on donations from the Muslim Brotherhood, which further Islamises the society.[186] These are the kind of conditions that led to the Arab Spring, starting in Egypt in late-2010, as people who'd been out of work for decades, and others who were in work under horrible conditions, revolted.

Libya was different. Gaddafi's warped version of socialism, the *Jamahiriya*, did have some benefits for the public. The fact that people benefited doesn't justify Gaddafi's dictatorship, because there were other approaches that could have been taken – a socialist democracy with a strong commitment to social security, for example. Gaddafi's model was contingent on oil sales. It led to the highest standard of living in Africa,[187] now wrecked by NATO.

You have remnants of British and French colonialism in Nigeria and Niger, respectively. Nigeria has low life expectancy and high infant mortality. This is dependent on class, as always. Then we can look at

South Africa, the supposed jewel in the crown of the new global economy, because it has a high GDP by Africa's standards. But it should always be remembered that GDP does not translate into equalised wealth. So just because a country does well macro-economically, a country like South Africa can still have a 50% poverty rate.[188] That's mostly black people, of course. Even under apartheid, which was a totally unjustifiable system, there was at least government provision for things like water. Now water is privatised and clean drinking water and indoor sanitation unavailable for many black South Africans.

The British Ministry of Defence in a projection cites Africa as, still, one of the poorest regions of the world. We hear a lot about 'failed states' but less about the reasons why they fail. The MoD says Africa might become a failed *continent* by 2036.[189] Africa's also home to where the major migration flows come from: sub-Saharan Africa. This is due to high levels of poverty, lack of government provision, and extreme fragility to climate change, and therefore acute vulnerability to crop failure. Though in the 1990s there was debt cancellation which went some way towards Africa's recovery—

So was the debt genuinely cancelled because of Bob Geldof, Bono, Live 8, etc.?

Many of the debts were cancelled, eventually. Grassroots and quasi-grassroots organisations and individuals, like rock stars, pushed for debt relief with some success. The US led the Highly Indebted Poor Countries Initiative and the Multilateral Debt Relief Initiative. This relieved about $100bn of debt across 26 countries. That's about the total assets of a single US bank, Goldman Sachs, alone, which indicates the power disparity between US financial institutions and entire countries, or even a continent in this case. The HIPCI and MDRI programmes erased about 70% of the debt, macro-economically. What was the real motive? Was it really because of Geldof? A paper for the US-led World Bank cites it as 'allow[ing] countries the opportunity to borrow again'. In other words to get them back into the US-led financial system. Poor countries are considered an investment risk and hence unprofitable. So by clearing their debts they get a better credit rating.[190]

But new debts followed. It's more a question of how debt is managed, what was the money spent on, etc. If the government borrows from itself via a nationalised central bank and invests in jobs, infrastructure, social security, and so on, there's no public burden of debt. Revenue is also raised by taxation. But that's not the system we have. The government issues bonds and private financial institutions buy them. But that's not how it has to be. In addition, there's a lot of propaganda against debt. People rail against central banks and government spending, even people who seem to be on the progressive or even 'anarchist' left, like David Graeber. He wrote *Debt: The First 5000 Years*, which is just propaganda against borrowing. In our current socio-political order we need to borrow to live. Ultimately, it's slavery. But within the current system it's necessary to buy things we need, like houses. It needn't be this way, but people like Graeber can't just pretend institutions don't exist.

We're all supposed to live in fear of debt. This is part of the propaganda that keeps the elite wealthy. Debt can be a good thing within the current system, depending on who you're borrowing from, what rate of interest they charge, how likely you are to pay it back, and what the money is spent on. But for it not to be slavery, it must be mutually agreed not necessitated by conditions set by others. Take Britain in the 1960s. Banks were well-regulated compared to the 1980s. People could borrow, wages were high – again, compared to the 1980s – and so people could get into temporary debt, pay it off, and enjoy some social mobility. By the '70s, that system was weakened and by the '80s it was destroyed. The crash of '08 has been blamed by many on debt, as opposed to deregulation.

In a fairer system, Africans could have borrowed to repair the damage wrought by colonisation, and the brutalities of decolonisation – the civil wars – and invested that capital in society. But what happened was that often corrupt dictators backed by the West borrowed and then the IMF came along and demanded that those economies disinvest in ordinary people and invest in businesses where the wealth goes into few pockets. That's called 'capitalism' or the 'free markets' but it's just organised plunder.

It irritates me when people say, 'Oh, your book is so timely!' There's *always* something important going on!

I generally agree but if you look at the '70s and '80s, with the exception of the Falklands and the so-called Troubles, most of what Britain was doing was under the radar. It wasn't relevant to the population because no one knew about it. Like sending troops to Sri Lanka and Colombia to train the militaries there. These weren't 'secret' wars in the sense that they were classified. They were 'secret' in the sense that no one bothered to report them, save the occasional article in the Associated Press, *New York Times*, or local papers where the training was taking place. So if someone produced a book about those or other countries where British Special Forces were operating, the response would have been bafflement, not praise of its 'timeliness'.

Tony Blair really transformed British foreign policy and put the whole issue of foreign policy into top gear. This coincided with the US post-Cold War agenda of 'Full Spectrum Dominance'. Wherever the US planned to go – Serbia, Afghanistan, Iraq – Britain followed. Before Blair, we had a mission in the Balkans, but not much else in terms of large occupation forces.

We helped to established a peace agreement in the Balkans, prior to the nightmare that was the 1999 NATO intervention in Kosovo.

That region, Yugoslavia and the Former Yugoslavia, was dominated by Serbia. The Serbs had the biggest military force, the most political influence, and they were allied politically to Russia. After the Soviet Union collapsed it was essential that eastern Europe wasn't going to be too much influenced by Russia or its allies. Serbia was one of Russia's footholds in or near Europe. Once the unifying force of the Soviet Union collapsed, Yugoslavia started to fall with it. The second major power there was Croatia, so there was major conflict between Serbia and Croatia. Serbia wanted to hold the region together because its elites were in a position of strength. Croatia wanted independence.

Britain had, on the surface, a mission as part of a broader United Nations peacekeeping effort in the region. NATO had an occupation force there. They sold it to the world as a moralistic intervention. But NATO had no UN mandate, any more than the Warsaw Pact would have had a mandate to get involved.[191] NATO was quite obviously against Serbia because that was the Soviet ally. So there was no balance in the moral equation to sending in NATO. It was a very selective concern. Obviously, the Serbs were committing atrocities – nobody disputes that – but so were the Croatians. Operation Storm (1995), for example, was a Croatian military operation which targeted Serb civilians. Where were the NATO forces to protect Serb civilians? The British media were so fanatically anti-Serbian that the supposedly left-wing *Independent* newspaper carried headlines like the 'Riddle of Serb exodus from Krajina'. It wasn't much of a riddle if you read human rights reports.[192]

At the same time in Bosnia, you had the US, British, and Israelis flying in *jihadis* to go and fight for Bosnian independence. So the remnants of 'al Qaeda', who we'd created in the late 1970s-'80s in Afghanistan, were recycled to fight in Bosnia. That's a case where

Britain created or at least empowered *jihadis* who then went on to train generations of terrorists at home. Abu Hamza of the Finsbury Park mosque, for instance, fought in Bosnia. The so-called security services gave him the rather unappealing codename, Damson Berry.[193] That wasn't Britain's aim – to create homespun *jihadis* – but the obvious effect that it had was inflating the *jihadi* presence in the region and thus around the world. Mark Urban of the BBC has a report asking if Bosnia is the 'cradle of modern jihadism?'. Try to find a single reference in the report of the US-British-Israeli role in facilitating it.[194]

And I guess the logic of that intervention led to Kosovo 1999, which seemed like a terrible idea. Is that your assessment?

There's a Belgian journalist, Michel Collon, who wrote that Kosovo was a 'prototype'. NATO laid a pattern for what we call 'intervention'. He's right.[195] In Libya and Syria, the pattern was repeated: Arm, train, and organise a significant nationalist militia, mainly comprised of terrorists. Get them to attack government and even civilian targets. When the government in power – usually a dictatorship – responds with violence, cry foul and claim that an 'ethnic cleansing' is taking place. Or chemical attacks, as in the case of Syria. Then NATO, with no legal mandate but a phony moral one, can go in and smash the country up. That's what happened in Serbia in 1999 and Libya in 2011. Syria is slightly different – no NATO involvement – but a similar pattern.

A small but significant number of Kosovar Albanians in the mid-1990s wanted independence from Serbia. Kosovo was a region of Serbia. It's now an independent state on the periphery of Europe. From about 1996, the British and Americans had been training and organising the Kosovo Liberation Army (KLA). The public relations firm Ruder Finn was brought in to give them a good image and make them look like a legitimate independence movement. The KLA did not represent the wishes of most Kosovar Albanians at that time. Quite the opposite. The leaders of the KLA were quite open about their plans: to attack Serb government and even civilian targets, provoke a response, and then use the counterattacks to build support for their cause from the UK and America – or 'international community' as it's called in the propaganda.[196]

The UN Security Council never authorised the use of force in Serbia-Kosovo and never authorised the NATO presence, which is where the pattern was repeated in Libya. The SAS were operating in Serbia in late-1998.[197] This was followed by the Račak massacre, in which Kosovar Albanian civilians were murdered. That was blamed on the Serbs. Rumours and outright lies about large-scale 'ethnic cleansing' started to circulate. It was true that there were disappearances. They're still digging up the bodies today of Kosovar Albanians killed by Serbs. So there's no denying that Milošević's Serb regime was terrible and committed war crimes, but it was not an 'ethnic cleansing'. And in fact the British House of Commons Library and other sources confirm that until March 1999, when the NATO bombing started, about 2,000 people on both sides – Serbs and Kosovar Albanians – had been killed.[198] That's a far cry from the tens of thousands of Kosovars that Foreign Secretary Robin Cook was talking about, or his American counterparts who were saying that hundreds of thousands had gone missing. These were just total lies. Outright propaganda. The House of Commons records say it was a civil war, not an ethnic cleansing, and that Milošević had authorised 'counter-offensive[s]', not attacks.[199]

There was an ethnic cleansing, however, when NATO started to bomb. At that point, Milošević started to drive out as many Kosovar Albanians as he could. So the NATO bombing triggered the ethnic cleansing. But that chronology – which we have from the best sources, the records of the governments launching the war – is inverted by popular historians and journalists. So it set the precedent for so-called humanitarian intervention. And one of the most chilling things about it was the Committee on Defence's report comparing Iraq 2003 with Kosovo 1999. They said that Iraq failed to build on the 'success' of Kosovo because so few people supported destroying Iraq as they had with Kosovo.[200]

People on the street or politicians may not know that much, but they think they're doing the right thing. To what extent do you think this is a cynical ploy by a couple dozen White Hall officials, and to what extent is it just stupidity among reasonably powerful people?

I wouldn't call it stupidity because there were clear military objectives. First of all, we should remember that this was a United States-led operation. They're the ones committed to what they call 'Full Spectrum Dominance' (1997) and Serbia was arguably the first major demonstration of this doctrine, outside of the blockade and no-fly zones in Iraq. The US bombed Afghanistan and Sudan in 1998, but not on the scale of Serbia in 1999. Kosovo is a key region in what strategists like Brzezinski call the 'game' for world domination.[201] As proof of that, even before the war began the US was building a permanent military base – one of the biggest in the world, Camp Bondsteel – right on the intersection of the oil and gas pipelines that go through Kosovo.[202] NATO's Secretary-general, Jaap de Hoop Schefer, told a conference that the energy industry had lobbied NATO to act in Serbia, long before he led NATO. 'Let's be glad that the gas is flowing again', he said.[203] So there are strategic interests there which the media ignore.

That's just greed and the desire to dominate. I wouldn't call it stupid. Pathological, for sure. The energy companies and military are at the top of the hierarchy. They've got the most power, strategic maps of where the world's resources are located, and they're going to try to set policies in those interests. Then there's the executive, Bill Clinton in the US at the time and Tony Blair here. We don't have internal records, or at least not many, so we have to try and build up a picture. But I assume from the limited evidence available that energy industry and military lobbyists told them that they must get involved and that it's good to get rid of Milošević. We know there was an MI6 plan to assassinate him and make it look like a car accident—

The same with Gaddafi and, I was going to say, Princess Diana...

There's some interesting questions about that—

It seems like the car 'accident' is quite a favoured plot. And, of course, Milošević died rather conveniently and abruptly in jail of heart attack.

That's right. Question marks hang over these events.

So returning to how acts of aggression get started: You have the hierarchy with the military and energy companies at the top, banks, too. Then there's the executive and the foreign policy wonks. Below them you've got the MPs, most of whom are pretty clueless about the way the world works. I did some campaign work in the run-up to the 2017 general election with a person who was an independent Parliamentary candidate. I didn't particularly support their policies but I wanted to help oust the local Tory MP. The person I was helping really didn't know much. I think that generalises. So from the point of view of the people who really set policy – the oil industry, the military, the secret services – that's perfect. They don't want people like Jeremy Corbyn as MPs – well-informed, pro-human rights, pacifistic Members of Parliament. That's obviously against their interests because people like that start raising questions. They're able to present facts that go against the standard line, that we're doing this in the interests of humanity.

The hierarchies are quire fluid. There's no central conspiracy in the way that someone like David Icke talks about. The people within it change. The nature of it changes. There's internal competition between departments and corporations. Brexit is a dramatic example of that. But just in terms of how policy gets set, this appears to be the way it works. The general public only get information from the media. That's a whole other question about how it happens or doesn't happen. Why aren't the media really questioning and putting these serious factual concerns to politicians? Within this very complicated mix, there's also self-belief. It's much easier to believe in the righteousness of your own state, culture, and foreign policy than to question whether what you're doing is right. And it's easy to fool yourself. As I say, Milošević was an oppressive leader. So it's easy to look at his horrors and exaggerate the importance of it and say, 'We must intervene'.

Humans also have a disconnect. When it's not you or me directly dropping bombs, it's much easier to disconnect and say, 'We'll intervene but we won't think about the consequences of dropping thousands of bombs'. In psychology, there's the now-classic 'trolley problem'. Most people think it's okay to pull a lever and divert a trolley car from a line where it will kill a dozen people. The lever diverts the trolley to another line, killing a single person. So you save six by killing one. But as a soon as people are asked, 'Is it okay to push someone onto the track to stop the trolley?', the majority say no.[204] There's a psychological disconnect. The lever somehow disconnects the person from their action. It's the same with bombing. Authorising it under the belief that it's a humanitarian intervention is fine, but not killing someone with your bare hands.

Sam Harris presents this solipsistic argument in his book, *The End of Faith.* He says it's somehow worse to kill face-to-face than with bombs.

But these things have to be thought through. When we bombed Serbia, NATO released tens of thousands of cluster bomblets, which are like mines but even worse because they have little parachutes and so the wind carries them. In addition to the 2,000 or so civilians who were killed as a result of the bombing, hundreds were injured by the bomblets alone. As the authorities dig up Kosovar corpses reinforcing how awful Milošević was, children are still getting injured and killed today by going out into fields, stepping on NATO cluster bomblets, and getting their legs blown off.[205] Where's the humanitarian aid to support prosthetics and psychological counselling in Serbia and Kosovo today?

You have to think through things like this. Assuming that it was a humanitarian intervention, which is a false premise in this case anyway, for reasons we've discussed, ask yourself, 'Is it better to bomb and save a few thousand lives, knowing that you're going to kill equal or greater numbers by bombing, or to let atrocities occur?' And what right, legally or morally, do we have to make those decisions? Had Serbia the power, it could have bombed Britain and pleaded humanitarian intervention to stop our blockade of Iraq, which was worse in reality than anything Milošević was doing and *accused* of doing in Kosovo. Then you've got to think about how serious you are about stopping atrocities. We know from the government's own records that the KLA were trying to provoke responses. So instead of bombing Serbia, withdraw support for the KLA.

In our culture, where everything has to be quick-thinking, fast-media create a sense of panic. Being told that a dictator is using chemical weapons or committing an ethnic cleansing creates an immediate, emotional kneejerk. To question that leads to accusations that you're an appeaser of violence or anti-British, or anti-American. There are so many factors. It's much easier for them to use violence than it is for us to justify peace.

I saw the film _Darkest Hour_ recently, which got me thinking. Firstly, can brutal people in power, like Churchill in 1940, do good things? He stopped the spread of Nazism. Secondly, in the case of World War 2, would you have gone to war at that point?

There's an article in the _New Statesman_ (Jan. 2018) by historian Adrian Smith about errors and omissions in the film, which I haven't seen. Smith's biggest gripes are with the portrayal of Foreign Secretary Halifax who is painted as a villain, and the inference that the Labour Party was unpatriotic – a propaganda smear made today.

To address the first point, can evil people do good? For me, it doesn't make much sense to talk about the responsibility of specific individuals when we're dealing with powerful institutions like nation-states. There are some cases, of course, where individuals give orders to commit atrocities, and those should be dealt with on a case-by-case basis. We're talking about the

Nazis, so people like Hoess, the commandant of Auschwitz, had personal responsibility for giving orders. But in the context of a question like, 'Does good come out of evil?', it's a question of unintended positive consequences. If we look at the typical evil leaders like Hitler and Stalin, you have to think in terms of the whole nation-state system. Yes, they are responsible for their own actions and did horrendous things – Hitler signed Action T4, to murder disabled children, to cite one of many. But if people like Hitler didn't have followers – those who supported their ideology, financed them, attended their rallies, and so on – they wouldn't be able to do anything evil on a large scale. They'd just be embittered lunatics ranting in a room somewhere—

That's what we are, aren't we?

We haven't laid out plans for world domination, yet.

Oh I don't know!

That may come as the evening progresses...

But seriously, when people build up a following, that's when it matters. It makes no sense to talk about individuals in this context, though they should be held accountable. What shape that accountability takes, we can discuss. We should look at the bigger picture. So forgetting about Churchill, was it good to go to war with Nazi Germany? There are unintended positive consequences that come out of the most horrendous things. For human beings, the worst period in history was the Holocaust. There is nothing that can justify it. One of the positive unintended consequences that came out of it was the fact that Zionist Jews were able to justify the creation of a Jewish homeland. Some ultra-right Zionists even made a deal with Nazis – the Haavara Agreement 1933 – to deport European Jews for colonisation in Palestine.[206] Most Jews at the time didn't want to go and colonise Palestine for a Zionist project. They wanted to live in the USA and Britain, but weren't allowed due to anti-immigration laws. The Zionists running European IDP camps were denying food to the healthiest Jews because they wanted what they called 'good human material' to go and colonise Palestine.[207] So they were exploited by Zionists. But one of the good things that came out of this unjustifiable horror story is that Jews have now ended up as the safest ethnic-religious minority in the world. They have their own highly militarised, nuclear-armed nation-state, whose existence is guaranteed by the world's superpower and whose existence is continuously justified by its leaders' rhetorical invocations of the Holocaust.

Then you've got unintended, *negative* consequences. The creation of the State of Israel cannot justify one of the major crimes of the post-War period: the expulsion of 700,000 Palestinians from their homes. So political consequences are extremely complicated, and even unintended, positive results for a second party can have subsequent, negative results for a third. And so on. Take another case, India. Indians benefited from Britain's diminished power that occurred as a result of World War 2, so they gained some independence as an unintended consequence of Britain entering the War and weakening its Empire. And, of course, Indians then had postcolonial problems of their own, from their own governments. But at least they were free from British rule. This benefited Hindus, mainly. There was a bloody civil war with millions killed and the creation of the independent states of Pakistan and eventually Bangladesh were the result. And so begins another cycle of positive and negative, like the Bangladeshi War of Independence from Pakistan (1971).

So if I am being fatalistic, we may be killing millions or even hundreds of millions of people but these people will die anyway. If we hadn't killed a million people in Iraq, maybe something hard to predict would have happened under Saddam Hussein instead. People like you say, 'We have to be responsible for the consequences of our actions', but who knows what the consequences are, or the consequences of our inaction?

It depends on who you're talking about, but no one we're discussing would 'die anyway'. The only people who would have 'died anyway' in Iraq without our blockade and invasion were the Kurds as a result of Saddam's genocide in the 1980s. But they didn't die in a vacuum. They died because we enabled Saddam Hussein to murder them. To give another example: Building up the Nazi war machine by selling Germany arms components in the early-'30s was not inaction. Selling Saddam weapons was not inaction. We know the consequences for Kurds when we supported Saddam in Iraq, for example. We can reasonably estimate at least the short-term consequences of withdrawing support for Saddam: the regime would have collapsed, as nearly happened in 1991 when the Shia and Kurds nearly overthrew him—

Yeah, but who knows what could have happened? Counter-factual histories are notoriously unreliable. Maybe the Kurds would have taken over Baghdad. Maybe if Saddam hadn't fought Iran with our weapons in the 1980s then Iran would have become more powerful in the Middle East – just as it had done post-2003.

Kurds were in no position to take over Baghdad. They didn't have the motive or the power. They had semi-autonomy in Iraqi Kurdistan, so maybe Kurdistan would have ceded. You can't just claim that would happen without understanding the political conditions at the time.

You're making a lot of assertions. In life, there are a million things that can happen, including unpredictable consequences. One perfectly predictable consequence of arming a dictator like Saddam is that he's going to commit mass murder, as he did. One possible consequence of building up a war machine in a politically fragile country like post-WW1 Germany is that a far-right government is going to come to power and use those weapons to oppress anyone who doesn't fit its ideology, as in fact happened. That's how we ended up with Nazism. It's a logical fallacy to say that a) we take an action and c) there are a million things that can happen as a result, good and bad. It misses b): the corollary that our actions have consequences. So if you can possibly have a morally responsible state – and that's an oxymoron in my view, because nation-state are basically death-cults – the state would consider the likely consequences of its actions. It's a logical gap to say, 'Let's not worry about our actions because we cannot be sure of what will happen'. That just doesn't make any sense, especially when we have real-world cases of what happened in history.

You don't like my question then?

I don't see the point of it because I was talking about the unintended consequences of a war. And the questions are tied together, about whether we should have fought a war with Nazi Germany. The fact is that until 1919, we imposed a naval blockade on Germany which destroyed much of the society. We made it impossible for Germany to reconstruct independent of us. We created the conditions that brought about the Nazi regime. We can't pretend we had no responsibility for partly creating the regime and then advocate violence to stop it, as if we're in some in some moral vacuum. That's another example of unintended consequences, stemming from WW1, and how those consequences helped lay the conditions for the creation of the Nazi Party and World War 2. It wasn't a case of, 'What didn't we do in WW1', but rather what *did* we do? And the conditions imposed on Germany after 1918 led to the ultimate nightmare of Nazism.

But you do sometimes need the big bad person to have the imagination to take an inspired risk. Just like

great sportsmen need to take risks. Churchill ultimately became our most revered statesman.

What 'inspired risks' were the British – the 'big bad person' of the day – taking when we imposed crippling conditions on Germany until 1919? Churchill described the blockade as intended 'to starve the whole population ... into submission'.[208] The National Archives describe it as a 'hunger blockade' and said the aim was to 'strangle the supply of raw materials and foodstuffs'.[209] Speaking of unintended consequences, they also note that Germany developed submarines – U-Boats – to counter the superior British Navy. Official British statistics put the German death toll at 700,000 as a result of the blockade. These were civilians.[210]

What 'inspired risks' did American banks take in buying out Germany's debts in the early-'30s? US corporations, including Ford, General Electric, Coca Cola, and Standard Oil, were investing in Germany because it was basically a captive economy thanks to WW1 and the Treaty of Versailles. It was a captive population. Inflation was out of control, sanctions were in place. What risks were they taking when they helped build the Nazi war machine by supplying iron and oil? What risks were GE taking during WW2, when they were sending instructions to US bombers with coordinates not to bomb their German subsidiary plants? This was pure profiteering. Britain did something similar. The Bank of England invested in what became Nazi Germany, so did British Steel.[211] The Western powers not only acted in ways that created horrendous conditions for ordinary German civilians, but they actually built up the Nazis' weapons. That history isn't taught.

So to answer my second question, what would you have done in 1940?

First of all I wouldn't have created the conditions in which the Nazis could come about in the first place, but—

Yeah, but everyone knows that. No one would do that.

But they did. That's history. You can't just pretend it didn't happen. And also, few people know about it, contrary to what you said. Only historians know that the Treaty of Versailles (1919) helped create impossible conditions for Germans, which crumbled the moderate institutions and led the way for the far-right. Even the majority of historians don't know about Western investment in Nazi Germany but it's in the Congressional and corporate records. You don't learn about it in school or on television. So how are people going to find out?

Yeah, but even a fifteen year old with a GCSE in History wouldn't do that these days, you know?

It *was* done again, in Iraq. Almost the same pattern. After a war – the Gulf War 1991 – crippling sanctions were imposed, then the invasion in 2003. This created the conditions for another far-right extremist organisation, Daesh. And it was predicted. Numerous intelligence agencies warned both the British and American governments that they would radicalise a generation by invading Iraq.[212] So I wouldn't have created those conditions in Iraq – firstly on humanitarian grounds, but secondly because when people are desperate enough they are more vulnerable to being exploited by fanatics. Ordinary Iraqi kids, 19–20-year-olds, who have nothing in their life are desperate to join such groups. In 2000s' Iraq, it developed into Daesh. In 1920s' Germany, it was the Nazis.

So Britain. 1940. You would have appeased the Nazis?

Appeasement is specific to Hitler's annexation of Sudetenland in 1938. PM Chamberlain co-signed the Munich Agreement (same year) allowing the annexation, which was wrong and something I wouldn't have endorsed. Hitler pretended that his invasion and theft of parts of Czechoslovakia was a humanitarian intervention to save German Czechs from the increasingly oppressive regime there. But that was 1938. You can't talk of appeasement in 1940. So let's consider Poland in 1939. It was understood at the time among the policymaking elite that Britain had no intention of living up to its international obligations to defend Danzig. There were secret negotiations between the Foreign Secretary Lord Halifax and an opponent of Hitler, but Churchill demoted Halifax when he took office.[213] So what was the result of not honouring our international commitments? It turned out to be the most catastrophic war in history. Hitler offered a peace treaty.

Britain could have used the League of Nations, which was the beginnings of international law—

But that's not going to work! Nazi Germany is the most powerful country in Europe, it doesn't give a monkey's about the League of Nations!

Obviously. Germany withdrew from the League of Nations in 1933 because the League refused to recognise it as a major player. The League could have recognised Germany. It didn't. Then Germany invaded Danzig, which was administered by the League. Had Germany's autonomy been recognised, it would have had to follow League rules. But that's not the point. My point is that if you're serious about pursuing peace, you exhaust all the non-military options before considering war. Incidentally, Churchill advocated such a policy, at least in hindsight. He said that WW2 could have been prevented 'without firing a single shot'.[214]

So in steps, we could have tried accepting Germany's offers, creating global conditions via the League of Nations to condemn Nazi Germany, building up the international pressure. That wasn't done. And I'm not sure that Nazi Germany was that powerful, because by late-1941 their incendiary bombs were pretty much depleted, they were rapidly losing their air power.[215] The US was getting the into war—

Yeah, but that required the US to be the big, bad bastard. What about Britain, when it fought alone in 1939–40. Should we have done that?

This gets back to international law. If you have international law, of course the Nazis won't abide by it. But it creates the conditions for international pressure against them. So it's a series of steps towards de-escalation, including withdrawal of support by our own companies operating in Nazi Germany. You proceed from there. I can only reiterate that Churchill himself said the War was unnecessary: 'There never was a war more easy to stop than that which has just wrecked what was left of the world from the previous struggle'.[216]

With regard to the US, if you could create conditions for international law, you could have had the US as a guarantor but that's not what they would do—

There's always this thing where it's possible to say it's the international system's fault, or the American's fault or whatever but essentially you're saying, as British Prime Minister in 1939–40 you would have pursued appeasement and stopped a set of British companies from investing in Germany?

First, as I said, appeasement was earlier and morally wrong. Second, you can't blame an abstract thing like 'international law'. You look to where responsibility lies, with people but more importantly the institutions they run. As far as continuing to profit from Nazi Germany, we're assuming British corporations were still doing it during the War. The record isn't clear on that. But we know that the US firm GE, to cite one of many, was still operating there—

And you're assuming that Nazi Germany was a bit weaker than it seemed and, what, it would just have gone away?

No assumption, historical record. As far as Germany 'going away', now you're jumping to the end of 1941, when Germany was weaker—

But you're shifting responsibility to US to take charge!

No. I'm not shifting responsibility to the US. I'm saying in any international coalition - and I'm talking about a peaceful one as a first step - there's your own responsibility and a joint responsibility if you're working with others. With regards to the Nazis growing, how can they grow if you withdraw your industries from their country? If those American companies were ordered by the US government to immediately withdraw all operations from Nazi Germany, as they were even operating during the War itself, you'd have had literally dozens of Nazi industries collapsing.

I think that's a really important point. But what about the British government? We couldn't even get the Americans into the War – a War which would profit them and ultimately did. What should Britain – not the world as a whole – what should *Britain* have done?

So are you saying that creating an international agreement wouldn't be taking action?

I'm saying it'd be taking action but that it wouldn't have a hope of working. If we're talking about living in the real world, and that we're responsible for the consequences of our actions, you'd have put in this motion through the League of Nations to get the US to withdraw its corporations from Nazi Germany and they'd have just said, 'No'.

No. That would not have required League of Nations approval, to withdraw domestic corporations from Nazi Germany. That decision can be made by the executive in any given country, to withdraw their firms from foreign nations.

We may have created the conditions that killed 50 million people but we may also have stopped Nazi Germany from killing another tens of millions of people, taking over the USSR and they would have established the most repulsive totalitarian dictatorship imaginable. Our country, our continent, and our world may never have recovered from that.

No. The Nazis tried to take over Russia and failed. In fact, the British had a plan, Operation Unthinkable, to rearm the Nazis to take over Russia on behalf of Britain and the US.[217]

Hmm. Okay. But I would still say in that narrow perspective that it would have been wrong to attempt

those measures economically and create an international consensus, because it would have failed.

We don't know because it wasn't tried. What was tried was violence. That, as you said, led to perhaps 50 million deaths.

Yes, but I am suggesting that even if British policy is consistently as horrible as you say, for that brief shining moment of irrational idiocy, Britain did the right thing.

By helping to build up the Nazis in the first place by investing in their regime? By refusing to pursue peaceful opposition to Nazi aggression? By blowing up Jewish refugee boats after World War 2 – Operation Embarrass – to blame Arabs?[218] Where's the good in any of that?

If Germany had invaded the UK, what would you have advocated?

At that point we could have fought a defensive war, which is very different to fighting an offensive war with a standing army. A standing army exists for conquest. The current Army was founded in 1660 and it (re)conquered Scotland and Ireland, subsuming them into the nation-state that eventually became the United Kingdom. The best way to defend ourselves – and defence is not what a standing army is for – is not to have a standing army. A well-organised, dispersed militia is the best way to defeat an enemy. This is what happened during the Vietnam War. The Viet Minh, or Vietcong as the US called them – because it sounded more communistic and easier to justify the war – was an army. But it operated like a militia. It was dispersed, had small units, fought in the jungle, and so on. Or when Hezbollah, the so-called Party of Allah, defeated Israel in Lebanon in 2006.

Historians regard these wars as defeats for the invading standing armies. Whether the US was really 'defeated' in Vietnam is another question, but militarily it was. As was Israel in Lebanon. But we're not doing that at all with the British Armed Forces. We have a standing Army, backed by a significant nuclear arsenal, which can only be for the purposes of conquest – since we're not ever going to be invaded, as long as we retain that arsenal. In the propaganda, Trident exists for defence. Maybe that's an unintended consequence, but the main reason for Trident is – as nuclear planners put it[219] – to allow us to act with impunity, with force, against non-nuclear states because we know they wouldn't dare retaliate.

So you're a pacifist?

In international relations, yes. But not an ultimate pacifist. I think that peaceful options should always be exhausted, especially now that we have weapons that could end all life as we know it. I certainly don't support the use of force for 'humanitarian intervention', for reasons we've discussed. If a state is under direct attack and there are no peaceful solutions, it can fight back. That's international law. But we have to ask whether states are legitimate entities. How can you fight back against a superpower? Is an army more effective in self-defence than a militia? Why do we need war at all since we have nuclear weapons, which act as both deterrents and enablers of lower-levels of conflict? These questions are not seriously tackled in media or scholarship, as far as I can see.

In personal affairs among family or neighbours, I'm not a pacifist. I think people should be able to sort out their own affairs without being threatened with the law or the coercion of state- or local police.

Build Unions Not Borders
FREEDOM OF MOVEMENT
OPEN THE BORDER
Labour Campaign for Free Movement

I like **JEREMY CORBYN** but I think he should be more like **TRUMP**. I'd like to see him **BUILD A WALL!** And then another wall, and another wall, and another wall. **THEN SOME ROOFS**. Do that a million times and solve the social housing crisis!

Chapter 7

Rue Britannia:
'Using the big stick'

Or: Why we train and arm death squads in the third world...

A lot of people will assume, and I kind of did until I read your book *Britain's Secret Wars*, that recent UK foreign policy is confined to overstretching itself in Iraq and that it is a little involved in Afghanistan but it hasn't really had any global reach since the 1940s, 1950s. But you're challenging that, aren't you?

The UK follows what its leaders call 'the national interest'. But 'national interest' doesn't mean in the interests of ordinary people. Most people are communal in their thinking, 'How does such and such policy affect me and my community?'. People are not generally nationalistic, unless motivated. So 'national interests' usually means in the interests of large corporations but also elements of the policymaking establishment, whoever they are at the time.

In the case of Iraq the so-called national interest was following the US lead in invading the country in 2003, even though the intelligence community predicted that doing so would increase the threat of terrorism against British citizens.[220] It was also predictable that invading would weaken Britain's position globally, as indeed it did. The Blair government proved once again to the US that Britain was willing to be a subordinate ally and support this internationally unpopular act of aggression. So from a political viewpoint, that was the 'national interest', showing loyalty to the US. From the point of view of corporations, the 'national interest' was maximising their profits. Contrary to what was reported about 'failures' in Iraq and so on, the oilfields were sold at auction to US and British companies, primarily. So BP won a contract to exploit the Rumaila oilfield in 2010 and another to exploit Kirkuk in 2018.[221]

Look at Britain's economy: 60% of GDP is dependent on trade and investment abroad,[222] so that immediately implies the UK needs a global reach to maintain 60% of its GDP. In various, open-source national security strategies, the British government talks about there being no economic security without military security. They talk about finance and diplomacy and 'soft power' and militarism as 'hard power'. Guys like Admiral Stanhope, former head of the Royal Navy, just a few years back spoke of 'wielding a big stick ... to compel others to act in a desired manner'.[223]

But where is all that money going, the 60% of foreign-generated GDP? It certainly isn't going into the pockets of British working people because the society is so unequal. If you look at the top ten corporations in terms of profits, a significant number tend to be oil companies and banks. Shell Oil is probably the biggest, but it employs a very small number of British people. Shell hardly uses British resources, oil and gas. It and its subsidiaries operate mostly in places like Nigeria. And they don't pay their fair share of corporate taxes,[224] so they're not contributing to society – in fact they, and we as consumers, are damaging society with pollution every time we buy their products.

So what exactly do these giant corporations contribute to the British economy? By supporting foreign policy through our taxes, we are essentially subsidising Shell Oil. Consider the case of Nigeria. Since at least the 1950s, when Nigeria was still an official colony, Shell has been exploiting Nigerian oil so much that it's made it impossible for itself to operate there. It creates a vicious cycle. Shell's subsidiary poisoned Nigeria's landscape and made miles of fertile land literally unliveable. Private gangs with no other income came along and sold oil on the black market. The state, armed and trained by Britain, responded with a heavy fist and launched a counterinsurgency war against the gangs.[225] And the cycle continues, to the point where now the civil war has made it impossible for Shell to operate. The company was allied to oppressive regimes, like that of General Abachca, who hanged dissidents – most famously Ken Saro-Wiwa – for opposing Shell's operations. The protestors were nonviolent, unlike the gangs. The British Ministry of Defence provides training for the Nigerian military, so in a circuitous way our taxes were a security subsidy for Shell to operate in Nigeria.

That's the 'national interest'.

The reason that people aren't aware of this systematic 'guaranteed access to and exploitation of resources', as the MoD calls globalisation, [226] is that it's not in the culture of the media to care about people in somewhere like Nigeria or Bangladesh. So if many of the 120 million Bangladeshis are living in poverty, working indirectly for Primark or whichever company, in slave labour-like conditions and so on, who cares? Unless there is some sudden, newsworthy tragedy, like a factory collapses and kills a thousand girls – and it often is girls, girls and young women working for many hours a day—

Has that happened?

Sure. It happened a few years ago, the Rana Plaza factory collapsed in 2013. It was headline news. But the fact that there are dozens of factories like this, where people die young not because the factories collapse, but because they don't make enough money to eat properly, having decent housing, and cover their medical costs – that goes unreported. The underlying, daily, abstract structure of oppression isn't newsworthy. It's harder, but not impossible, to visualise and present to news consumers a structure of oppression. But it's easy to present them with photos and footage of a collapsed building, even though the former is far more destructive in terms of numbers of people hurt. It just takes longer.

I bought clothes from Primark literally today. What would be the alternative to having shops like that? If

we got rid of Primark would there be slightly more expensive clothes, or much more expensive clothes? Would it screw up everything in the country? Would we end up as poor as Bangladesh, or whatever?

Of course not. The UK is not a poor, devastated former colony consisting largely of flood plains. In the UK, the so-called 'ethical market' is worth £81bn. So that's an economy in itself. This has grown by nearly half in less than a decade. The *Financial Times* says '[b]usinesses are seeing the appeal' of the ethical market. The same report cites a survey by Nielsen, that 66% of respondents would pay more for 'sustainable goods'. Rob Harrison of Ethical Consumer says: 'if you don't look around to check ethical risk in your supply chain, people will discover issues like child labour or pollution in China and you'll have a front-page scandal'.[227] So exploiting people is fine, but the risk of getting caught is too high, so it's better to treat people with minimal decency for good publicity.

This shows the divide between elites – corporate elites in this case – and ordinary people. It's also worth noting that young people are far more switched on and compassionate. The new market in ethical consumption – which barely existed 20 years ago – is being driven by Generations X and Y, and Millennials (*FT* article cited earlier). That's why they have to be demonised in the media and culture as narcissists – the 'Twitter generation' – and 'snowflakes'.

We should also remember that the top British corporations don't contribute much to the economy anyway, in terms of employing British people or paying taxes. And the ones that do, like Primark or ASDA, have very low wages for their workers. Low wages is a method of internal exploitation. So you have cheap labour abroad to produce the products – clothes in the case of Primark, then the Ministry of Defence guards the seas so that the container ships can bring those products back to the UK. Then, covert special operations forces train death-squads in the countries where the products come from – the Rapid Action Battalion in the case of Bangladesh. This is to ensure unions are crushed if they organise against this system. Once the clothes, or whatever product it is, comes to Britain you have people working for almost nothing in those shops. It's often old people, usually women, at the tills who would like to retire, who are struggling to get by on a state-pension.

So we should unionise at home to demand better wages. That may hurt Primark's profits, but profit for corporations is not the economy. The economy can include the wages saved or spent by working people. Domestic unions can form associations with foreign ones, as in the case of Colombia which has links to British unions. That raises awareness about abuses. As far as the source of exploitation is concerned, when people are made aware of it, most are in favour of ethical consumption. But that's harder when you don't have much money.

And you don't think that would wreck the economy? Might it even improve it?

I mentioned the 'ethical market'. But unless we define 'the economy', it's difficult to say whether or not fair wages and ethically-sourced products would cause harm. But the kind of clothing shops we're talking about are just a small fraction of the macro-economy. So we're talking specifically about consumer prices. Most consumers won't be particularly affected if clothing is made in more ethical conditions and retail prices go up by, say, 30% because companies have to produce at home and pay their staff more than they pay people in Bangladesh. I say 'most' because people at the very bottom of the income scale in the UK would be hit. But the supermarkets, including clothing retailers, are engaged in price wars anyway, trying to out-do each other with promotions. 'Let's make everything as cheap as possible' – that's the philosophy. The price of cheapness is exploitation abroad and at home to some degree.

Most people have far too many clothes, anyway. We live in a disposable culture. Almost half of adults in the UK have clothes they don't wear – that's about 700 items of clothing per person getting moth-eaten. So girls are slaving in sweatshops and political opponents are getting their brains blown out in Bangladesh, in part, so that British people can have clothes they don't even wear. That's the 'free market'. A study by Marks & Spencer says that people take on average 15 minutes each morning choosing what to wear.[228] Incidentally, a couple of decades ago, M&S sponsored a book by Chatham House about British foreign policy which talked about child labour, and said that 'exploitation may be a *necessary* stage in the evolution of capitalist societies' (their emphasis). But the authors also say that third world countries can't develop ('evolve') or they'll challenge the supremacy of the West. So log-

ically that means exploitation is necessary in perpetui-
ty.[229]

In addition, Oxfam says that clothing has become
the most wasteful consumer product, with hundreds of
millions of tonnes of clothing being thrown away every year, instead of being recycled.

There are all sorts of ways for people to buy af-
fordable clothing without resorting to the exploitation
of foreign labourers and domestic retailers. One way is
to equalise the economy, to share more evenly the
wealth of the upper 1%, as people call it. But that's not
in the interests of the class structure. The people at
the top don't want to permit that because they'd lose
their status. It sounds obvious, but think about the
wider implications. In the 1940s, for example, sociali-
sation of the economy was absolutely necessary because the country had been so wrecked by the War.
Even the Conservatives recognised that because they
continued nationalisation, for a while. So the country
was rebuilt and rebuilt for the better, with the NHS,
social security, and so on. This required higher taxes
on the rich and state controls over industry.

The Conservatives were worried about their class –
the rich – losing its status. A.H. Halsey's book on
Change in British Society (OUP) points out that the top
1% lost a tiny fraction of its wealth between the end of
the War and the 1970s, when the neoliberal programmes were implemented. The elites were terrified
about this. Literally terrified. They felt their wealth
slipping away, even thought it was a tiny percent. It's
like taking sweets away from children. They went into
a tantrum. In international relations there's a term for
it: the threat of a good example. It's Oxfam's phrase

about Nicaragua and how the country developed rapidly when, for a brief period, it escaped the sphere of US influence. But it generalises to power. The elites of Britain felt really threatened by socialism – remember what we were saying earlier about their paranoia. So they organised in their own class interests. It was call the New Conservativism. People like Nigel Lawson were telling party members that you can't have state provision for the poor,[230] all the while the poor provide circuitous – and sometimes blatant –subsidies for companies like Shell.

So can you give us a rundown of the kind of countries in which Britain is involved? Your work shows how the spread of British power is much greater than most people know.

'Involved' is a vague term, as is 'Britain'. There's a British person in every country in the world. So I assume you mean the state. Britain has embassies in most foreign countries. So the question is how much harm is Britain doing? That's hard to measure, for reasons we've discussed. But if our policies are hurting even one person, we should be concerned. That's even more true when they're hurting millions, as is the case. Our Middle East policies are a clear example of that. So let's contextualise the question. Offhand I can think of 'involvement' in terms of privatisation, subversion, policing, military training, and arms supplies. If I've left out something obvious, let me know. So within this framework, what does Britain do?

Privatisation: There's DFID, the Department for International Development. It used to be the Overseas Development Administration. It's a scam organisation that – under the cover of an aid programme – privatises assets in foreign countries for the benefit of British corporations. This is another way in which British taxpayers are getting fleeced and even worse poor people abroad are getting seriously hurt. One particularly obvious case was the Victoria Project in Sri Lanka in the '80s. It was a hydroelectricity project which displaced 30,000 people and cost British taxpayers £100m.[231] Today, DFID operates in about 30 countries.[232] And there's a direct correlation with policing, which I'll come onto. The people working in DFID at the lower levels, like the daughter of a friend of mine, think they're doing humanitarian work by raising the standards of 'backward' countries by, for example, pressing for laws that give rights to women or workers. They don't see the bigger picture, that these Westernised foundations are laid to advance London-based businesses.

There's also a sinister move to integrate so-called 'aid', which means investment, with militarism. This is what ideologues call the 'iron fist' and the 'velvet glove'.[233] DFID became a close partner of the National Security Council. It's described as a 'battleship' in Parliamentary hearings.[234] In 2011, it really integrated with the Foreign Office and the MoD, 'three pillars' of 'stability' as the government calls it. And to makes its image more appealing to NGOs with whom it partners, it's been further rebranded 'UK Aid'.

Subversion: Britain interferes in elections and with propaganda systems abroad via organisations like the British Council and the Westminster Foundation for Democracy – innocent-sounding entities. But behind the façade, they meddle in other countries' affairs. The British Council, for instance, says it operates in over 60 countries and does some good work, for displaced persons in Sri Lanka,[235] for example – displaced in part because of our support for the military, one might add. Take their operations in Libya, for example. As you know, we smashed up Libya, overthrew the dictatorship, and replaced it with something arguably worse: gangsters and *jihadi* factions warring with each other. What our leaders want to impose on Libya is some kind of political order that will benefit British corporations. How do you do that when you wreck a society with militias and aerial bombardments? Well, the British Council in Libya tested the waters. It asked Libyans what they thought of their political systems and media.[236] This information then feeds back to the Foreign Office which can strategise its next operations there. That's 'soft power'.

Or consider the Westminster Foundation for Democracy (WFD). This organisation works in over 20 countries. Consider the dire situation with Russia. The last thing we should be doing in this taut atmosphere is provoking Russia by interfering in the political affairs of its neighbours. 'Georgia is steadily progressing towards becoming a democratic state which shares the values of the European Union', says the WFD's website. The job of the WFD, for which taxpayers pay, is to assist this transition from the Russian sphere to the Western sphere of influence.[237]

Policing: Britain has policing missions all over the world, where British officers train their foreign counterparts in how to oppress unruly elements, which are usually people fighting for social justice. We're not the only ones. The US does, of course, so does Germany, Italy, and others. But if we're interested in making the world a better place, we should be concerned with what our leaders are doing, not solely to what extent. A few years ago a citizen filed a FOIA request and found out that the College of Policing is training officers in over 60 countries, many of them dictatorships like China[238]—

But aren't they doing a good thing by providing human rights training – raising those countries up to our standards?

There's a correlation. Every time the UK provides 'human rights training' as the government calls it – in Bangladesh, Colombia, Somalia – rights groups like Amnesty or Human Rights Watch report increased human rights abuses. I've documented this elsewhere.[239]

But returning to my point, there's policing the third world – making sure the 'savages armed with ideas', as Churchill called them,[240] aren't able to act on those ideas, like shaping the politics of their societies in ways to benefit their domestic populations, not consumers like us.

Military training: I don't think there's any information about how many forces around the world the UK trains. One of the most egregious things our elites are doing at the moment is training the Burmese Army while it carries out ethnic cleansing against the

Rohingya people. These are a people trapped between two artificial state lines, the Bangladeshi line and the Myanmar line. This is what happens when you create nation-states. People suffer. There's an independence movement which uses violence against the state, so the state is cracking down on the independence movement. But as is the case in counterinsurgency operations – Ireland during the so-called Troubles, 1950s' Kenya, Sri Lanka in the '80s and '00s, anywhere you can think of – the civilians pay the price. So before the ethnic cleansing started in Myanmar or Burma as we still call it, the UK announced its intention to train the Burmese Army – to give them 'human rights training', of course.[241] You can find the occasional article here or there – mainly in the right-wing press, interestingly enough, or perhaps not so interestingly – but try finding sustained reminders and analyses of these facts in the broadcast media, the media that reach the majority of the public. It's the same with Channel 4, for instance. They broadcast a documentary, *Sri Lanka's Killing Fields*. Does it mention Britain's role in training and arming the regime?

Arms supplies: That takes us to the arms industry. Britain arms everyone you can think of, including Iran and North Korea.[242]

We sell weapons to North Korea?

Yes, the list is quite astonishing. They get around this by issuing 'dual use' licenses, things that could be but are not necessarily used for military purposes, or licenses for 'non-lethal' equipment, like helmets and radios.

A helmet never killed anyone.

No, but anything that strengths a military oppressing its own or another population except in direct self-defence is immoral. And it's not only non-lethal stuff. We export chemicals, too.

How can they keep a straight face?

We are supposed to be horrified by Syria's chemical weapons, but the then-Foreign Secretary William Hague told Parliament that Britain sold chemical precursors to Syria.[243] Why aren't we equally horrified that our own governments sold the very chemicals used in the alleged attacks and don't even resign, let alone face disciplinary or legal action—

I know someone in the Foreign Office who I like and trust, a nice man, who said Hague was the inheritor of the 'ethical foreign policy', that he had a heart, and did a highly competent job. How can they maintain that bullshit? Or do you ever doubt your analysis on this? Could you be wrong?

It's hard to be wrong when they're admitting it. The 'ethical foreign policy' actually originated with Thatcher of the Conservatives, not Robin Cook of New Labour who spoke of the 'ethical dimension'. Thatcher said there has to be a 'moral basis' for foreign policy,[244] like selling Saddam even more weapons so he could kill more Kurds or selling billion-dollar arms systems to the Saudis from which Thatcher's son personally profited – which isn't even illegal in this country. Other, even more obscure examples include Thatcher sending the SAS to Colombia to train the military, which in turn trained death-squads, and her authorisation of special forces to train the Sri Lankan military in its war against Tamils. Robin Cook, Britain's Foreign Secretary under New Labour, came to power as sanctions were destroying Iraq. Another example of our ethical foreign policy.

So returning to them admitting things. In 2014, Hague said it in Parliament – that we exported weapons to Syria. He was referring to chemical stockpiles in the 1980s, but also more recently than that; about the exporting of machine parts that could have been used in Syria's chemical weapons production as late as the mid-2000s.

Surely a government in Britain could be a lot more popular by not exploiting the world?

They care about power, not popularity. They count on getting votes by scaring the public and demonising their opponents, not by making themselves look good. If they cared about popularity, they'd follow what the polls say: They'd get the private interests out of the NHS, renationalise most industries and services, not invade sovereign nations, and so on. The fact that they're not doing it shows they have higher priorities than popularity. And few Britons know or care about foreign policy, anyway.

In the case of the current Tory government, what's really interesting is the fact that Tory members halved since Cameron came to power in 2010.[245] Why? Because the party is so beholden to large corporations, particularly in the financial sector, which supplies half of its funding, that even Tories are getting exasperated with the lack of democracy in their own party.[246] So the party leaders don't even care about being popular among their own grassroots constituents, let alone the public. Their real constituents are the business community.

Governments also don't care about popularity when they have a weak and divided opposition. The big business class, like Shell, didn't oppose the New Labour government (1997–2010) because it was openly pro-business. They are terrified of Corby's Labour Party because it is openly against neoliberalism. But the corporate media, and even state media, have done a fantastic job of taking a party – Labour under Corbyn in this case – whose actual policies are *supported* by the majority of the public, and making it look ridiculous and unelectable.

But someone like Boris Johnson, doesn't he want to get re-elected? Or is this idea of craven politicians seeking electoral support a bit of a myth?

If we're talking about members of Parliament, even the worst Tory will get re-elected in a safe Tory seat. The 'worst' for its constituents could mean soft on migration and voting against benefit cuts. But that's ideology. Vote for the Tory, even if they're soft, because it's still better than Labour. The same goes for Labour. Ben Bradshaw MP for Exeter, for instance, is one of the worst. He's abstained from voting in favour of social security and in his ministerial roles justified arms exports to Israel, Nepal, and others.[247] But the attitude of the public is, 'Oh, well. He's not a Tory so vote for him'. But in contested constituencies, MPs have a battle between their cabinet and appeasing their grassroots, as opposed to corporate, constituents. Then you have pure careerist politicians like Blair and Cameron. They didn't go back to being MPs. They went off to get lucrative deals in the private sector.

So it's more about controlling and managing society than it is about electability. As long as the party itself can govern, which means as long as the class interests are safe, it's okay. With someone like Boris Johnson, he's paid to write for the *Telegraph* and was born into wealth and privilege. I doubt he's kept awake at night worrying about his political career when he can fade back into that privilege, hence his resignation over May's allegedly soft Brexit in July 2018. When he was Mayor of London, someone told him that he's insulting the poor because of his 250k a year salaries as a columnist. He replied: £250,000 a year is 'chickenfeed'.[248] When they have that kind of mentality it's less about politicians staying in power and more about enforcing their class system. There are plenty of replacements from the same class. Think of it as bacteria: an unconscious, self-organising, self-interested system. That's how many systems seem to operate.

So could we just elect a Labour government and that will sort out all the problems?

There's no one solution to all our problems, much less from political parties, even progressive ones. We're in a dichotomy because on the one hand, we shouldn't be delegating responsibility to others to sort out our problems. But on the other, law – or more specifically, law enforcement – restricts us from taking matters into our own hands; spontaneously building houses for the poor on the acres of unused land owned by the rich, for example, or going on permanent rent strikes against landlords.

Then there's the question of conflicting interests. Britain is a country like any other. It has a large population that has diverse objectives and needs. Take the example of tenant seizures of landlord properties. Very few Britons would support that because fairness and justice when it comes to housing is not part of our culture. It's axiomatic that people should be allowed to not only own several properties but exploit the poverty of others who can't get onto the housing ladder. How is a centralised politician taking their orders from London supposed to appease both the tenant and the landlord? No single political party can appeal to everyone's needs, unless they make conditions so unliveable that everyone has to depend on that party simply to survive. That's what dictators do. Then we're assuming that Labour or whichever party actually has the interests of the public at heart. But, like a microcosm of the nation-state, a political party is an amorphous mix of concerns, goals, and interests; some of which are shared, others are not. So there are internal divisions which make the party look less appealing to the electorate.

Consider the technical question about how you're going to get there. In the last election, Labour got just 3% of the vote-share less than the Tories, but Labour ended up with 262 seats in Parliament and the Tories got 318. We've got a Tory government for the sake of a three percent difference in vote share.[249] This is because the people in power arranged a political system in which majoritarian democracy is fragmented across unequal Parliamentary representation. Plymouth, for instance, is a city of a quarter of a million people, but it has just two constituencies – three, technically, but one is within the boundary of South Hams. This creates problems for tenants. I remember when I rented there, just inside the boundary of Plymouth, Housing Benefit was accessible because it was Plymouth City Council. But for people renting inside the South Hams District Council, Housing Benefit was harder to claim because it was a Tory council. So by including the South Hams MP within the Plymouth boundary, it splits the vote in favour of the Tories. When you look at smaller constituencies, like East Devon, which is traditionally Tory, it's much smaller. So the Tories take advantage of having more numerous constituencies with smaller numbers of constituents than big towns and cities. This goes on all over the country. We have such a limited understanding of how our democracy works – and I'm no different, I'm still figuring it out because there are no books or media analyses of it – that we let the politicians in London erode our representation.

So even if you could get a large number of people to share the same interests, people in power find ways to split the vote, as with local boundary changes and so on.

But people like Nigel Lawson, Ken Clarke, they don't seem evil. Same with Boris Johnson. These people seem capable of having an emotion. How can you explain why they're so horrific?

They don't see themselves as horrific. Who does? A good example of this recently is Iain Duncan Smith, who left his office at the Department for Work and Pensions. He oversaw many of the cuts to social security under the pretext of austerity. Smith was interviewed by the BBC about these criminal cuts to public spending. Literally criminal. According to DWP figures, which they initially tried to hide, thousands of people died after having their benefits stopped.[250] In the interview, Smith starts to cry. But he wasn't crying for people whom he'd sent to their graves, he was crying because he felt so pleased that he had helped people into work. He related a story of a woman who had spent all her life on benefits and thanked him because now, she suddenly had the dignity of getting a job.[251]

Is there any truth in that? I know people trapped on benefits – it's not great for anyone...

Most people on social security are either retired – they've work hard most of their lives and are enjoying their retirement, which they've earned – or they're in work and are simply not being paid enough to survive. Next comes disabled people. Then you've got people between jobs. Fraud accounts for less than 1% of claims.[252]

The propaganda is that benefits are a drain on society and are designed for scroungers. The fact is that social security is a subsidy for corporations. When corporations know that their workforce survives partly on government payments – people in work also claiming benefits – they know that they don't have to pay their staff high or even liveable wages, the government makes sure their workers stay afloat. And they don't have to provide a decent pension. Governments want to keep corporations happy by not legislating to force them to pay their workers a living wage. It's the same with Housing Benefit – it's just a state subsidy for private landlords. If you trace the money further, it's also a subsidy for banks, because banks are the ones who lend to landlords so they can buy. As a tenant, you're not allowed to claim housing benefit to pay off a mortgage. But the landlord is allowed to do that by having a tenant, many of whom are claiming Housing Benefit. The fact that the entire society is run on this kleptocratic model is bad enough. But the fact that no one seems to notice is an impressive achievement of propaganda. The whole notion of social security is part of the incredible illusion in which we live.

KEEP HUMA
ON LEADS

I believe in the

SURVEILLANCE STATE. If you've got nothing to hide, you've got nothing to fear. And just to make sure that the **GOVERNMENT HAS EVERY POSSIBLE PIECE OF INFORMATION ON ME**, every month I make sure I package up my turds and cum rags and send them off to GCHQ and 10 Downing Street.

Chapter 8

Beware the eggheads

Or: How professors shape policy...

Name some of the people behind the scenes and how academics fit in.

You can look at the structure of the way the US works, because that's the world superpower. Back in the 1960s, the Joint Chiefs of Staff – the heads of all of the armed forces – sat around and plotted terror attacks on Americans which they would blame on Cuba. That was Operation Northwoods, now declassified.[253] So the Joint Chiefs of Staff are some people behind the scenes. We've mentioned the oil companies, so the executives, and more likely the geostrategists they employ who sit around studying the maps and cultural geography of the world.

In terms of people in academia who are sympathetic to power. Zbigniew Brzezinski, for example, started off in universities and business, headed the Trilateral Commission, became an advisor to President Jimmy Carter. He helped organise the *Mujahideen* – the so-called 'freedom fighters' whom the US and Britain trained and armed to lure the Soviets into invading Afghanistan in the late-1970s. Arthur Schlesinger is another case. He was an historian by profession and an advisor to President Kennedy. Francis Fukuyama worked at the State Department and went on to write books generally supportive of US foreign policy. Historian John Lewis Gaddis was invited to read parts of his book to the George W. Bush administration at the White House. Samantha Power started off as a journalist-academic-propagandist and went on to act as Obama's ambassador to the UN.

In the UK, we've got guys like Niall Ferguson, an outright racist who called Iraq a 'sun-scorched sandpit' and referred to the Middle East's 'retarded political culture'.[254] He even went on television with a documentary about Chile under Pinochet – whom the British protected in his later years – saying that it's a difficult choice, but Pinochet's torture machine was worth the pain because it transformed Chile into a neoliberal economy.[255] The astonishing thing about it is that nobody notices when a respected academic goes on television and advocates torture. Ferguson had a top academic position at both Oxford in the UK and Harvard in the US. He's written official histories for the Rothschild family. Now he's got a job as a kind of advisor to the Bilderberg Group, which meets behind closed doors each year – though some meetings may soon be broadcast to improve the Group's image – so that the people who really run the world, the upper classes in business, can talk off the record. Ferguson is a really extreme case because he's so right-wing. But this generalises to the so-called liberal intelligentsia.

The Royal Institute for International Affairs (Chatham House) frequently hosts discussions and conferences. It's basically a think-thank for foreign policy. To give an example of how that works: Back in 2010, Barclays bank, BP oil, and BAE weapons – all the b's – funded a series of papers on the future of British foreign policy.[256] They or Chatham House, it's not clear who, because we don't have access to the pay slips – hired a couple of academics to write assessments of the shape of global order and Britain's role within it. Presumably, these companies wanted to academics to come up with intellectual justifications for why we need weapons systems, to take oil resources, and put the money in private banks. The subtitle of their paper was *UK Foreign Policy in an Age of Uncertainty*. They said that the British public were basically pacifistic, but pacifism isn't good for the economy because so much of our trade and investment is tied up overseas. So to overcome this dichotomy they said that the government should sell foreign policy as 'managing global risks on behalf of British citizens'. This was one of several papers that was circulated among the foreign policy planners and ended up shaping the government's official National Security Strategy (NSS). The NSS was called *A strong Britain in an age of uncertainty*. It even used the same language as the main document on which it was based. The only difference was the that NSS was a glossy brochure aimed at MPs, cabinet ministers, and the media, with all the references on how to deceive the public removed.

That's a specific case of the hierarchy at work. A small concentration of very wealthy corporations hiring or working with academics to write policy that serves their interests. The academics find ways of selling the agenda as being in the interests of the British public. And then you get the really sanitised version being presented to MPs in the form of the official NSS. All the references to deception omitted, the NSS – in any given year – just runs through a list of things we need to be scared of: climate change, which is ironic, given BP's involvement, at least in the 2010 case; instability caused by globalisation, again ironic given Barclays' involvement; well-armed nation states, think BAE systems; terrorists, cyber-attacks... Just anything to keep people frightened and justify the centralisation of power and spending tax money on Armed Forces.

I was outside a nightclub the other evening for graduation day and an international relations (IR) graduate was asked by a young Royal Air Force (RAF) guy why he had studied that topic. He replied, 'So I can tell you which countries to bomb'. And although he then feigned that he was joking, he really wasn't joking. I remember it was quite a disturbing scene, with the RAF guy looking uncomfortable and harassed while his 'friend' smoked a cigarette and concluded, 'Yeah, but some countries really do need bombing'. So are academics more important than we realise in shaping policy?

They're a sort of interface between government and corporations. Read the front matter of dry, boring academic books on British foreign policy and you'll get an idea of who sponsors them. The fact that the government sponsors them means that the government wants intellectual outcomes favourable to its interests. Plymouth University's Jamie Gaskarth, for instance, writes in his Acknowledgements: 'I have relied heavily on the generosity of officials in the Foreign and Commonwealth Office and the Ministry of Defence'. For the book, he interviews people like Malcolm Rifkind and Mark Malloch-Brown. And what conclusions does he draw? Exactly what you'd expect: that the so-called 'intervention' in Libya 'derived its authority from UN Security Council Resolutions 1970, 1973 and 2009'.[257]

Never mind that the government won't release the full opinion of the Attorney-general because they know full-well it was an illegal war. Well, that's not a scholar, that's a propagandist – no critical thinking. Or I should say, critical thinking within limits, like the question, 'Was Libya a mistake?'. It's a cushy job, to get paid in a respectable position to spout government propaganda. But high status means that people take you seriously, unfortunately. So these sort of books lay the intellectual foundations that allow war crimes to be committed. And Gaskarth's far from being the only one.

We should also remember that intellectuals have a history of supporting those in power. Francis Bacon was arguably Britain's first scholar of Empire an advisor to queen Elizabeth. He pioneered what we now call 'just war theory', writing: 'a just fear of an imminent danger, though no blow given, is a lawful cause of a war' (*Of Empire* 1612). That became the 'preventive war doctrine' of George W. Bush in 2003. Then there's Thomas Hobbes who famously wrote *The Leviathan* (1651). The book gave those in power the intellec-

tual justification to maintain the state to act as a unifying force because it's a dangerous world out there.
Hobbes was given a pension by Charles II, whom he
taught as a boy. And it's not just the UK. Aristotle famously tutored Alexander the Great.

In the 1980s, the French intellectual class bol-
stered US efforts to undermine the Soviets by turning
against 'communism' – as if the Soviet Union was real
communism – and embracing 'capitalism' – as if the
system of organised plunder we have today is real capitalism. There's an interesting CIA report, now declassified, which goes into depth about the importance of
the French intellectuals of the period in shaping cultural and political thought.[258] At the same time, the
MoD in Britain was waging a virtual war against anti-
nuclear activists, including the Greenham Common
movement led mainly by women. They were spying on
them, countering their intelligence, and so on.[259] The
Thatcher government assisted these general efforts to
maintain the power of a privileged few by cutting back
on Bradford University's peace studies programme. So
academics who do think critically can have a harder
time finding work. That's not to pity them. In Saudi
Arabia they can get decapitated or flogged.

Turning to the present: It doesn't look good to
have big business directly dictating policy. Sometimes
it happens and it gets exposed, as in the case of BP
lobbying memos to Tony Blair expressing their desire
for Iraqi oil. Well, those got released thanks to the
dedicated efforts of a conscientious citizen, Greg
Muttitt, and they prove what we already knew: that
invading Iraq was mostly about the oil.[260] It shows in
whose interests the government works, how undemo-

cratic it is, and so on. So if you can create a veneer of intellectual legitimacy, it looks less bad.

In the UK, there's no real class of intellectuals like there is, or was, in the USA, where you had the 'mandarins' – like Schlesinger, Fukuyama, and so on. But if you look at the kind of strategy documents that I've been talking about, it tends to be the usual Oxbridge set, the professors at Oxford and Cambridge. They come from the upper classes and are simply representing their class interests. They're exactly the kind of people who go into the oil industry, and similar professions, as advisors and so forth, or into the higher levels of politics and the military. So it's a pool of self-interest. And the ones who go into academia are hired by people from the same class working in corporations to formulate policy and give it a veneer of intellectual legitimacy. Their views filter down to the cabinet. The cabinet then, I suppose, puts the final result through the public relations filter and you get the glossy pamphlets that make policy a bit more palatable to the general public. The final filter is the media, which take the glossy version and report it, marginally, to news consumers.

So academics create the intellectual conditions that justify the actions of elites in the minds of the general public – especially since those actions are generally against the public interest and in the interests of the upper classes.

Can't we just get lucky one day and a nice guy will get to head MI6 or whatever?

Anybody that seems to portray any kind of humanity within the system – never mind the façade shown to the public – or act in ways that appear to be against what's called the 'national interest' isn't going to last very long. Their promotions will stall, they'll get deselected, or whatever happens in their particular organisation.

I was surprised that somebody like whistleblower David Shayler was able to get a job in MI5 handling sensitive information. Unfortunately, he's since gone mad. Maybe something was done to him as a warning against other whistleblowers, but that's just speculation. At the time, he seemed to be a genuine person with a conscience who exposed MI6's financing of terrorist groups. He went to prison for other revelations. His life was destroyed. You can't imagine someone like that getting to the top of MI5 or MI6.

I was talking with my Tory councillor friend about Britain having mercenary forces and she said, 'Well, every country does that!' How bad is Britain? Is it one of the worst countries?

Imagine somebody on trial for murder saying, 'Well, lots of people commit murder'. The court wouldn't even laugh if that was uttered as a defence. So to say that everybody's got mercenary forces is not much of an argument.

In terms of being 'the worst', that's difficult to measure. We were talking earlier about the underlying structures of the global economy, which set conditions for famine, poverty, low life expectancy, high infant mortality, and so on. We can try and tally up those deaths, but how do you do it? For example, with pollution the United States is the world's worst polluter, per capita. Bangladesh, let's say, has millions of climate refugees because the country is basically marshland, rivers, tributaries, and so on. It's very prone to rising sea levels. So if you were to somehow create a model of global emissions that factored in US pollution to climate change, how do you say that a particular percentage of sea-level rise is caused by another particular percentage of US emissions, and therefore causes this particular percentage of Bangladeshi climate refugees?

On the other hand, it's easy to make the world seem more complicated than it is. In one of those dry, academic books on British foreign policy in the mid-2000s – again, supported by the elites it praises, Paul D. Williams agrees that thousands of Afghan civilians died in the bombing in 2001. But he says that pinpointing Britain's direct responsibility is difficult.[261] So from this justification for war crimes by the intelligentsia, we have the outright denial that dropping bombs makes our country directly culpable.

Generally, there's a correlation between the amount of power a person or institution has and their ability to do damage. Except in really obvious cases, like controlling children's behaviour so that they don't put themselves in danger, power is inherently abusive. As an aside, people with power often think of everyone else as children who have to be controlled. Colonial records speak of Iraq as a naughty child that needs 'spanking'.[262] The idea that one mentally functioning adult should have power over another is an abusive dynamic. That's why it's important to keep relationships – with partners, friends, colleagues – as equal as possible.

So with that in mind, how bad is Britain? Britain is nothing now compared to what it was in the days of Empire. As its power diminished, so too did its capacity to do as much harm in proportion to that diminishment of power. The United States is the world superpower, so its potential to do harm is much greater. People would argue that its potential to do good is also strong. But that ignores power being inherently abusive, except in very specific cases. The US today is dropping the most bombs of any nation, it's polluting the most per capita, it's maintaining and expanding a very destructive economic programme called neoliberalism. Asia had, until recently, avoided the neoliberal programmes. Europe, since the Maastricht Treaty 1992, has been a neoliberal economic bloc. And this is harming people, too. So the US is probably the worst. Not because the people running the US are particularly evil. They're not like Nazis. But they have so much power, that anything they do is going to have significant ripple effects across the world.

How much difference does evilness make? The people running Britain may be doing evil things, but what about those who are not consciously cruel or manipulative? You know, people who just like eating strawberries at Wimbledon and owning Aga ovens.

They can be both cruel and manipulative and enjoy eating strawberries. It depends which moral equation you're using.

Take a car accident. Deliberately running someone down in a car with the intent of murdering them, assuming they've done nothing serious to you or your family, and assuming it's not an act of self-defence, is wrong. It's murder. We'd also agree that accidentally running someone over, knowing you've done it, and driving off – hit and run – is also wrong. You've let fear get the better of you and you should have stayed and called an ambulance, and the police. So those two things – murder and hit-and-run – are different. One was deliberate and the other was so negligent that most people would consider it almost as bad as deliberate. However, if you accidentally run someone over and kill them, but you do the right thing – call the ambulance and police, apologise to the family, feel bad for the rest of your life – most people agree that it's tragic but morally acceptable. So that's one moral equation.

But now consider another: murder, negligence or genuine accident, the outcome is the same. Someone has died. So it doesn't matter to the corpse what the intention or circumstances were. It does seem to matter to the family. People who have lost loved ones in car accidents seem to find more solace when the perpetrator expresses genuine regret and guilt.

So if we compare foreign or domestic policy to the car accident analogy, there's intended and unintended consequences. In Iraq in 2003, it was an intention to commit mass murder. That was called Shock and Awe. Although it was consciously devised, it was intended to be less cruel than letting the war drag on. The objective was to kill a lot of people very quickly, traumatise the nation into surrendering, and then avoid even more civilian deaths and deaths of US military personnel – the latter being more important to the war planners. So inside the minds of the planners, it was a perfectly legitimate, moral strategy. To the objective observer, it's psychopathic. The US or Britain had no legal or moral right to do anything in Iraq, let alone wipe out thousands of people in the first few days of bombing. So they weren't consciously cruel or manipulative in their own minds, quite the opposite. And neither were the Nazis. The Nazis genuinely believed that the Aryan race was the best thing in the world and that it was under threat from everyone, especially Jews. Speaking of intellectuals and power, even apparently intelligent people like Martin Heidegger believed this. So they devised all sorts of plans to – in their own sick heads – protect themselves and save the Fatherland from the rodential barbarians. But as with the Shock and Awe example, to an outside observer, like a student of history, it is pure psychopathy – of the worst kind.

Then you've got unintended consequences that result from inhumane policies. Going back to the car analogy, such policies result in outcomes that might as well have been intentional. For example, thousands of people died in the UK when their social security was cut by the government. They government didn't intend to kill them. They just wanted to keep Britain an attractive place in which to invest by signalling that they were reducing the deficit. Reducing the deficit means carrying on with the neoliberal programmes. It means demonstrating to investors that you can kick the public in the face and make them pick up the tab when the gravy train derails. The implication there is the same as with the car accident. If you create conditions in which your actions are going to lead to deaths, it doesn't make too much moral difference to the victims or outsiders whether the outcome was intentional.

Also, the nation-state, the neoliberal economy, etc., are rather abstract concepts. It's easier for the brain to cope with thinking of a hitman taking out a target than it is to visualise a complex and often contradictory system like an economic structure, even though the hitman might kill someone and an economic cutback might do the same.

I can just about drum up some pride watching England during the football World Cup. How much better would Britain have to be for you to have pride in your country?

The nation-state is just a romantic idea. Pretty emblems, like flags and songs, form people's perceptions of what the 'nation' is. The 'nation' includes your culture, like sports and language. There's a strong ethnic element, even in ethnically diverse nations because the nation is abstract enough to project your own ideas into it. A nation can be whatever you want. So I understand the appeal, but when you recognise it as a construct, it can no longer have appeal because it's not a real thing.

In addition, you're born into this complex series of things called a nation-state. You have no say about anything that goes on within it. Any kind of democracy has to be fought for. The nation-state usually means the capital city, which is where the money and power lies, in both senses of the word. It's where elites, some of them elected representatives, make the laws that you have to follow. So instead of the UK, we're mostly taking about London. The idea of national pride is extremely dangerous, for one thing. We've seen throughout history what it can lead to. Even if you had a relatively peaceful, so-called neutral nation-state like Switzerland – which, in reality, wasn't so neutral because it was laundering money for the Nazis,[263] but that's another story – where does the pride come in? Can you be proud of what other people do? If so, should it extend from friends and family to political leaders, who are strangers, even ones you didn't vote for? Well, then we're talking about being proud of *individuals*, rather than an abstract thing called a nation.

I can imagine being proud for a brief period, localised in space and time, and in very specific circumstances. For example, when you're being attacked by an outside force, you're confronted with a choice. Come together as something – in this case the nation-state, though in the past it might have been a kingdom – and defeat the enemy. Or don't come together because you oppose the idea of a nation-state or king, etc. In that context, it makes sense to support the nation. That's how the elites of today keep the nation together, in part, by finding foreign threats against which we must come together.

I can imagine that many Indians were very proud of India when they kicked the British out in 1947. Or the Algerians were proud when they kicked out the French in '62. But then, what do we mean by 'the Indians' or 'the Algerians'? This puts the diverse ethnicities and cultures of those countries into the pigeonhole of national homogeneity. Do we mean the collaborator classes who were happy to keep the British and French in their respective countries? Do we mean the Muslims of India, many of whom became Pakistanis in the bloody civil war? How many of them would have preferred to have remained under British rule than be victims of mass killings? Maybe many Pakistanis felt proud eventually about having a nation-state where they could be safe from Hindu nationalism?

But what about former PM John Major's vision of a Britain of warm beer and cricket? The good things about Britain?

It's just more deception, to point to the supposed greatness of your own nation, whichever nation that may be. It makes your public think that you've reached the pinnacle of civilisation, so there's no point even thinking let alone fighting for something better.

We're often told that Britain is the 'world's oldest democracy', but the colonial planners knew that wasn't true. When they tried to impose the British way of life – meaning their own   on Afghans, Australians, Nigerians, they wrote papers explaining that it was difficult because no one recognised anyone as a leader.[264] So these communities, tribes we call them, were direct democracies. These were the real oldest democracies. That's an example of where we're supposed to be proud of something that is patently false. And it's not only false, it's dangerous for the people in Whitehall, or even in your local council, to give people the idea that they could control their own little community and not be ruled by a central power. So it's better to feed illusions about being the oldest democracy. The implication is that, as the oldest, we set the standard so it can't get any better than us.

I don't want to romanticise so-called tribes. They had and have serious problems. They were patriarchies, fought violently with rival communities, and so on. But they had freedom – as far as it's possible to be free in material reality and as a biological organism. These 'tribes' didn't understand the concept of borders or land ownership, or representative democracy. They were really the last free peoples. Some, like the Hadza of what is now Tanzania or the Awá of South America have retained that freedom, but they're living precariously now, as civilisation approaches and gradually destroys them. And to call these early peoples Australians and Nigerians is a disservice, because it was pre-nation-state. The borders and political systems we now call Australia and so on were constructs imposed by the British.

Another example of construction of national pride is the National Health Service. I'm writing a book at the moment about privatisation. The publisher is asking me to big up the notion that the NHS is the envy of the world. Well, that's just not true. Obviously, there's no point comparing our superior healthcare system to Iraq's or Nigeria's. That's not sensible. Of course it's going to be the best compared to those. Let's compare it to a nation that has similar standards of living, France or Germany. My partner's French. If you ask her family, 'Do you sit around envying the NHS?', they'll laugh at you. First of all, most French people have had no experience of the NHS. Secondly, how are they going to know about it, except through visits to the UK or friends living here? They'll know about it through their own propaganda, French TV and newspapers. Is the French propaganda system really going to say, 'Our system is crap, let's mimic the Roast Beef?'. Of course, not – any more than ours is going to say, 'Let's copy the Frogs'. So when you've got two competing narratives, how do you make a sensible evaluation? One way is to look at international surveys. They show that ranking health systems among comparably developed nations – except the US, which is universally panned for having a terrible health system – is impossible because so many measures are used. For general performance, the NHS comes top or close to the top. But for patient care, it ranks near the bottom. On measures like prevention and mental health, it's also ranked low. But on affordability, it's high.

So to drill it into people's heads – that we're the oldest democracy or we've got the best health service – is just mind control.

Wouldn't it be nice, though? To be proud of your country? Isn't it natural to love a group, whether it's seven people or 70 million people?

That gets back to the communities that I was talking about. Taking the innate drive to identify with a group and broadening it to a nation-state to serve elite interests is where it becomes a weapon. Our instinct is to the group because the group ensures our own survival. So that commitment is innate. But there's nothing innate about committing yourself to a nation-state because it's an artificial creation, and one that's quite recent in the history of humans. It was only a couple of centuries ago that nation-states were formed by elites for elites. Ordinary people don't recognise them. That's why you've got independence movements, like Scottish nationalism or Catalonian nationalism.

Scots and Catalonians were absorbed into the wider nation-states of the UK and Spain, respectively. They have regional accents that might as well be dialects, and there are dialects that are entirely different languages. If they achieved independence, they'd become their own nation-states, but within those you'd get regionalism. Even within England, so not including Northern Ireland, Scotland, and Wales, you've got small movements that support regional independence, like freedom for Cornwall. And of course public opinion polls say time and time again that most people think London has far too much power,[265] that local representatives are more trusted than national ones.[266] This is a reflection of the unnatural conditions into which we are forced and against which people struggle.

It's not the same for everyone. Some people, of course, love the unifying concept of a nation, as long as you conform to it. But what about those who don't conform? Why should they be excluded from the thing(s) referred to as a 'nation'? There are people all over the world, like the Pashtuns of what is now Afghanistan and Pakistan, who found themselves on different sides of state borders, which they still refuse to recognise, because the British came along and imposed those borders. They are now unnaturally called Afghan Pashtuns and Pakistani Pashtuns, depending the side of the line that someone else drew – literally with a pencil – on which they find themselves.

This generalises. The migration flows of today are not solely about desperate people looking for work, though that's a big part, of course. It's in the nature of humans to travel and be nomadic. That's how our species populated the Earth, by moving around. We left Africa – we assume it's Africa, there's perhaps some evidence that it might have been somewhere else initially,[267] but certainly Africa as well – about 100,000 years ago and spread all over the place. It's in people's nature to breed with different ethnic groups, trade with or assimilate into different cultures, blend languages, and so on. The nation-state makes this very difficult. And as the neoliberal programmes come into being, which say that your only value is how much can someone else profit from you, that natural urge to travel is getting harder and harder, as border security tightens. You're permitted entry on the basis of whether you can serve an economic system, not because you're a free human being.

So to divide us up into nation-states is a weapon used by elites. There's a book by Eli Saga, *At the Dawn of Tyranny*, where he goes through the history of what became nation-states to trace the origins of social control and ask why so many people succumb to control by so few. He uses the unassimilated kingdoms of the British and other empires as a guide to how the pre-historical kingdoms probably looked. It starts off with a few dominant elites assimilating another community, or 'tribe', and they use violence against others in the tribe, and before long you've got a complex hierarchy with a few violent people at the top controlling everyone else with a combination of force, law, and money – whether the money is food or shells or coins, it doesn't matter. The ever-growing society conforms to that particular culture.[268] Then you get city-states, as in Babylon and Greece. This system spreads and develops into empires.

So you're saying there's a justification for national pride in a war, but now since the end of the World Wars, it's outdated?

I don't think that it's outdated because it was never legitimate. One of the cases that is really quite frightening and demonstrates the insanity to which otherwise normal, rational people can be driven, is the case of World War 1 of interactions between British and German soldiers in the trenches.[269] You were talking about football. Well, here you had cases where in between the fighting, the German and British troops would lay down their arms and have a game of football! When it was time to fight again, they'd stop playing and go and kill each other. That tells you that if you take the war and nationalism elements out of the equation, they're just normal guys who want to have fun and enjoy life.

You've said to me that politics is deliberately made complicated.

There are different layers to this. If we're talking about domestic politics, the objective of people in power is to take as much power from you as possible, until a tipping point is reached where you've nothing to lose, so you either vote for people they regard as extremists, like a far-right or far-left candidate, or have a revolution. So the system pushes people as far as it can. Sometimes it pushes people too far and you get Jeremy Corbyn, a serious contender. But most of the time it's about maintaining the status quo.

How do they do that? In many ways. At the local level, you can't just get funding for a community project. You've got to apply for grants. The Treasury in London determines how much money they give for projects like that. Local bureaucracies make the final decisions. You have local council elections but the council depends on money from London. It has ways of raising its own money, through taxes or investing in Icelandic banks, we've now learned,[270] and that raises the issue of corruption. So anything to keep people from getting directly involved. Having representatives elected in periodic elections instead of direct action. That's at the local level. Then there's local media. The BBC and ITV have regional news, which from what I've seen in Devon is a joke. There's almost no content relevant to ordinary people's lives. Just trivia. Then there's local print media, which is often a subsidiary of right-wing, London-based corporations. So you get the usual content: human interest stories, crime, almost nothing about how the system works and what you can do about it. There needs to be democratisation of the media, where people get involved in creating media content in a cooperative, not some fragmented thing like the internet.

At the national level, it's even worse. For one thing, there's the question of how votes are distributed across Parliamentary seats in proportion to the vote-share. So the Tories and Labour are about 50-50 in terms of the sheer number of people who voted for one or the other party – with a small margin of percentage difference. But that doesn't translate into a roughly equal number of seats in Parliament. Then you've got boundary changes to give the Tories more votes. Next comes the issue of political funding. The Tories are 50% funded by financial institutions.[271] Not even banks – we're talking financial institutions like asset companies, liquidity firms, pensions companies, and hedge funds. There's a concentration of power behind the scenes, too. This is alienating even traditional Tory members. As I said, since Cameron came along, Tory membership halved. Literally halved. Studies have shown that many Tories at the grassroots simply don't feel listened to by the Tory elite, the Camerons and the Mays. So until Corbyn came along – the unifying external threat – grassroots Tory members were leaving in droves. The Tory elite is paying attention to its real constituents, the financial sector, not the grassroots constituents.

So there is alienation even among rich people. They're in a political battle with the super-rich. This possibly explains why even the Tories under May with her Brexit strategy, if you can call it that, have alienated business. There are companies that make tangible things, like Airbus, BMW, and Siemens, who are worried about a hard Brexit. May & Co. don't *appear* to be acting in their interests, though we don't have access to internal records. Why? I suspect it's because the Tories are so beholden to the financial sector. There are others, like certain hedge funds – not all of them – that want a hard Brexit. These institutions, unlike Airbus and the rest, make money from money, with financial instruments, bond procurements, etc., not from physical products.

So among all this extreme complexity, there's the question of how this is portrayed to the average BBC- or Sky News audience. It's just really boring. There's a huge focus on minutia which avoids the bigger picture. Did such and such politician live up to their promise on a particular issue? The behind-the-scenes operations, like hedge funds or what boundary changes imply for democracy, are not covered. Or if they are, it's very marginal. There is no broader analysis of, say, the neoliberal structure and how our society compares with other so-called developed nations. So we get no sense of perspective.

Media have the ridiculous phrase 'objectivity', which means the media allow the government to have its say on a particular issue. Then they'll bring in a member of the opposition who usually disagrees. And that's it. They don't have a broad range of representatives. They don't have a guy from a hedge fund sitting there telling you how they're screwing up the economy. Or a trade union representative. Sometimes they'll invite Len McCluskey of Unite the Union, or equivalent, but it's tokenistic and not sustained. The tone is also negative, 'Who are you to be representing people?'

They don't have a fisherman from a village who's convinced that EU fishing quotas have made him redundant. So that upsets the nationalistic right which accuses the BBC of being too left-wing. They don't have an analyst explaining that Britain doesn't follow many of the EU's directives, anyway. So people don't understand what little control Brussels actually has over us. They don't have people describing the horrendous conditions of living with social security cuts. Again, you can always find exceptions and contradictions to what I've just said, but it's a fact that these voices don't form the general content or shape the direction of the media. It's a top-down, dictatorial message: The government says this, the opposition doesn't agree. And that's it.

So when you try and balance this 'objectivity' by running a story or broadcasting a documentary exposing, say, social security cuts, that's called 'being polemical'. The BBC is not thought of as polemical for parroting the government line and the line of the opposition and mostly excluding all other voices. It's called objective. The whole broadcast news system is set up to present complicated situations in a one-dimensional and boring way – like focusing on executive decisions as opposed the underlying causes of those decisions.

One of the consequences of this entire system – the lack of local democracy, the centralisation of power in London, and poor presentation of this to the public via the media – is that people are disengaged. Be it going to the polls or having grassroots activities, people are alienated from the political system, which is what elites want; unless it produces so much alienation that their system collapses. Another factor that political elites rely on is the working culture. People are so exploited now that they just don't have time to get involved or to really educate themselves about things. Laws against trade unions have meant that we have some of the lowest levels of unionisation in Europe.[272] That means that working people don't get to meet with union representatives and learn more about the intricacies of how things work. It's not part of the office culture – or wherever you work – to talk about politics, because it's so divisive and boring. So you can't get information, organise, formulate strategies, share ideas and so on.

With the new 'gig economy', you have an extremely precarious workforce – called the precariat by political scientists[273] – who have zero-hours contracts. That's about 1.8m people.[274] There are tenants on short-term tenancies. Rental agency fees are now astronomical and they're reluctant to let to people on social security. Councils have introduced 'bidding systems', where you can't just wait on a list for a council house, you have log on each morning and bid for a property.[275] These are just ways of putting people in competition with each other. Worker against worker, landlord against tenant, renter against renter. Being in competition with other people is against everyone's interest, except the interest of the elites. When people are competing with each other, they're not getting together to challenge the power of the few. This has made the entire social structure extremely fragile.

So in this situation, there's not much of a threat of political engagement because people have got too much to do in their working lives. And the media don't systematically reflect these concerns.

PEACE
CIDER
AND
SOCIALISM

Conclusion

What can we do?

Or: How to be active and *stay on your arse!*

We're always being told, 'It's a dangerous world out there'. Is it?

It's a *very* dangerous world. But not for the reason's we're told. The standard reasons we're given are that Russia is coming to get us, terrorists are coming to get us, and so on. There's a huge gap between the rhetoric and the reality.

Back in 1997, one of the Chatham House books I mentioned said that Britain is not in any danger in terms of being invaded or having its territories conquered. They asked, therefore, should we become 'friendly hedgehogs' – their phrase – mind our own business but have a enough of an armed force in case we're directly attacked.[276] Well, that sounds sensible. And in fact polls around that time suggested that most British people thought that we should be 'friendly hedgehogs'. They asked if Britain should be more like Sweden and similar countries in terms of its foreign policy, and the majority said yes.[277] But we live in a democracy, remember, so public opinion counts for nothing.

So the Chatham House authors in 1997, again academics, asked this question and concluded, no. Obviously we should keep trying to dominate as much of the world as possible, even though we're a much smaller power now. They said that Britain is safer than it's ever been. We don't have international competition that can pose an existential threat. We find the same things more recently. Evidence presented by Oxbridge academics to Parliament in the formulation of the NSS 2015 said that Britain doesn't have peer competitors and this is, in their words, 'a nice problem to have'.[278] Well, if it's 'nice', why is it a 'problem'? It's a problem because if there are no real enemies, how do you justify a continuation of aggressive policies and significant military spending? So from that point of view, it's not a dangerous world.

However, from the point of view of objective sanity, it's extremely dangerous. You've got the US, a nuclear power, trying to dominate other nuclear powers in what strategists call 'conflicts short of war'. And specialists understand how grave the situation is. *The Bulletin of the Atomic Scientists* was set up by people who had worked on the Manhattan Project, developing nuclear weapons. That organisation continues today. It has a symbolic Doomsday Clock. Midnight means the end of the world. The hands can be set back and forth, depending on how close they think we're getting to terminal disaster. When Trump came to power, it was set to 2 ½ minutes to Midnight. That's because of the tensions with Russia over Ukraine and Syria. But also because of Trump's commitment to making climate change worse. A year later, the hands were set to 2 minutes to Midnight – the closest they've been since the Soviets detonated the hydrogen bomb in the 1950s.[279]

If we lived in a sane world, first of all this wouldn't have happened. Secondly, as it is happening, it should be all over the front pages every day until people protest enough to de-escalate and even denuclearise. But the media don't seem concerned about their own survival.

So the real threats, namely the *insane* behaviour of our leaders, is omitted from political discourse and even thought. Who even *thinks* about such things, except dedicated groups the Campaign for Nuclear Disarmament? But the very minor, almost non-existent threats, like Russia's strategic moves. We're supposed to be terrified. And all the while, the real dangers are not discussed.

A lot of people don't connect with politics, both because they think there's nothing they can do as one person but also because the system is rigged against them anyway. You're a miserable bastard but I imagine your research has led you to consider solutions. Is that correct?

There are plenty of solutions and people are acting on them. A lot of it happens unconsciously. The culture changes and it becomes taboo to think certain thoughts. But solutions implies we're all the same and have the same goals in mind. I've said throughout the course of our discussions that I think the nation-state system is completely artificial and that national culture doesn't make sense. It tries to fit complex, contradictory local communities, like your neighbourhood and mine, into macro-systems. There's already enough complexity and disagreement among neighbours. So by the time you get to the national level, it's a nightmare to try to manage.

Despite that, there are basic human concerns we all share: wanting to survive is one. But how do we get a community and thus national consensus that climate change is a threat to life as we know it, as are neoliberal policies, and nuclear weapons?

But change is constant and it can happen quite unconsciously without too much effort from the likes of you and me. Look at ethical consumption, which was a tiny market twenty years ago. Now it's a pretty serious market for businesses. That's mostly being driven by young people. No one knows why but something happens to the brain as you get older. You get more right-wing. The really important intergenerational cultural changes are usually made by under-35s – not in every case, of course, but generally speaking. They're the ones who now care most about buying ethically-sourced products. It used to be that corporations entirely maximised profit by cutting corners and sourcing unethically. They still do. But now their profits can be potentially harmed by consumer boycotts. So more corporations now have to avoid participating in human rights abuses if they want to maintain a good public image. Or look at transgender rights, which were almost non-existent ten years ago.

These grassroots changes are important. People like Alex Jones want you to believe that progressive social change is a plot funded by George Soros. More broadly, the Iraq War (2003) was probably the first war that was protested *before* it officially began. I say officially because as we've discussed, there were near-daily no-fly zone bombings and the naval blockade. So the 2003 invasion was an escalation. But the people protesting it didn't know that. The protests in the UK alone numbered about 1 million, mostly in the capital. That sent a message to the war planners that the public wasn't going to tolerate wars of this kind—

But it didn't stop the war.

That's irrelevant. Elites who have spent years covertly planning a full-scale military occupation of a poor, devastated oil-rich nation aren't going to change their plans just because you stand on the street for a couple of hours with a placard. It was such a shame that first-time demonstrators were put off by the fact that their protest had no immediate effect. But to expect a war to be stopped on the basis of a single protest, or even a hundred protests, is totally unrealistic. If you enter political activism you have to do it with the understanding that you're volunteering to be part of a long-term shift in the culture, one that says no to wars of aggression, yes to transgender rights, or whatever it may be.

These kind of intergenerational protests have significant effects over time. The bombing of Iraq in 2003 and the aftermath killed a million people. It didn't kill the 3 million who died in Vietnam, Laos,

and Cambodia. The protests of the late-1960s and ear-
ly-1970s really constrained US action for future wars
like Iraq. We can't prove it but the protests over Iraq
probably led the governments in the US, Britain, and
France to go easier on Libya when they wrecked the
country in 2011. They killed about 30,000 people. That
isn't to suggest for one second that killing even one
person is okay, but it shows that ongoing cultural
changes brought about in part by protest can have positive long-term consequences in constraining government actions.

**Someone from the posh houses near our Occupy
meeting came up to us to share a cider. He was sort
of angry from the beginning. He said he supported
our anti-war aims but felt we were wasting our time
because we hadn't stopped the Iraq War. My response at the time was to say that people power
didn't stop Iraq in 2003 but may well have stopped
the Bush administration attacking Iran in 2007/8.**

I'm not sure they really wanted to try occupying Iran
the way they did with Iraq. Certainly there's a plan to
do it. But there's a plan for everything. Iran's Air
Force can be taken out, no problem. But then you've
got a long ground war. Iraq was very different. There
was a comparatively short Gulf War (1991), which
wiped out about half of Iraq's military capability. It
mostly involved saturation bombing, though not on
the scale of Vietnam. Next came the blockade which
reduced Iraq's military capability to the point where
once the US and Britain invaded in 2003, they didn't

face the Iraqi Army. They faced pockets of organised resistance, like the Mahdi Army. Iran is very different. The sanctions are brutal but not yet on the level of Iraq. There's far more diplomacy, albeit US-EU-centric. Iran does not control Lebanon's Hezbollah militia as the propaganda says, but Iran no doubt has some significant allies. A proxy war, where the US might get a newly 'liberated' Iraq or even Israel or Saudi Arabia to fight Iran cannot be ruled out.

With regard to protest, we don't really know if the threat of people on the street was the decisive factor there, since the administration was already aware of how such a war would have been even worse than Iraq, including for American soldiers – which is the main humanitarian aspect they actually care about; not because they care about soldiers, but because it makes the government lose votes if too many of 'our boys' are dying. The protests in the US and Britain over Iraq in 2003 sent a strong message to the powerful because a mass protest is just one step away from an encampment, like Occupy, which came next after the financial crisis. An encampment is just one step away from taking over offices and banks. And that's what really terrifies the elites – direct democracy. They even call it 'civil disobedience'. But if the country is the society, the 'civil', how can the society disobey itself? It can't. The logical conclusion we draw from that is that the country is the elites that run it, not the society.

There were 250,000 people on the street in London recently for the Donald Trump visit. Commentators

can simply say, 'Well that's just a tiny fraction of the population and it's just the usual rabble anyway'. But I think it is ultimately a threat of force. If you regularly have a million people on the street you could see the take-over of offices of state. It may be a soft threat of force, but nonetheless...

Resorting to violence is about the worst thing protestors can do.

First of all, it's immoral. Violence is what the government is doing: invading countries, stealing meagre benefits from poor people, sending in the cops to beat you up and toss you in jail. What's the point of becoming the thing you hate? Many revolutions throughout history have produced equally bad or worse versions of what came before: the Bolsheviks in Russia which led to Stalin, Che in Cuba which led to Castro, Mao in China, and so on. These psychopaths rode the wave of popular discontent and tried to hold onto power by working with the very nation-state system that had gone before. The only thing that's going to work is a decentralised community-based system, where governance is mutually agreed by local participants, as had been the case for tens of thousands of years until the agricultural age and settled city-states dawned.

Second, if you use force to get your way the authorities will use more force. There's no evidence to support the idea that the African National Congress's bombing campaigns in the '80s actually helped their position against Apartheid domestically or internationally. There are cases where violence *has* worked, so it's a mixed bag. The Ploughshares group in the 1990s was led by three women. They broke into a BAE Systems hangar and destroyed the nosecone of a Hawk jet with hammers. Their defensive was that of using a minor crime - breaking and entering and criminal damage - to prevent a major one, namely the UK's unlawful supplying of military equipment to Indonesia during its war crimes against East Timor. And they won.[280] So did the Elbit 9 in 2014, who were nonviolent. These were rooftop protestors who occupied the roof of UAV Engines near Birmingham because it was making drone parts for Elbit, which was allegedly using drones in Israel's destruction of Gaza in 2014. Because neither the company nor the government would release information about export licenses - probably because doing so would implicate them in war crimes - the case of racially-aggravated trespass was dropped.[281]

Third, if you use violence you risk turning the public against you. That's why the police use provocateurs like these black-clothed, masked idiots in Antifa who make the progressive left look like the very fascists they claim to oppose.[282] Depending on the issue, protestors usually have the public interest at heart, so it's essential from the point of view of elites to alienate the public from the protestors, the people actively working in their interests. Provocateurism is one way of doing it - getting undercover cops to vandalise property or attack other cops and blame the left. Suppose some of the people in Occupy - legitimate ones - had actually broken into a bank and said, 'Right. We're going to run it now'. Without serious planning and an understanding of the economy, that would last about 10 minutes. The public supported the ideals of

Occupy – opposition to the greed of the entire financial system – but Occupy weren't really able to articulate their aims. So if Occupy took over certain institutions, the public would turn against them because of the novelty of the situation and the impracticality of it. On the other hand, if Occupy had a platform, say a series of plans that people in their local communities had worked out and wanted to see implemented, that could have worked.

Making a civilised society from the grassroots up?

Yes, but not by just signing a petition or even a hundred. Or attending a single protest or even 50. It has to be many things and sustained—

That sounds really tiring, Tim. What can someone reading this do tomorrow that's easy and can help?

It depends who they are. You're assuming that the people reading this are like us. That they support Corbyn and would want to see changes implemented that set the conditions for greater changes in the future. But maybe people don't agree with us. Maybe they hate Labour. Maybe they want direct anarchy now. I was involved in the Stop the War Coalition. Some of the very people – this is at the local level, not the national group – who were against the invasion of Iraq in 2003 supported the destruction of Libya in 2011. They had what the UK MoD calls '[h]umanitarian fatigue'.[283] The mood at the time was one of weariness: Weariness that the invasion of Iraq had dragged on, that the financial crisis had wiped out people's wealth and jobs, that the Tories had beaten Labour in the 2010 general election so we knew what was in store economically, and now another war. So some people convinced themselves that Gaddafi needed to be removed for the good of the Libyan people. They could ignore the reality. I attended an Amnesty International AGM in Plymouth and the person presenting it said, 'We've liberated Libya'. I couldn't believe it.

So what to do with people like that? Even people we assume are on our side? The only thing that can work there is education. We should also be aware of how right-wing the alternative media are becoming. Take say the Richie Allen Show. It's the most listened to independent radio show in Europe. It's been running for a few years and was a very mixed bag. Initially sponsored by David Icke, it had all the usual guff about reptilians and people like Jordan Maxwell saying that Steven Spielberg can summon demons in the desert.[284] But it also had some serious, progressive political analysis from guests like Medea Benjamin of Code Pink, Kerry-Anne Mendoza of TheCanary.co, Tommy Sheridan the poll tax protestor, and so on. I was on the show back in 2016. Then it gradually drifted more and more to the right. The presenter wouldn't return my emails. Guests like me are excluded. Now the show is beyond idiocy. The only guests are climate change deniers like Lord Christopher Monckton and Piers Corbyn (Jeremy's brother), anti-Semites like Gilad Atzmon[285] and Alison Chabloz, BNP and UKIP candidates (David Furness and Anne Marie Waters (now ex-UKIP)), and people like David Vance of Biased BBC, who actually believes that the BBC is a

Marxist entity! You'd think with all that's going on in the UK, the presenter would invite teachers, nurses, firefighters, union representatives, and so on. But no.

There's a disturbing language creeping into these kind of shows. Whenever someone voices a concern that an abuse of human rights is taking place, they're labelled 'virtue signallers'. So you should shut up and not speak out against injustice, otherwise you're just a narcissist engaged in 'virtue signalling'.

So what can be done easily? I'd say join a worthwhile organisation for a cheap cost, like the Campaign for Nuclear Disarmament. Have fun at protests where you can. And send letters and Freedom of Information Act requests to push for more accountability if an issue annoys you. Some of them seem pretty obvious to me – like a few years ago I read a report saying that the MoD executes thousands of animals each year, including primates, just to test their new weapons. That's got to be worth a quick letter?

Yes, although again I think we have to underscore it all with education. People will say, 'Why campaign for disarmament? We need nuclear weapons'. They have to be educated about the dangerous posed by intercontinental ballistic missiles. Others will say, 'Yeah, it's bad to raise monkeys in horrendous conditions, torture them, and murder them with chemical weapons, but we need to keep ourselves safe – the Russians are coming!'. People like that need to understand the broader geopolitical context. Here's where academics – people supposedly trained in research and critical thinking – can play a crucial role in reaching out. But do we care? Can we be bothered?

Endnotes

[1] Mark Curtis (2018) *Secret Affairs: Britain's Collusion with Radical Islam* London: Serpent's Tail, (2004) *Unpeople: Britain's Secret Human Rights Abuses* London: Vintage, (2003) *Web of Deceit: Britain's Real Role in the World*, (1998) *The Great Deception: Anglo-American Power and World Order* London: Pluto Press, (1995) *The Ambiguities of Power: British Foreign Policy Since 1945* London: Zed Books.

[2] Aidan Hartley (2008) *Dispatches: The Warlords Next Door* Channel 4 and (2008) 'The Terror of Tesco's Finest...' *Daily Mail* http://www.dailymail.co.uk/home/moslive/article-1020934/The-terror-Tescos-finest--forklift-driver-Leicester-Somalias-feared-general.html.

[3] Miller's most important work is his document (2014) *Britain's Dirty War Against the Tamil People, 1979–2009* Bremen: International Human Rights Association https://www.tamilnet.com/img/publish/2014/07/britains_dirty_war.pdf. Miller has also published information via *Vice* (2016) 'Exclusive: Secret Documents Reveal How Britain Funded Possible War Crimes in Sri Lanka' https://www.vice.com/en_uk/article/dp5beq/sri-lanka-british-police-training-phil-miller. It was a late as 2018, nearly a decade after the ethnic cleansing that the mainstream – the *Guardian* in this case – finally took some notice. But even then, Miller could only publish on historical crimes committed in the late-1970s and '80s. This focus on the past instead of contemporary events is typical of media criticism. See his (2018) 'Files on Tamil Tigers and MI5 in Sri Lanka erased at Foreign Office' *Guardian* https://www.theguardian.com/world/2018/may/23/

files-on-tamil-tigers-and-mi5-in-sri-lanka-erased-at-foreign-office.

[4] Nafeez Ahmed (2015) 'The circus: How British intelligence primed both sides of the "terror war" ' *Middle East Eye* http://www.middleeasteye.net/columns/circus-how-british-intelligence-primed-both-sides-terror-war-55293733. See also his (2017) 'ISIS recruiter who radicalised London Bridge attackers was protected by MI5' *Insurge Intelligence* https://medium.com/insurge-intelligence/isis-recruiter-who-radicalised-london-bridge-attackers-was-protected-by-mi5-232998ab6421.

[5] Technically, Ahmed was never on the *Guardian* payroll. He was working freelance, but they ended the blog: 'we took the decision to end the blog when a number of his posts on a range of subjects strayed too far from this [environmentalism] brief'. GNM Press Office (2014) 'Statement in response to a blog post by Nafeez Ahmed' *Guardian* https://www.theguardian.com/gnm-press-office/2014/dec/05/statement-in-response-to-a-blog-post-by-nafeez-ahmed. Nafeez Ahmed (2014) 'Palestine is not an environment story' *Insurge Intelligence* https://medium.com/insurge-intelligence/palestine-is-not-an-environment-story-921d9167ddef.

[6] This is called the Israel lobby theory, which has been in existence since at least the 1980s. The theory was revived by Walt and Mearsheimer after the invasion of Iraq in 2003. See, for instance, Paul Findley (2003 [1985]) *They Dare To Speak Out: People and Institutions Confront Israel's Lobby*, New York: Lawrence Hill Books. The main text, however, is John J. Mearsheimer and Stephen M. Walt (2008) *The Israel Lobby and US Foreign Policy* London: Penguin.

The Israeli lobby theory has infected thinking about British foreign policy, such as it is. *Lobster Magazine* editor Robin Ramsay writes:

> the new factor in the rise of NuLab [New Labour], was not the American state, which was doing what it had always done since about 1950, but the role of the state of Israel.

Now let's be careful here. This is not about Zionism or even Judaism: this is about the actions of a state, the Israeli state.

Tony Blair joined the Labour Friends of Israel, LFI, when he became an MP in 1983. The LFI used to boast about this on its Website but it's long since been removed. LFI became significant in the Parliamentary Labour Party chiefly because Israel was one of Tony's things and ambitious politicians try to kiss the appropriate arses.

In 1994, then Shadow Home Secretary and LFI member Tony Blair went on an Israeli-funded visit to the Holy Land; and when he returned, an Israeli diplomat in London introduced him to Michael Levy, a retired Jewish businessman and fund-raiser for Jewish charities. When John Smith died and Blair became leader of the party, Levy began fund-raising not for the Labour Party but for Blair. Most of the early money came from Jewish businessmen in England. With his own sources of money – initially Jewish money – Blair became financially independent of the Labour Party and he could afford to hire his own staff – Alistair Campbell and Jonathan Powell – and essentially behave like an American presidential candidate. NuLab was born and one of its parents was Israel. This looks like a fairly simple operation: Israel identifies Blair as very pro-Israel and the Israeli embassy in London connects him to the Israeli lobby in Britain – for the future.

This is an example of the kind of thin evidence cited in support of the theory. Robin Ramsay (2012) 'The rise of new Labour' (sic) *Lobster* (63): http://www.lobster-magazine.co.uk/free/lobster63/lob63-new-labour.pdf.

[7] This is the belief of followers of Lyndon LaRouche. See his journal, *Executive Intelligence Review*.

[8] For instance, Richard Gott (2011) *Britain's Empire: Resistance, Repression and Revolt* London: Verso.

[9] (2012) *Cruel Britannia* London: Portobello and (2016) *The History Thieves* London: Portobello.

[10] In the UK, the burden of proof lies on the accused, not the accuser, which is contrary to common law. The UK has been condemned by the United Nations Committee on Human Rights. See Duncan Campbell (2008) 'British libel laws violate human rights, says UN' *Guardian* https://www.theguardian.com/uk/ 2008/aug/14/law.unitednations.

[11] Robert Barrington of Transparency International writes:

> The Panama Papers and Paradise Papers have shown how much illicit wealth is channelled via Britain's Overseas Territories and Crown Dependencies, and how the system can be played to rig regulations in weak jurisdictions. The free interplay between London and numerous secret jurisdictions, sharing a common language, legal system and history, has provided the perfect enabling environment for money laundering.

(2017) 'London, the money-laundering capital' *The World Today* London: Chatham House https://www.chathamhouse.org /publications/twt/london-money-laundering-capital.

[12] The Centre for Economic and Business Research reckons that '[a] rapidly growing population, relatively low taxes and independence from the ailing Eurozone will make Britain the most successful economy in the West after the United States over the next fifteen years' (*Telegraph*'s paraphrase). Matthew Holehouse (2013) 'Britain "will become biggest economy in Europe" ' *Telegraph* https://www.telegraph.co.uk/finance/ economics/10537773/Britain-will-become-biggest-economy-in-Europe.html.

[13] Cabinet Office Minister David Lidington standing in for PM May told Shadow Foreign Secretary Emily Thornbury, standing in for leader of the opposition Jeremy Corbyn:

> The reason we are proposing to treat services differently is that it is in services that regulatory flexibility matters most for both current and future trading opportunities. Although the EU *acquis* [*acquis communautaire*—acquired body of EU law] on goods has been stable for about 30 years, the EU

> *acquis* on services has not been, and the risk of unwelcome
> EU measures coming into play through the *acquis* on ser-
> vices is much greater.

Lidington (2018) 'PM's questions: Engagements' House of
Commons Col 962 Vol 644 https://hansard.parliament.uk/
Commons/2018-07-11/debates/618591DE-F425-4889-90F7-
799814300C4D/Engagements.

[14] This question doesn't seem to have been studied much in academia. Consider for instance Investopedia:

> The exact meaning and usage of the term has changed
> throughout time. In its earliest sense, neoliberalism referred
> to an economic philosophy popular among 1930s European
> liberal scholars, a sort of middle road between classic liber-
> alism and socialist planning. The use and popularity of the
> term "neoliberal" declined steadily, specifically in the 1960s.
> Neoliberalism gained popularity again in the 1980s, con-
> nected to Chilean economic reforms issued by Augusto Pi-
> nochet. During this time, the term gained a negatively slant-
> ed connotation and was used primarily by critics of market
> reform. The meaning of the term also shifted to indicate a
> more radical laissez-faire capitalist pool of ideas.

Investopedia (no date) 'Neoliberalism'
https://www.investopedia.com/terms/n/neoliberalism.asp.

[15] Economist J.K. Galbraith, for instance, writes about the misuse
of Adam Smith's theories on what became capitalism by what
Galbraith calls 'free market' ideologues. See, for instance, his
1998 (Fortieth Anniversary Edition) *The Affluent Society* Bos-
ton: Mariner, pp. 21-22, 26.

[16] Victor D. Lippit, for instance, writes that 'Ricardo believed that
the competition over the economic surplus' supposedly resulting from competition – competition being a facet of classical
capitalism, 'would be carried out between the landowners and
the capitalists' (2005) *Capitalism* London: Routledge, p. 108.

[17] E.D. Steele writes:

> If there was so little to choose between Palmerston and Gladstone in their understanding of how free trade and security were related, [liberal Richard] Cobden's doctrine of non-intervention definitely took second place to practical politics.

(1991) *Palmerstone and Liberalism, 1855–1865* Cambridge: Cambridge University Press, p. 201. Historian Dominic Green writes: 'Palmerston believed in Free Trade and gunboat diplomacy, not territorial conquest' (2008) *Armies of God: Islam and Empire on the Nile, 1869-1899: The First Jihad of the Modern Era* London: Arrow Books, p. 11.

[18] T.J. Coles (2016) *The Great Brexit Swindle* West Sussex: Clairview Books, pp. 2, 110n4.

[19] A report by the Institute for Public Policy Research notes that one:

> widely discussed reason for the decline of manufacturing as a share of the economy is the shift towards higher levels of service inputs into manufacturing firms. Over the period 1992 to 2000, National Statistics input-output tables indicate that the share of services in UK manufacturing firms' gross inputs rose from 17 per cent to 20 per cent.

Richard Brooks and Peter Robinson (2011) *Manufacturing in the UK* London: IPPR, p. 14 https://www.ippr.org/files/images/media/files/publication/2011/05/manufacturering_in_uk_1285.pdf. Ron Martin blames Labour and the Tories, writing:

> since 1979, the Conservative governments' policies designed to achieve national economic revival, appear instead to have increased the regional divide in Britain and to have created a new 'politics of inequality' ...
>
> [T]he rapid and sustained de-industrialisation of the nation's manufacturing base ... has led to a fall in manufacturing employment of more than 2.8 million (36 per cent) since 1971, most of this having occurred since 1971.

(1988) 'The political economy of Britain's north-south divide'
Transactions of the Institute of British Geographers 13(4): 389-
418.

[20] The European Economic Monetary Union, the Schengen agreement, and the Charter of Fundamental Human Rights and
Freedom, Security and Justice are the major ones. Mark Briggs:
'The UK is not the only country to which EU legislation selec-
tively applies, but – with exceptions in four key areas – it is the
member state with the most opt-outs' (2015) 'Europe 'à la
carte': The whats and whys behind UK opt-outs' EurActiv
https://www.euractiv.com/section/uk-europe/linksdossier/
europe-a-la-carte-the-whats-and-whys-behind-uk-opt-outs/.

[21] William Turvill (2017) 'Financial and professional services industry contributes £176bn to the UK economy' *CityA.M.*
https://web.archive.org/web/201704250553937/http://www.ci
tyam.com/263446/financial-and-professional-services-
industry-contributes.

[22] Secretary of State for Foreign and Commonwealth Affairs
(2012) *Review of the Balance of Competences between the
United Kingdom and the European Union* Cm 8415 London: The
Stationary Office https://assets.publishing.service.gov.uk
/government/uploads/system/uploads/attachment_data/file/
35431/eu-balance-of-competences-review.pdf.

[23] Conservative Party *Manifesto 2015*:

> The EU is too bureaucratic and too undemocratic. It inter-
> feres too much in our daily lives, and the scale of migration
> triggered by new members joining in recent years has had a
> real impact on local communities. We are clear about what
> we want from Europe. We say: yes to the Single Market. Yes
> to turbocharging free trade.

London: Conservative Party HQ, p. 72 https://www.bond.org.
uk/data/files/Blog/ConservativeManifesto2015.pdf.

[24] Quoted in T.J. Coles, *Brexit Swindle* op cit., pp. 101-02.

[25] See T.J. Coles (2017) *President Trump, Inc.* West Sussex: Clairview Books, pp. 24-25.

[26] Percentage of Jews who vote for Democrats: Gore 79%, Kerry 74%, Obama 78%, Obama (2012) 69%. Pew Research Center (2012) 'How the Faithful Voted: 2012 Preliminary Analysis' http://www.pewforum.org/2012/11/07/how-the-faithful-voted-2012-preliminary-exit-poll-analysis/.

In 2016, 71% of Jews voted Clinton. Gregory A. Smith and Jessica Martínez (2016) 'How the faithful voted' Pew Research Center http://www.pewresearch.org/fact-tank/2016/11/09/how-the-faithful-voted-a-preliminary-2016-analysis/.

[27] 'Asked who they would support in next month's general election, 69 per cent of Jewish voters said they would support the Tories. Only 22 per cent said they would vote Labour'. Marcus Dysch (2015) 'Huge majority of British Jews will vote Tory, JC poll reveals' *Jewish Chronicle* https://www.thejc.com/news/uk-news/huge-majority-of-british-jews-will-vote-tory-jc-poll-reveals-1.66001.

[28] 'Just 13 per cent of British Jews plan to vote for Jeremy Corbyn's Labour Party next week, an exclusive JC poll has revealed. Theresa May's Conservatives have the support of 77 per cent of Jewish voters'. Marcus Dysch (2017) 'Labour support just 13 per cent among UK Jews' *Jewish Chronicle* https://www.thejc.com/news/uk-news/labour-support-just-13-per-cent-among-uk-jews-1.439325.

[29] *Jewish World Review* notes that until the 1970s, most Jews in Britain were relatively poor and supported the Labour Party. But under the pro-Israeli PM Thatcher, support shifted to the Tories. But it shifted back again to Labour under Tony Blair. Jon Mandelson then of Labour Friends of Israel, said that Blair 'attacked the anti-Israelism that had existed in the Labor Party [sic]'. Richard Allen Greene (2000) 'British Jewish vote undergoes shift' *Jewish World Review* http://www.jewishworldreview.com/0501/uk.jews.asp.

That being said, New Labour endured a couple of weeks of criticism after portraying then-Tory leader Michael Howard allegedly as a Shylock-type figure in campaign posters. Matthew Tempest (2005) 'Blair combats anti-semitism [sic] claim'

Guardian https://www.theguardian.com/politics/2005/feb/18/election2005.uk.

[30] The Jewish *Evening Standard* reporter Oliver Finegold asked Livingstone: 'How did tonight go?'
Livingstone: 'Have you thought of having treatment?'
Finegold: 'Was it a good party? What does it mean for you?'
Livingstone: 'What did you do before? Were you a German war criminal?'
Finegold: 'No, I'm Jewish. I wasn't a German war criminal'.
Livingstone: 'Ah ... right' (ellipsis in original).
Finegold: 'I'm actually quite offended by that. So, how did tonight go?'
Livingstone: 'Well you might be, but actually you are just like a concentration camp guard. You're just doing it 'cause you're paid to, aren't you?'. *Guardian* (2006) 'Transcript' https://www.theguardian.com/society/2006/feb/25/localgovernment.politicsandthemedia.

[31] Reuters:

> Many of the National Militia's members come from the Azov movement, one of the 30-odd privately-funded "volunteer battalions" that, in the early days of the war, helped the regular army to defend Ukrainian territory against Russia's separatist proxies. Although Azov uses Nazi-era symbolism and recruits neo-Nazis into its ranks, a recent article in *Foreign Affairs* downplayed any risks the group might pose, pointing out that, like other volunteer militias, Azov has been "reined in" through its integration into Ukraine's armed forces. While it's true that private militias no longer rule the battlefront, it's the home front that Kiev needs to worry about now.

> Josh Cohen (2018) 'Commentary: Ukraine's neo-Nazi problem' Reuters https://www.reuters.com/article/us-cohen-ukraine-commentary/commentary-ukraines-neo-nazi-problem-idUSKBN1GV2TY.

32 *Times of Israel* (2014) 'Saudi Arabia: Israelis banned, but Jews now allowed to work here' https://www.timesofisrael.com/saudi-arabia-jews-now-allowed-to-work-here/.

33 Paul Mason:

> ... a law passed by Poland's right-wing government in January 2018 ... makes it illegal to assert that either "the Polish state or the Polish nation" participated in the Holocaust. Offenders are liable to three years' imprisonment. Its passage triggered a diplomatic outcry both from Israel and the US, and has left many of Poland's 20,000-strong Jewish community apprehensive.
>
> Why? Because it is a fact, meticulously documented by new research over the past ten years, that while some Poles courageously defended Jews during the Holocaust, others killed them, denounced them or joined in the Nazi-orchestrated manhunt for them.

(2018) 'Poland is rewriting history – and the consequence is the rise of anti-Semitism' *New Statesman* https://www.newstatesman.com/world/europe/2018/06/poland-rewriting-history-and-consequence-rise-anti-semitism.

34 Shami Chakrabarti found:

> The Labour Party is not overrun by anti-Semitism [sic], Islamophobia or other forms of racism. Further, it is the party that initiated every single United Kingdom race equality law. However, as with wider society, there is too much clear evidence (going back some years) of minority hateful or ignorant attitudes and behaviours festering within a sometimes bitter incivility of discourse.

(2016) *The Shami Chakrabarti Inquiry* London: Labour Headquarters https://labour.org.uk/wp-content/uploads/2017/10/Chakrabarti-Inquiry-Report-30June16.pdf.

35 According to the data collection site, TheyWorkForYou.com, Mann voted for war on six out of 11 occasions (one abstention), voted for the invasion of Iraq in 2003 (five votes in total), voted against investigating the war (13 times against, one ab-

stention, one vote for), voted for replacing Trident with a new weapons system, but voted against war on Daesh on 2 out of three occasions. TheyWorkForYou.com (no date) 'John Mann: How John Mann Voted...' https://www.theyworkforyou.com/mp/11093/john_mann/bassetlaw/votes.

[36] The leaked cables say:

> Labour Prospective Parliamentary Candidate for Burton Ruth Smeeth (strictly protect) told us April 20 [2009] that [PM Gordon] Brown had intended to announce the elections on May 12, and hold them after a very short (matter of weeks) campaign season. Labour had been "just" 7 points behind the Conservatives in some polls taken right after the G-20 Summit, which other Labour contacts had told us was close to an acceptable standing from which to launch a campaign, but the drop in Labour's poll numbers following Smeargate [New Labour's plan to smear opponents] forced Brown to abandon his plan, a despondent Smeeth said. (Note: This information has not been reported in the press. End note.)

(2009) *UK political snapshot: Gloomy budget and a new scandal torpedo Brown's poll numbers* 09LONDON956_aPublic https://search.wikileaks.org/plusd/cables/09LONDON956_a.html.

[37] Nick Couldry (2016) *From Watchdog to Attack Dog* London: London School of Economics http://www.lse.ac.uk/media-and-communications/assets/documents/research/projects/corbyn/Cobyn-Report.pdf. Justin Schlosberg (2016) *Should he stay or should he go? Television and Online News Coverage of the Labour Party in Crisis* London: Media Reform Coalition and Birkbeck University of London http://www.mediareform.org.uk/wp-content/uploads/2016/07/Corbynresearch.pdf. Robert Piazza and Paul Lashmar (2017) 'Jeremy Corbyn according to the BBC: ideological representation and identity construction of the Labour Party leader' CADAAD http://www.lancaster.ac.uk/fass/journals/cadaad/wp-content/uploads/2017/12/08-Piazza-Lashmar.pdf.

[38] YouGov and the Campaign Against Antisemitism (2015) *YouGov/Campaign Against Antisemitism Survey Results*

https://d25d2506sfb94s.cloudfront.net/cumulus_uploads/document/921pn4p2fh/CampaignAgainstAntisemitismResults_MergedFile_W.pdf.

39 A Campaign Against Antisemitism/YouGov poll from 2017 found that 68% of Labour supporters 'endorse' no anti-Semitic statements compared to 60% of Tory voters. Thirty-two percent of Labour supporters '[e]ndorsed at least one statement' compared to 40% of Tory voters. CAAS/YouGov (2017) *Antisemitism Barometer 2017* https://antisemitism.uk/wp-content/uploads/2017/08/Antisemitism-Barometer-2017.pdf.

40 The 2015 YouGov poll finds that 58% of Britons 'have a negative impression' of Roma/Gypsies. A further 40% have a negative perception of Muslims. (It is worth remembering that most Muslims in the UK are ethnic Pakistanis and Bangladeshis, so when the poll says 'Muslims', it could be read racially as Pakistanis and Bangladeshis). Nine percent of Britons have a negative perception of homosexuals and 8% have a negative perception of black people. Seven percent of Britons have a negative perception of Jews. Will Dahlgreen (2015) 'Roma people and Muslims are the least tolerated minorities in Europe' YouGov https://yougov.co.uk/news/2015/06/05/european-attitudes-minorities/.

41 UNITE the Union (2016) *A dossier on racism in the Conservative Party* http://www.unitetheunion.org/uploaded/documents/(JN7434)%20A4%20Tory%20Racism%20Brochure%20SIN11-26629.pdf.

42 Dan Sabbagh (2018) 'Sayeeda Warsi calls for inquiry into Islamophobia within Tory party' *Guardian* https://www.theguardian.com/politics/2018/jul/04/sayeeda-warsi-calls-for-inquiry-into-islamophobia-within-tory-party.

43 Peter Moore (2016) 'How Britain voted' YouGov https://yougov.co.uk/news/2016/06/27/how-britain-voted/ and BBC News Online (2016) 'EU referendum: Results' https://www.bbc.co.uk/news/politics/eu_referendum/results.

44 For a breakdown of the figures, see Liisa Talving and Sofia Vasilopoulou (2017) 'What do British citizens think about the rights of EU citizens in the UK as part of the Brexit divorce?' London

School of Economics http://blogs.lse.ac.uk/brexit/2017/12/14/
what-is-the-opinion-of-british-citizens-on-the-rights-of-eu-
citizens-in-the-uk-as-part-of-the-brexit-divorce/.

[45] Lord Ashcroft (2016) 'EU Referendum "How Did You Vote" Poll'
https://lordashcroftpolls.com/wp-content/uploads/2016/06/
How-the-UK-voted-Full-tables-1.pdf.

[46] Tim Ross '…revealed' https://www.telegraph.co.uk/news/poli
tics/david-cameron/11924603/David-Camerons-four-key-
demands-to-remain-in-the-EU-revealed.html.

[47] For example, The American Federation of Labor and Congress of
Industrial Organizations says of the North American Free Trade
Agreement (NAFTA):

> NAFTA caused massive employment-related demographic
> shifts, both within and between countries. In Mexico, subsi-
> dized agricultural imports from the United States sparked
> unprecedented migration. The country lost 1 million jobs in
> corn alone between 1991 and 2000, and an additional mil-
> lion in the agricultural sector as a whole.

(2014) *NAFTA at 20* Washington, DC: AFL-CIO, p. 5 aflcio.org/
sites/default/files/2017-03/March2014_NAFTA20_nb.pdf.
The same organisation says of the TPP:

> The TPP categorically fails to protect workers in the Pacific
> Rim.
> As currently drafted, the TPP would increase corporate
> profits and power while exposing working people to real and
> predictable harm, including lost jobs and lower wages. Mi-
> grant workers already are subject to extreme rights viola-
> tions in some TPP countries, and this new trade deal would
> make it even harder for many families to find decent work at
> home.

AFL-CIO (2017) *Trading Away Migrant Rights: How the TPP
Would Fuel Displacement and Fail Migrant Workers* Washington, DC: AFL-CIO, p. 3 https://aflcio.org/sites/default/files/
2017-03/MigrantReport_nb.pdf.

[48] Maude Barlow (2015) 'Why Canada is one of the most sued countries in the world' *Global Justice Now* http://www.globaljustice.org.uk/blog/2015/oct/23/why-canada-one-most-sued-countries-world.

[49] Office of the United States Trade Representative (2015) 'Fact Sheet: Investor-State Dispute Settlement (ISDS)' https://ustr.gov/about-us/policy-offices/press-office/fact-sheets/2015/march/investor-state-dispute-settlement-isds.

[50] By 1992, intra-firm investment flows (e.g., Ford Europe to Ford USA) accounted for 40% of all US 'trade', compared to foreign investment flows, which accounted for only 10%. See Peter F. Cowhey and Jonathan D. Aronson (1992) 'A new trade order' *Foreign Affairs* January-February.

[51] See Kevin Bales's important book (2016) *Blood and Earth: Modern Slavery, Ecocide, and the Secret to Saving the World* New York: Spiegel & Grau, pp. 16-32.

[52] Sean Starrs (2015) 'China's rise is designed in America, assembled in China' *China's World* 2(2): 9-20 and Starrs (2013) 'American Economic Power Hasn't Declined—It Globalized! Summoning the Data and Taking Globalization Seriously' *International Studies Quarterly* 57(4): 817-30.

[53] The Government Office for Science (UK) states:

> Government was more interventionist until the 1970s, with nationalisation common, industrial subsidies widespread and regional policy often important. Government intervention has since fallen, but macroeconomic policies, privatisation, and joining the EEC all affected manufacturing ...
>
> [T]he EEC6 [i.e., the six initial members] became more important than "British" countries only after Britain joined the Common Market in 1973. With the consolidation of Germany as the manufacturing hub of Western Europe, this has led to a substantial UK rebalancing away from manufacturing towards services, where the UK has a strong comparative advantage.

Stephen Broadberry and Tim Leunig (2013) *The impact of Government policies on UK manufacturing since 1945* Government

Office for Science London: Stationary Office https://assets.pub lishing.service.gov.uk/government/uploads/system/uploads/ attachment_data/file/277158/ep2-government-policy-since-1945.pdf.

[54] On beef, see T.J. Coles (2016) *The Great Brexit Swindle* West Sussex: Clairview Books. On Indian technology and visas, see Stuart Lauchlan (2018) 'UK and India sign new tech alliance – a model for post-Brexit Britain?' *diginomica/government* https://government.diginomica.com/2018/04/19/uk-india-sign-new-tech-alliance-model-post-brexit-britain/. On GMOS, the House of Commons says:

> Witnesses highlighted products produced with different methods of farming across the globe that included, higher level of pesticides use, genetically modified organisms (GMOs), growth hormones, animal cloning and cultured meat. Two high profile examples are hormone-treated beef and chlorinated chicken.

House of Commons Environment, Food and Rural Affairs Committee (2018) *Brexit: Trade in Food* Third Report of Session 2017–19 HC 348 London: Stationary Office, p. 12 https://public ations.parliament.uk/pa/cm201719/cmselect/cmenvfru/348/3 48.pdf.

British Summer Fruits (2017) *The impact of Brexit on the soft fruit industry* http://www.britishsummerfruits.co.uk/media /TheAndersonReport.pdf. The report says: 'At present machines for the robotic picking of Soft Fruit are not commercially available' (p. 20). So the solution, ironically, is provided by the Secretary of State for Justice, David Gauke, who writes:

> The fact is, prisons have the potential to provide many loyal and hard-working recruits. Some employers see that, but others still need to change their thinking. The dynamics of the labour market should focus the minds of employers. We have a thriving jobs market and demand for workers in some sectors is very high. Leaving the European Union is al-

so likely to have an impact on the workforce in sectors such as catering, construction and agriculture.

(2018) 'Foreword' in *Education and Employment Strategy* Ministry of Justice London: Stationary Office, https://assets.publ ishing.service.gov.uk/government/uploads/system/uploads/ attachment_data/file/710406/education-and-employment-strategy-2018.pdf.

[55] See, for instance, T.J. Coles (2017) *President Trump, Inc.* West Sussex: Clairview Books and T.J. Coles (2019) *Privatized Planet* Oxford: New Internationalist.

[56] *Bloomberg* reports:

> The manufacturing mini-renaissance continues. Over the past year, according to today's employment report from the Bureau of Labor Statistics, the sector has added 222,000 jobs, 1 resuming a recovery that had paused in 2015 and 2016 amid strength in the dollar and weakness in the U.S. oil and gas industry.

Justin Fox (2018) 'Manufacturers Are Hiring, and Hiring' *Bloomberg* https://web.archive.org/web/20180309215947 /www.bloomberg.com/view/articles/2018-03-09/manufactur ing-keeps-adding-jobs-amid-trump-s-tough-talk.

But *Bloomberg* also reports:

> The U.S. economy is growing, but workers are seeing less and less of the benefits. Since the Great Recession, real gross domestic product per capita has increased substantially, but real compensation per hour — which includes benefits like health care — hasn't grown at all.

Noah Smith (2018) 'How about a free market for wages?' *Bloomberg* www.bloomberg.com/view/articles/2018-07-25/states-should-ban-contracts-barring-workers-from-joining rivals. (As if we don't already have a 'free market' for wages.)

[57] Trump:

> I think NATO is going to be very, very effective. I'm very impressed with — and really know, and he's a friend mine —

> but Secretary General Stoltenberg has done a fantastic job
> and putting it all together. And we were the ones that really
> — we gave him an extension of his contract, as you know. I
> think he's done a really good job.

Donald Trump (2018) 'Remarks by President Trump at Press Conference After NATO Summit' Estonia: US Embassy in Estonia https://ee.usembassy.gov/remarks-by-president-nato-summit/.

[58] Trump:

> ... we still have to figure out what's going on with the pipeline, because the pipeline is coming in from Russia ...
>
> [M]aybe everybody is going to have a good relationship with Russia so there will be a lot less problem with the pipeline. But, to me, that was a very major point of contention. We discussed it at length today. Germany has agreed to do a lot better than they were doing, and we're very happy with that.

Ibid.

[59] See T.J. Coles (2018) *Real Fake News* Ontario: Red Pill Press, Chapter 7.

[60] For example: J. Boone Bartholomees (ed) (2010 4th) *The U.S. Army War College Guide to National Security Issues Volume 1: Theory of War and Strategy* Strategic Studies Institute Pennsylvania: U.S. Army War College and Michael I. Handel (1991) *Sun Tzu and Clausewitz: The Art of War and On War Compared* Strategic Studies Institute Pennsylvania: U.S. Army War College.

[61] Mark Leonard and Nicu Popescu (2007) 'A Power Audit of EU-Russia Relations' European Council on Foreign Relations, Policy Paper, p. 1 http://www.ecfr.eu/page/-/ECFR-02_A_POWER_AUDIT_OF_EU-RUSSIA_RELATIONS.pdf.

[62] 'Anglo-Russian relations were severely strained; what was in effect a cold war lasted from the late 1820s to the beginning of the next century'. The Crimean War seems to have set a precedent for today. James writes:

> [It] was an imperial war, the only one fought by Britain
> against a European power during the nineteenth century,
> although some would have regarded Russia as essentially an
> Asiatic power. No territory was at stake; the war was under-
> taken solely to guarantee British naval supremacy in the
> Mediterranean and, indirectly, to forestall any threat to In-
> dia which might have followed Russia replacing Britain as
> the dominant power in the Middle East.

Lawrence James (1997) *The Rise and Fall of the British Empire*
London: Abacus, pp. 180-82.

[63] Churchill said in 1920:

> All these strikes and rumours of strikes and threats of strikes
> and loss and suffering caused by them; all this talk of revolu-
> tion and "direct action" have deeply offended most of the
> British people. There is a growing feeling that a considerable
> section of organized Labour is trying to tyrannize over the
> whole public and to bully them into submission, not by ar-
> gument, not by recognized political measures, but by brute
> force ...
>
> But if we can do little for Russia [under the Bolsheviks],
> we can do much for Britain. We do not want any of these
> experiments here ...
>
> Whether it is the Irish murder gang or the Egyptian
> vengeance society, or the seditious extremists in India, or
> the arch-traitors we have at home, they will feel the weight
> of the British arm.

Winston Churchill (1920) *Bolshevism and Imperial Sedition.*
Speech to United Wards Club. London: The International
Churchill Society
https://winstonchurchill.org/resources/speeches/1915-1929-
nadir-and-recovery/bolshevism-and-imperial-sedition/.

[64] The fake letter says:

> A settlement of relations between the two countries [UK
> and Russia] will assist in the revolutionising of the interna-

> tional and British proletariat, ... [and] make it possible for us
> to extend and develop the propaganda and ideas of Lenin-
> ism in England and the colonies.

It also says that 'British workmen' have 'inclinations to com-
promise' and that rapprochement will eventually lead to domestic '[a]rmed warfare'. It was leaked by the services to the
Conservative party and then to the media. Richard Norton-
Taylor (1999) 'Zinoviev letter was dirty trick by MI6' *Guardian*
https://www.theguardian.com/politics/1999/feb/04/uk.politic
alnews6 and Louise Jury (1999) 'Official Zinoviev letter was
forged' *Independent* http://www.independent.co.uk/news/off
icial-zinoviev-letter-was-forged-1068600.html. For media coverage at the time, see James Curran and Jean Seaton (1997)
Power without Responsibility London: Routledge, p. 52.

[65] Paul F. Walker (2017) 'A Century of Chemical Warfare: Building
a World Free of Chemical Weapons' Conference: One Hundred
Years of Chemical Warfare: Research, Deployment, Conse-
quences pp. 379-400 and Giles Milton (2013) *Russian Roulette:
A Deadly Game: How British Spies Thwarted Lenin's Global Plot*
London: Hodder, eBook.

[66] 'The Russian Federation has shown repeatedly that common
values play almost no role in its consideration of its trading
partners', meaning the US and EU. 'It often builds relationships
with countries that most openly thwart Western values of free
markets and democracy', notably Iran and Venezuela. 'In this
regard, the Russian Federation behaves like "Russia Incorpo-
rated." It uses its re-nationalized industries to further its
wealth and influence, the latter often at the expense of the EU
and the U.S.'. Colonel Richard J. Anderson (2008) 'A History of
President Putin's Campaign to Re-Nationalize Industry and the
Implications for Russian Reform and Foreign Policy' Senior Service College, US Army War College, Pennsylvania: Carlisle Barracks, p. 52.

[67] Daniel R. Coats (2017) *Statement for the Record: Worldwide
Threat Assessment of the US Intelligence Community* Senate
Select Committee on Intelligence, Washington, DC: Office of

68 the Director of National Intelligence, pp. 18-19
https://www.dni.gov/files/documents/Newsroom/Testimonies
/SSCI%20Unclassified%20SFR%20-%20Final.pdf.

68 US Space Command (1997) *Vision for 2020* Colorado: Peterson
Air Force Base https://ia802705.us.archive.org/10/items/pdfy-
j6U3MFw1cGmC-yob/U.S.%20Space%20Command%20Vision
%20For%202020.pdf.

69 The document also says: 'a replay of the West-sponsored coup
against pro-Russian elites could result in a split, or indeed multiple splits, of the failed Ukraine, which would open a door for
NATO intervention'. Pavel K. Baev (2011) 'Russia's security relations with the United States: Futures planned and un-
planned' in Stephen J. Blank (ed.) *Russian Nuclear Weapons:
Past, Present, and Future* Strategic Studies Institute Pennsylvania: Carlisle Barracks, p. 170, www.strategicstudiesinstitute
.army.mil/pdffiles/PUB1087.pdf.

70 *Forces Network* (2016) 'British troops to deploy to Poland'
https://www.forces.net/news/tri-service/british-troops-
deploy-poland.

71 For example, Nate Jones, Thomas Blanton and Christian F. Os-
termann (2016) 'Able Archer 83: The Secret History' Nuclear
Proliferation International History Project Washington, DC:
Woodrow Wilson International Center for Scholars
https://www.wilsoncenter.org/event/able-archer-83-the-
secret-history.

72 It was reported in the ultra-right, neo-con press at the time
that:

> [Russian] President Dmitri Medvedev announced in his first
> state-of-the-nation address plans to deploy the short-range
> SS-26 ("Iskander") missiles in the Russian exclave of Kalinin-
> grad if the U.S. goes ahead with its European Ballistic Missile
> Defense System (BMDS). Medvedev told parliament that the
> deployment would "neutralize" U.S. plans for a missile de-
> fense shield based in Poland and the Czech Republic [now in
> Romania), which the U.S. claims as vital in defending against
> missile attacks from 'rogue states' such as Iran.

Neil Leslie (2008) 'The Kaliningrad Missile Crisis' *The New At-
lanticist*, available at http://www.atlanticcouncil.org/blogs/
new-atlanticist/the-kaliningrad-missile-crisis.

73 For example, a Parliamentary inquiry into British-Russian relations says of the newly-imposed US-British ally in Ukraine:

> President Poroshenko's Government is more openly com-
> mitted to economic reform and anti-corruption than any
> previous Ukrainian Administration. The reform agenda has
> made considerable progress and has enjoyed some success-
> es including police reform, liberalisation of the energy mar-
> ket and the launch of an online platform for government
> procurement …
>
> The annexation of Crimea also resulted in a ban on im-
> porting products from Crimea, on investing in or providing
> services linked to tourism and on exporting certain goods for
> use in the transport, telecoms and energy sectors.

House of Commons Foreign Affairs Committee (2017) *The
United Kingdom's relations with Russia* Seventh report of session 2016–17, HC 120 London: Stationary Office, pp. 28, 31
https://publications.parliament.uk/pa/cm201617/cmselect/cm
faff/120/120.pdf.

74 The *Daily Mail* obtained US Defense Department documents
that appear to confirm another failure in 2011. The error that
occurred in 2011 was the same as the one that occurred in
2016, namely a navigational problem. '[A] news blackout had
been enforced', says the newspaper. Rebecca Taylor (2017)
'Trident nuclear missiles suffered navigation problems five
YEARS before the malfunction covered up by Number 10 while
MPs voted on its renewal' *Daily Mail* http://www.dailymail.co.
uk/news/article-4168010/Trident-navigation-issue-five-YEARS-
malfunction.html. For the 2016 failure, see Jon Rosamond
(2017) 'Royal Navy Trident missile "malfunction" prompts
claims of U.K. government cover-up' *U.S. Naval Institute News*
https://news.usni.org/2017/01/25/royal-navy-trident-missile-
malfunction-prompts-claims-u-k-government-cover and Barbara Starr and James Masters (2017) 'US official confirms Trident

missile failure' CNN https://web.archive.org/web/20170123 155833/https://edition.cnn.com/2017/01/23/europe/trident-missile-failure-theresa-may/index.html.

[75] The UK MoD says:

> nuclear possession *may* lead to greater adventurism and irresponsible conventional and irregular behaviour, to the point of brinkmanship and misunderstanding …
>
> Various doomsday scenarios arising in relation to these and other areas of development present the possibility of catastrophic impacts, ultimately including the end of the world, or at least of humanity. (Emphasis in original)

Ministry of Defence (2007 3rd) *The DCDC Global Strategic Trends Programme: 2007–2036* Swindon: Developments, Concepts and Doctrine Centre, pp. 72, 83. https://ia800407.us.arc hive.org/18/items/20072036UK_201606/2007-2036%20UK .pdf.

[76] Ministry of Defence (2015) *Strategic Trends Programme: Future Operating Environment 2035* Swindon: DCDC p. 18 https://assets.publishing.service.gov.uk/government/uploads/ system/uploads/attachment_data/file/646821/20151203-FOE_35_final_v29_web.pdf

[77] Michael J. Mills, Owen B. Toon, Julia Lee-Taylor and Alan Robock (2014) 'Multidecadal global cooling and unprecedented ozone loss following a regional nuclear conflict' *Earth's Future* 2(4): 161-76.

[78] John Haltiwanger (2017) 'Trump has dropped record number of bombs on Middle East' *Newsweek* https://web.archive.org/ web/20170919194118/www.newsweek.com/trump-era-record-number-bombs-dropped-middle-east-667505. Jessica Purkiss, Jack Serle and Abigail Fielding-Smith (2017) 'US counter terror air strikes double in Trump's first year' The Bureau of Investigative Journalism https://www.thebureauinvestig ates.com/stories/2017-12-19/counterrorism-strikes-double-trump-first-year. Josh Smith (2018) 'U.S. bombs dropped in Afghanistan at highest since 2010, under new Trump strategy' Reuters www.reuters.com/ article/us-afghanistan-airstrikes/u-

s-bombs-dropped-in-afghanistan-at-highest since-2010-under-new-trump-strategy-idUSKBN1CG0O0.

[79] '[T]he loss of the UK could leave the EU significantly reduced as a defence and security actor', says the RAND Corporation. At present, British taxpayers foot the bill for Europe's 'security', meaning the security of private corporations which rely on militarism to enforce the global economy. RAND continues: 'Brexit raises questions about the EU's future credibility and ambition in this field … particularly if Europe hopes to be a counterbalance to US influence within NATO, or to Russia and China'. James Black, Alex Hall, Kate Cox, Marta Kepe and Erik Silfversten (2017) *Defence and security after Brexit: Understanding the possible implications of the UK's decision to leave the EU* Cambridge: RAND Europe https://www.rand.org/content/dam/rand/pubs/research_reports/RR1700/RR1786z1/RAND_RR1786z1.pdf.

[80] At the NATO 2014 Summit in Wales, PM Cameron said: 'Britain is one of only four countries that currently spends 2% of its GDP on defence. But others will now do more'. David Cameron (2014) 'NATO Summit 2014: PM end of summit press conference' No. 10 Downing Street https://www.gov.uk/government/speeches/nato-summit-2014-pm-end-of-summit-press-conference.

[81] The report says:

> At the heart of the BBC's journalism is a well-trained journalistic workforce. In a fast-changing world, life-long training at every level is vital. Competence based training should be the key to competence based promotion. We recommend that the BBC establishes an industry-wide, residential college of journalism under the leadership of an academic principal.

> *The Neil Report* (2004) 'Statement by the Board of Governors' http://downloads.bbc.co.uk/aboutthebbc/insidethebbc/howwework/reports/pdf/neil_report.html.

[82] One Joyce Brown filed a FOIA request with the Foreign and Commonwealth Office (FCO). This is what they said: 'As of 31 March 2018, the total sum of funding that the British Govern-

ment has supplied to the White Helmets is £38,425,591.23'. FCO Near East Department (2018) FOIA 2000 Request Ref: 0400-18, available at https://www.whatdotheyknow.com/req uest/477177/response/1154293/attach/html/3/FOI%200400% 2018%20Response.pdf.html.

83 McCormack wrote: 'It is also an established fact that a) the White Helmets are basically Al Q (they provide most of the re-porting from Jihadi held areas and b) that hospitals are used as bases by these groups' (Twitter 5 Feb. 2018 https://twitter. com/McCormack_Tara/status/960527482502991875).

84 Emily Buchanan (2014) 'How the UK taught Brazil's dictators interrogation techniques' *BBC Magazine* https://www.bbc.co.uk/news/magazine-27625540.

85 *National Post* (2014) 'Watch as Russia Today presenter quits on live television over Moscow's actions in Crimea' https://nationalpost.com/news/russia-today-presenter-abby-martin-says-she-isnt-going-to-crimea-no-matter-what-her-bosses-say.

86 Oren Segal of the Anti-Defamation League says the alt-left is '[a] made-up term'. The ADL's Mark Pitcavage says: 'there are ex-tremists on the left, including very problematic ones. But the "alt left" is not a thing. It's just an insult'. Assistant Professor of Political Science at the University of Alabama concurs: 'There is no such movement as the alt-left'. All quoted in Joe Sterling and Nicole Chavez (2017) 'What's the "alt-left"? Experts say it's a "made-up term" ' CNN https://edition.cnn.com/2017/08/16/ politics/what-Is-alt-left/index.html.

87 RT (2013) 'Israeli settlers slam govt for lives left in limbo over holy land grabs' https://www.youtube.com/watch?v=4PDUrsz9eLw.

88 On quantifying the effects, Linda Risso cautions:

> Scholars can do nothing more than rely on anecdotal and partial information; as a result, their conclusions can only be careful educated guesses, which often do not stray far from the perceived success of the practitioners of the time.

Risso (2013) 'Radio Wars: Broadcasting in the Cold War' *Cold War History* 13(2): 149.

[89] RT (2011) 'New face of Chechen capital' https://www.rt.com/news/chechen-republic-grozny-city-181/.

[90] So-called al-Qaeda in Iraq leader Musab al-Zarqawi was allegedly stationed in Fallujah. But military documents show that he was a phantom menace largely concocted by the US to justify the ongoing violence in Iraq in general:

> Our own focus on Zarqawi has enlarged his caricature, if you will -- made him more important than he really is, in some ways ... The long-term threat is not Zarqawi or religious extremists, but these former regime types and their friends. (Col. Derek Harvey)

One document said:

> Villainize Zarqawi/leverage xenophobia response ... The Zarqawi PSYOP program is the most successful information campaign to date ... Through aggressive Strategic Communications, Abu Musab al-Zarqawi now represents: Terrorism in Iraq/Foreign Fighters in Iraq/Suffering of Iraqi People (Infrastructure Attacks)/Denial of Iraqi Aspirations.

Thomas E. Ricks (2006) 'Military plays up role of Zarqawi' *Washington Post* https://web.archive.org/web/20060617001236/http://www.washingtonpost.com/wp-dyn/content/article/2006/04/09/AR2006040900890.html and https://web.archive.org/web/20121026062243/http://www.washingtonpost.com/wp-dyn/content/article/2006/04/09/AR2006040900890_2.html.

[91] The report admits that the US simply rebranded the opposition: 'Elements of Abu Musab al-Zarqawi's network (called Jama'at al-Tawhid wa' al-Jihadh or JTJ at the time, now referred to as al-Qaida in Iraq) were also present'. National Ground Intelligence Center (2004) 'Complex Environments: Battle of Fallujah' United States Army, available at http://www.expose-the-war-profiteers.org/archive/government/2006/20060331.pdf.

[92] See Human Rights Watch (2003) *Violent Response: The U.S. Army in al-Falluaja* (sic) https://www.hrw.org/report/2003/06/16/violent-response/us-army-al-falluja.

[93] For the harrowing details, see Office of the Special Inspector General for Iraq Reconstruction (2008) 'Falluja Waste Water Treatment System Falluja, Iraq' (sic) Arlington: SIGIR http://www.dtic.mil/dtic/tr/fulltext/u2/a529001.pdf.

[94] C. Busby et al. (2010) 'Cancer, infant mortality and birth sex-ratio in Fallujah, Iraq 2005-2009' *International Journal of Environmental Research and Public Health* 7(7): 2828-37. S. Alaani et al. (2011) 'Uranium and other contaminants in hair from the parents of children with congenital anomalies in Fallujah, Iraq' *Conflict Health* 2(5): 15.

[95] Curtis, *Unpeople* op cit.

[96] On the 950th anniversary of the Battle of Hastings, *The Economist* (24th Dec.) said that 'Norman rule reshaped England', adding with typical pro-imperial zeal: 'while the blood and guts were horrifying, the conquest also did a lot of good. It transformed the English economy. Institutions, trade patterns and investment all improved'. This exemplifies the adulation of power on the part of the intelligentsia (who are British in this case), even when the intelligentsia derive from an ethnic 'stock' that was conquered; hence the great love of the Roman Empire among the elites of the British Empire, who sought to use Rome as a model. Harry De Quetteville, who is of Norman 'stock' (whatever that may mean genetically), says in the *Telegraph* that, 'We Normans made England what it is today' (5 Jan.). The Normans brought '[r]ape, pillage and subjugation ... It is as if Islamic State had arrived on the beach, smashed their way past every defence, and imposed a kind of fundamentalist medieval misery'. But, following the standard imperial line, it wasn't all bad: 'the Norman legacy has lasted longer than that, and more gloriously', such as formalised land ownership (as opposed to freedom) and parliament (as opposed to direct, tribal democracy). The BBC (Bitesize, 'The Norman Conquest') teaches children studying for their GCSEs to think dialectically about conquest. Either it's good or bad: 'What is your interpre-

tation of the Norman Conquest? Who did you want to win – Harold or William – and why?' [emphasis in original]. How about a lesson on the history of ordinary Britons and Normans who wanted neither king nor parliament?

[97] Imposing historical boundaries on events and their consequences is not an exact science. Nevertheless, generalising timeframes can help us to understand things. Nationalism goes hand in glove with feelings of cultural, religious or ethnic superiority. The leading scholar of nationalism, Hans Kohn, writes that Cromwell 'more than any other awakened the consciousness of the English people as the chosen people', by linking England to ancient Israel. Quoted in Krishan Kumar (2003) *The Making of English National Identity* Cambridge: Cambridge University Press, p. 128.

[98] David Miles debunks homogeneity in his (2006) *The Tribes of Britain: Who Are We? And Where Do We Come From?* London: Phoenix.

[99] For example: Gilbert Burnham, Riyadh Lafta, Shannon Doocy and Les Roberts (2006) 'Mortality after the 2003 invasion of Iraq: a cross-sectional cluster sample survey' *The Lancet* 368(9545): 1421-28. Opinion Research Business (2008) 'Update on Iraqi Casualty Data' http://www.opinion.co.uk/Newsroom details.aspx?NewsId=120. For a critique, see Michael Spagat and Josh Dougherty (2010) 'Conflict Deaths in Iraq: A Methodological Critique of the ORB Survey Estimate' *Survey Research Methods* 4(1): 3-15.

[100] Physicians for Social Responsibility, Physicians for Global Survival and IPPNW (Germany) (2015) *Body Count: Casualty Figures after 10 Years of the "War on Terror"* http://www.psr.org/assets/pdfs/body-count.pdf.

[101] Gunter Lewy disputes the idea that the Nazis tried to exterminate all Gypsy-Roma, as they had with respect to Jews. See his 'Gypsies and Jews Under the Nazis' *Holocaust and Genocide Studies* 13(3): 383-404.

[102] See the metadata: Colin Rowat (2001 2nd) 'UN agency reports on the humanitarian situation in Iraq' *Campaign Against Sanctions on Iraq* Cambridge: Cambridge University, pp. 1-33,

http://citeseerx.ist.psu.edu/viewdoc/download?doi=10.1.1.49
2.7935&rep=rep1&type=pdf. The British government's Select
Committee on International Development accepts that at least
200,000 infants had died by 1999, based on independent US
university studies. See its (1999-2000) 'The Impact of Sanctions: Other Special Circumstances: Children' International Development: Second Report para. 54 https://publications.parlia
ment.uk/pa/cm199900/cmselect/cmintdev/67/6707.htm.

[103] Michael Spagat claims that the 1995 UN Food and Agricultural
Organisation report on Iraqi infant deaths was based on Saddam's propaganda:

> In 1995 the United Nations Food and Agriculture Organisa-
> tion (FAO), in cooperation with Iraq's Ministry of Agriculture
> and Nutrition Research Institute (NRI), organised a child nu-
> trition and mortality survey of Baghdad. The Iraqi ministry
> provided the interviewers for this survey, in contrast to the
> more independent IST survey that had supplied its own in-
> terviewers.

Spagat (2010) 'Truth and death in Iraq under sanctions' *Significance: The Royal Statistical Society* September: 117-18.
Sources: None. But Spagat's logic collapses his own case. Suppose he's right and Saddam chose the families that the team
interviewed. If Saddam selected over 2,000 starving children,
the data would have yielded 100% starvation. But there were
starving and non-starving children interviewed. *The New York
Times* (careful to blame the 'Security Council' not the US) said:
'Dr. Fawzi, who surveyed 2,120 children under 10 years of age
in 25 neighborhoods in Baghdad in August, said 28 percent
were stunted in growth, up from 12 percent in 1991'. If Saddam had picked the families, as Spagat claims, he would have
chosen far more than three in 10 starving children to show the
epidemiologists. Barbara Crossette (1995) 'Iraq sanctions kill
children, U.N. reports' *New York Times*
https://www.nytimes.com/1995/12/01/world/iraq-sanctions-
kill-children-un-reports.html.

Elsewhere, Spagat has written that the sanctions 'caused a lot of pain', but: 'I just think it's a myth that economic sanctions caused a spike in child mortality that led to hundreds of thousands of deaths and that replacing sanctions with war could (or did) lead to an improvement for Iraq's children'. Quoted in Joe Emersberger (2013) 'Exchange with Michael Spagat re "The Iraq Sanctions Myth" ' *Z Blogs* https://zcomm. org/zblogs/exchange-with-michael-spagat-re-the-iraq-sanctions-myth-by-joe-emersberger/.

[104] There are efforts to challenge this. See, for instance, Commission on Security and Cooperation in Europe (2015) *A Century of Denial: The Armenian Genocide of the Ongoing Quest for Justice*, 114th Session United States Congress, Washington, DC: Government Printing Office https://chrissmith.house.gov/upl oadedfiles/2015.04.23_a_century_of_denial-_the_armenian_ genocid_and_the_ongoing_quest_for_justice.pdf.

[105] Geoff Simons, London: Palgrave Macmillan.

[106] *LA Times* (28 March 1992). The Teddy campaign was launched by an American nurse, Dianne Judice, who had lost her son to leukemia and was empathising with Iraqi children; the ones with cancer couldn't even get painkillers due to the blockade. Voices in the Wilderness was led by Kathy Kelly, who now co-ordinates Voices for Creative Non-Violence.

[107] For example, Denis Halliday (1999) 'The impact of the UN sanctions on the people of Iraq' *The Journal of Palestine Studies* 28(20): 29-36.

[108] On the comparison to Greece and Burundi, see Patrick Cockburn (2007) *The Occupation* London: Verso, p.15. On the comparison to Congo, see Clare Short MP's letter to PM Tony Blair, released as evidence to the Chilcot Inquiry, available at www.web.archive.org/web/20140207111506/http://www.iraq inquiry.org.uk:80/media/44220/050303short-blair.pdf.

[109] Jeremy Scahill (2011 2nd) *Blackwater: The Rise of the World's Most Powerful Mercenary Army* London: Serpent's Tail, chapter 17.

[110] It didn't necessarily work. Iraq was accused of selling oil to countries to which the US objected, notably Russia. See Paul A.

Volcker, Richard J. Goldstone and Mark Pieth (2005) *Manipulation of the Oil-for-Food Programme by the Iraqi Regime Independent Inquiry into Committee into the United Nations Oil-for-Food Programme* https://web.archive.org/web/200607111941 09/http://www.iic-offp.org/documents/IIC%20Final%20Report %2027Oct2005.pdf.

[111] Bender writes that 'sanctions are believed to have been very effective in limiting Iraq's ability to rebuild conventional forces that were essentially cut by 50% as a result of the Gulf War'. He also writes:

> A primary US interest has been to maintain access to the vast supplies of inexpensive and readily available oil from the Gulf, a critical commodity to the economies of all industrialized nations. A second, related interest has been to preserve regional stability by preventing the emergence of a regional power unfriendly to US interests.

Lt. Col. William J. Bender (2002) *Strategic Implications for U.S. Policy in Iraq: Why Now?* USAWC Strategy Research Project Pennsylvania: US Army War College, pp. 11, 4 http://www.dtic.mil/dtic/tr/fulltext/u2/a402145.pdf.

[112] See the now-defunct organisation's document, Thomas Donnelly (2000) *Rebuilding America's Defenses: Strategy, Forces and Resources For a New Century* The Project for the New American Century, Washington, DC: PNAC, p. 14 https://web.archive.org/web/20021112224032/http://www.n ewamericancentury.org/RebuildingAmericasDefenses.pdf.

[113] For example: 'The UK continues to play an important role in training and mentoring the Iraqi Army and Police. It is unclear how its trainers will be supported once UK force levels are reduced further'. House of Commons Defence Committee (2007) *UK Land Operations in Iraq 2007* First Report of Session 2007-08 HC 110, p. 3 https://publications.parliament.uk/pa/ cm200708/cmselect/cmdfence/110/110.pdf.

And less than 10 years later:

> The British army has helped train more than 6,500 person-
> nel in Iraq to date ... Britain is set to pledge several dozen
> more troops to support the Iraqi Security Forces (ISF) as
> they take the fight to Daesh ... It will bring the total number
> of UK personnel involved in training inside Iraq to over 300,
> and the total engaged in theatre to over 1,000.

Ministry of Defence and Michael Fallon (2016) 'UK to increase training to Iraqi forces' https://www.gov.uk/government /news/uk-to-increase-training-to-iraqi-forces. With regards to naval operations post-'withdrawal':

> In Iraq, the UK Training and Maritime Support Agreement
> came into force and the majority of forces withdrew in July
> 2009. They have also undertaken the other military tasks re-
> quired of them in the year. The proportion of forces de-
> ployed on operations and other military tasks decreased
> from 17% in the last quarter of 2008-09 to 14% in the last
> quarter of 2009-10, largely due to the withdrawal from Iraq.

Ministry of Defence (2010) *Consolidated Departmental Re-source Accounts 2009-2010* HC 258 London: The Stationary Office, p. 126 https://assets.publishing.service.gov.uk/governm ent/uploads/system/uploads/attachment_data/file/27065/mo d_ra0910.pdf.

[114] In 2007, Iraq's National Security Advisor, Mowaffaq al-Rubaie, said: 'permanent forces or bases in Iraq for any foreign forces is a red line that cannot be accepted by any nationalist Iraqi'. Peter Graff (2007) 'Iraq rejects permanent U.S. bases: adviser' *Reuters* https://www.reuters.com/article/us-iraq-bases/iraq-rejects-permanent-u-s-bases-adviser-idUSL08647786200 71211.

Eight years later, it was reported:

> The United States and Iraq have agreed on five military ba-
> ses to become permanent locations for 3,100 US troops in
> Iraq, a senior Iraqi military official has revealed. "Both par-
> ties, Iraq and the US, have previously agreed on the loca-

tions for the US troops," the official from the Iraqi Ministry of Defence told al-Araby al-Jadeed.

Othman al-Mukhtar (2014) 'US to control five military bases in Iraq' *Al-Araby* https://www.alaraby.co.uk/english/news/2014/11/9/us-to-control-five-military-bases-in-iraq.

[115] 'Over the years many victims of torture have been Shia Muslims from Baghdad or from Southern Iraq'. Amnesty International UK (2001) 'Iraq: Stop the Torture' https://www.amnesty.org.uk/press-releases/iraq-stop-torture.

[116] Early polling is hard to find, but consider the US State Department's internal poll which found that 65% of Iraqis wanted an immediate US withdrawal in 2006. Amit R. Paley (2006) 'Most Iraqis Favor Immediate U.S. Pullout, Polls Show' *Washington Post* https://web.archive.org/web/20060928015012/http://www.washingtonpost.com/wp-dyn/content/article/2006/09/26/AR2006092601721.html.

[117] SCL was 'providing the strategic management of the first democratic elections in Iraq' (their website) quoted in PowerBase (no date) 'SCL Elections' http://powerbase.info/index.php/SCL_Elections.

[118] Amnesty wrote in 2010:

> Rape or the threat of rape. Beating with cables and hose-pipes. Prolonged suspension by the limbs. Electric shocks to sensitive parts of the body. Breaking of limbs. Removal of toenails with pliers. Asphyxiation using a plastic bag[s] over the head. Piercing the body with drills. Being forced to sit on sharp objects such as broken bottles. These are just some of the torture methods used against men, women and children by Iraqi security forces.

Amnesty International (2010) *New Order, Same Abuses* https://www.amnesty.org/download/Documents/40000/mde140062010en.pdf.

Many quite the literally the same abuses. Compare the above to Amnesty's report from 2001 (op cit.), written during the Saddam years:

> Other methods of torture include extinguishing of cigarettes on various parts of the body, extraction of finger nails and toenails and piercing of the hands with an electric drill. Some have been sexually abused and others have had objects, including broken bottles, forced into their anus. In addition to physical torture, detainees have been threatened with rape and subjected to mock executions.

[119] See, for example, on the dual-use technologies Mark Phythian (1997) *Arming Iraq: How the U.S. and Britain Secretly Built Saddam's War Machine* Chicago: Northwestern University Press.

[120] Tariq S. Al-Hadithi, Jawad K. Al-Diwan, Abubakir M. Saleh and Nazar P. Shabila (2012) 'Birth defects in Iraq and the plausibility of environmental exposure: A review' *Conflict and Health* 6(3): https://www.ncbi.nlm.nih.gov/pmc/articles/PMC3492088/.

[121] Human Rights Watch (1992) *Endless Torment: The 1991 Uprising in Iraq and Its Aftermath* New York: Human Rights Watch https://www.hrw.org/legacy/reports/1992/Iraq926.htm.

[122] BAE Systems, for instance, regularly supports Chatham House research into foreign policy. That research often ends up in the official *National Security Strategy*.

[123] Human Rights Law Centre (2017) 'UK High Court finds that arms trade to Saudi Arabia can continue' https://www.hrlc.org.au/human-rights-case-summaries/2017/10/13/uk-high-court-finds-that-arms-trade-to-saudi-arabia-can-continue.

[124] As Home Secretary, Theresa May set up the College of Policing, which trained police in Indonesia, Botswana, and elsewhere – mostly Middle Eastern countries. Lucas Amin (2017) 'UK police earned millions training officers in repressive regimes' *Guardian* https://www.theguardian.com/law/2017/sep/15/uk-police-earned-millions-training-officers-in-repressive-regimes.

[125] These are drawn from government figures. Tom Dunlop (2016) 'UK is second largest global arms dealer' *UK Defence Journal* https://ukdefencejournal.org.uk/uk-is-second-largest-global-arms-dealer/.

126 The public agreed that '[w]ars the UK has supported or fought ARE responsible, at least in part, for terror attacks against the UK', 53% to 24%. Matthew Smith (2017) 'Jeremy Corbyn is on the right side of public opinion on foreign policy: except for the Falklands' YouGov https://yougov.co.uk/news/2017/05/30/jeremy-corbyn-right-side-public-opinion-foreign-po/.

127 For example, the Skripal poisonings:

> The poisoning of Sergei and Yulia Skripal in Salisbury in early March afforded Theresa May a chance to look prime ministerial, with 53% of Brits saying they thought she had handled the crisis well. Corbyn, by contrast, was only seen by 18% as having responded to the crisis well.

Matthew Smith (2018) 'The public sees Theresa May more favourably than Jeremy Corbyn for the first time since the election' YouGov https://yougov.co.uk/news/2018/04/09/public-sees-theresa-may-more-favourably-jeremy-cor/.

128 Extensive details and sources are available in T.J. Coles (2016) *Britain's Secret Wars: How and Why the United Kingdom Sponsors Conflict Around the World* West Sussex: Clairview Books, chapters 1-2.

129 Nafeez Ahmed (2017) ' "Sorted' by MI5: How UK government sent British-Libyans to fight Gaddafi' *Middle East Eye* http://www.middleeasteye.net/news/sorted-mi5-how-uk-government-sent-british-libyans-fight-gaddafi-1219906488.

130 *Foreign Policy* (2017) 'Here's how the global GDP is divided up' https://foreignpolicy.com/2017/02/24/infographic-heres-how-the-global-gdp-is-divvied-up/.

131 For example Antony C. Sutton (1968) *Western Technology and Soviet Economic Development* California: Hoover Institution on War, Revolution and Peace. Sutton's findings were endorsed as accurate by future-National Security Advisor to Jimmy Carter, Zbigniew Brzezinki (1969) *Between Two Ages: America's Role in the Technetronic Era* New York: Greenwood Press, p. 135n.

132 Estimates vary between 17% and 22%. For example London's Economic Plan (no date) 'The Development of London's Economy' http://www.uncsbrp.org/economicdevelopment.htm and

Jon Kelly (2015) 'London-centric' BBC News Online https://www.bbc.co.uk/news/resources/idt-248d9ac7-9784-4769-936a-8d3b435857a8.

[133] The annual intelligence report to Congress confirms that China's reach is regional, not global. See Daniel C. Coates (2018) *Statement for the Record: Worldwide Threat Assessment of the US Intelligence Community* Office of the Director of National Intelligence Washington, DC: Government Printing Office https://www.dni.gov/files/documents/Newsroom/Testimonies/2018-ATA---Unclassified-SSCI.pdf.

[134] This resolution calls on both sides to resolve the issue under the principle of decolonisation: United Nations (1965) General Assembly Resolution 2065(XX) https://documents-dds-ny.un.org/doc/RESOLUTION/GEN/NR0/218/28/IMG/NR021828.pdf?OpenElement. This resolution expresses 'gratitude' to Argentina, not the UK, for its respecting the previous resolution and criticises the fact that no progress had been made, which can only mean that the UK stalled: United Nations (1973) General Assembly Resolution 3160 (XXVIII) https://documents-dds-ny.un.org/doc/RESOLUTION/GEN/NR0/282/32/IMG/NR028232.pdf?OpenElement.

[135] The full quote from the Foreign Office archives reads: 'It is not easy to explain our possession of the islands without showing ourselves up as international bandits'. Quoted in Nick Davies (2009) *Flat Earth News* London: Vintage, p. 145.

[136] Christoph Bluth (1987) 'The British Resort to Force in the Falklands/Malvinas Conflict 1982: International Law and Just War Theory' *Journal of Peace Research* 24(1): 5-20. W. Michael Reisman (1983) 'The Struggle for the Falklands' *The Yale Law Journal* 93(2): 287-317. Peter Calvert 'Sovereignty and the Falklands Crisis' *International Affairs* 59(3): 405-413.

[137] The UK's *Strategic Defence and Security Review* said a few years ago:

> The UK currently ... has a major military presence in Germany, with 20,000 service personnel and their families based there. For more than 50 years the Federal Government has

supported the British military presence providing essential training and operational opportunities as well as basing. The presence of the British military has played an important role in demonstrating Alliance solidarity, and has also been a symbol of steadfast UK-German friendship. But there is no longer any operational requirement for UK forces to be based there.

HM Government (2010) *Securing Britain in an Age of Uncertainty: The Strategic Defence and Security Review* Cm 7948, p. 28 https://assets.publishing.service.gov.uk/government/uploads/system/uploads/attachment_data/file/62482/strategic-defence-security-review.pdf.

[138] United Nations Security Council Resolution 503 (1982).

[139] A *Guardian*/ICM poll taken in 2012 found that 61% of respondents thought that 'Britain should protect the Falklands so long as the islanders want protecting, no matter what the cost'. The phrase 'nuclear war' was not used, but 'no matter what the cost' implies it. Tom Clark (2012) 'Britain should protect Falkland Islands "at all costs," say 61% of voters' *Guardian* https://www.theguardian.com/uk/2012/mar/20/falkland-islands-guardian-icm-poll.

[140] Johnson's comments could be read either way, as racism or sarcasm against then-PM Tony Blair, or both:

> It is said that the Queen has come to love the Commonwealth, partly because it supplies her with regular cheering crowds of flag-waving piccaninnies; and one can imagine that Blair, twice victor abroad but enmired at home, is similarly seduced by foreign politeness.
>
> They say he is shortly off to the Congo. No doubt the AK47s will fall silent, and the pangas will stop their hacking of human flesh, and the tribal warriors will all break out in watermelon smiles to see the big white chief touch down in his big white British taxpayer-funded bird.

Johnson (2002) 'If Blair's so good at running the Congo, let him stay there' *Telegraph* https://www.telegraph.co.uk/comment/

personal-view/3571742/If-Blairs-so-good-at-running-the-Congo-let-him-stay-there.html.

141 Johnson (2002) 'Cancel the guilt trip' *The Spectator* http://archive.spectator.co.uk/article/2nd-february-2002/14/cancel-the-guilt-trip.

142 '[I]f the spoils' of the US Empire 'went, as they traditionally do, to the victor [in Iraq], what share would the victor's spear-carrier get?', referring to Britain. Niall Ferguson (2004) *Colossus* London: Allen Lane, p. 161.

143 Britain Israel Communications and Research Centre (2017) 'UK financial contributions have successfully funded police and weapons training programmes for PA forces' London: BICOM, p. 13 http://www.bicom.org.uk/wp-content/uploads/2017/07/UK-paper-FINAL-Supporting-a-two-state-solution-effective-UK-policy-to-boost-Israeli-Palestinian-relations-1.pdf.

144 David Cameron (2011) 'Speech to Conservative Spring Conference'. Available at https://www.newstatesman.com/2011/03/enterprise-government-party.

145 The FT interviewed Kagame and included a little about his background: '1990: Kagame is training at a US military academy in Fort Leavenworth when he is called to Rwanda after the death of a comrade who was leading an invading Tutsi force. He takes control of 2,000 rebels'. Davi Pilling and Lionel Barber (2017) 'Interview: Kagame insists "Rwandans understand the greater goal" ' *Financial Times* https://www.ft.com/content/a2838936-88c6-11e7-bf50-e1c239b45787.

146 BBC News Online (2007) https://www.bbc.co.uk/news/10479882. The disgraceful article is a classic example of un-objective objectivity. The obviously favourable article is 'balanced' with some negative comments. For example:

> [Kagame's] opponents accuse him of being the latest in a long line of authoritarian rulers in Africa, who will win the 4 August [2017] election after his regime brutally suppressed the opposition and killed some of his most vocal critics - a charge his allies vehemently deny.

Imagine the BBC quoting Gaddafi's victims and adding the qualifier, 'Gaddafi's supporters deny the charges'. That is not how to evaluate a situation. An honest reporter would go to a third source, like Amnesty International, and see what they report. This is routinely done by the BBC in Syria, for instance, citing Human Rights Watch reports documenting abuses by Bashar al-Assad (an enemy). The BBC does in fact include an Amnesty statement in its Kagame (an ally) piece, but adds the qualifier 'for'. So 'for' Amnesty, Kagame is a dictator. But 'for' his supporters, he's not. Suddenly, the alleged objectivity principle is abandoned and any opinion, even those of respected rights groups is subjective and therefore irrelevant. Imagine the BBC writing the following about Gaddafi (an enemy)'s Libya: 'For leading rights group Amnesty International, the election is taking place in a "climate of fear created by years of repression against opposition politicians, journalists and human rights defenders" '. The article then goes on to justify Kagame's actions:

> For the president, it would signal that his biggest political mission - to end the ethnic divisions that caused the genocide - had failed.
>
> And probably this fear, more than any other, is driving him to repel threats to his rule.

Again, imagine the BBC saying the same of Gaddafi.
[147] Cameron reminded the Kuwaiti regime, which Britain arms and trains, that the UK sacrificed lives (meaning the lives of lower-class British servicemen) for Kuwait (meaning Kuwaiti oil) when Saddam invaded. So now Kuwait must make sure the country is open for business. Bearing in mind that this was taking place in the context of the Arab Spring, when the British establishment feared that its allies might be overthrown in a popular revolution, Cameron told the Kuwaiti regime:

> It is not for me, or for governments outside the region, to pontificate about how each country meets the aspirations of

its people. It is not for us to tell you how to do it, or precisely what shape your future should take.

David Cameron (2011) 'Prime Minister's speech to the National Assembly Kuwait' Cabinet Office https://www.gov.uk/government/speeches/prime-ministers-speech-to-the-national-assembly-kuwait.

[148] According to the International Crisis Group, which has links with energy companies: 'By the second half of the [1990s], a group of senior officials … convinced Qaddafi of the need to rebuild relations with the international community'. Gaddafi's son, Saif, was the frontman for these changes, but: 'the reformist current always was tightly controlled, and the reform process was highly orchestrated, in effect an affair of marginal and cosmetic rather than radical or wholesale changes'. International Crisis Group (2011) *Popular Protest in North Africa and the Middle East (V): Making Sense of Libya* Report No. 107 http://citizenshiprightsafrica.org/wp-content/uploads/2016/06/ICG-Making-Sense-of-Libya-2011.pdf.

[149] Then-US Secretary of State Hillary Clinton's advisor, Sidney Blumenthal, wrote an unclassified but confidential email to Clinton:

> During mid-September 2011 French President Nicolas Sarkozy and British Prime Minister David Cameron traveled to Tripoli to meet with and express support for the leaders of the new government of Libya under the National Transitional Council (NTC). According to knowledgeable individuals, as part of this effort, the two leaders, in private conversations, also intend to press the leaders of the NTC to reward their early support for the rebellion against Muammar al Qaddafi. Sarkozy and Cameron expect this recognition to be tangible, in the form of favorable contracts for French and British energy companies looking to play a major role in the Libyan oil industry. According to this source, Sarkozy feels, quite strongly, that without French support there would have been no revolution and that the NTC government must demonstrate that it realizes this fact. For his part, Cameron

appears most concerned that despite British support for the rebels during the fighting, certain members of the NTC remain focused on the fact that the British government and oil industry had good relations with the Qaddafi regime, particularly the firm British Petroleum (BP).

Sidney Blumenthal (2011). Email to Hillary Clinton https://wikileaks.org/clinton-emails/emailid/12900.

[150] 'Israel has been a major arms supplier to Sri Lanka's government, as well as providing it with strategic military advice. With permission from the United States, Israel has sold Sri Lanka consignments of Kfir jets and drones'. Krisna Saravanamuttu (2013) 'Israel advises Sri Lanka on slow-motion genocide' *Electronic Intifada* https://electronicintifada.net/content/israel-advises-sri-lanka-slow-motion-genocide/12644.

This is nothing new. In the 1980s, when UK special forces were providing training, the Israelis were, too:

Israeli intelligence agents and former British Army commandos are training Sri Lanka's security forces as part of a new drive by the Government to combat a violent Tamil separatist movement in the north, the country's National Security Affairs Minister says ... [F]ormer members of Britain's Special Air Service, now working for a private security company based in the Channel Islands off Britain, had already trained a group of paratroopers who took part in a recent antiterrorist operation. They performed "quite well," and "have come back for further training," he said ... A British diplomat said he did not know much about the British training team although he confirmed that they were here.

Sanjoy Hazarika (1984) 'Israel said to aid Sri Lanka forces' *New York Times* https://www.nytimes.com/1984/08/26/world/israel-said-to-aid-sri-lanka-forces.html.

[151] Icke:

Are you ready for this? I wish I didn't have to introduce the following information because it complicates the story and opens me up to mass ridicule. But stuff it. If that is where

> the evidence takes me, that is where I shall go every time ... Putting together the mass of evidence, views, research and opinions, that I have read or heard almost daily these past years, I feel the Anunnaki are a race from a reptile genetic stream. In UFO research these have become known as reptilians. Nor am I alone in this view. I have personally been staggered by how many people today are open to these possibilities and, indeed, are coming to the same conclusions through their own research. These include many who would have laughed at the very idea not so long ago.

David Icke (1999) *The Biggest Secret* Arizona: Bridge of Love, p. 19. Icke is still pursuing the reptiles – not the only inter-dimensional beings controlling us, he says. David Icke (2018) 'Laugh All You Like - Possession and Reptilians are REAL - The David Icke Dot-Connector Videocast' *David Icke Dot-Connector* https://www.youtube.com/watch?v=yCuEpcciuCs.

[152] The National Archives (no date) 'The struggle for democracy: Getting the vote: Voting rights before 1832' http://www.nationalarchives.gov.uk/pathways/citizenship/struggle_democracy/getting_vote.htm.

[153] Two academic researchers write:

> the heyday of conspiracy rhetoric in the British parliament occurred in the two decades 1916–35, a period coinciding first with WW1 and then with an intensification with the struggle for independence in Ireland, India, and in other colonies of the British Empire.

Andrew McKenzie-McHarg and Rolf Fredheim (2017) 'Cock-ups and slap-downs: A quantitative analysis of conspiracy rhetoric in the British Parliament 1916–2015' *Historical Methods* 50(3): 159.

[154] Central Intelligence Agency (no date) 'Concerning Criticism of the Warren Report' #1035-960. Available at http://www.jfklancer.com/CIA.html.

[155] Cass R. Sunstein and Adrian Vermeule write:

> [S]ome conspiracy theories, under our definition, have turned out to be true. The Watergate hotel room used by Democratic National Committee was, in fact, bugged by Republican officials, operating at the behest of the White House. In the 1950s, the Central Intelligence Agency did, in fact, administer LSD and related drugs under Project MKULTRA, in an effort to investigate the possibility of "mind control." Operation Northwoods, a rumored plan by the Department of Defense to simulate acts of terrorism and to blame them on Cuba, really was proposed by high-level officials (though the plan never went into effect).

Sunstein and Vermeule (2008) 'Conspiracy Theories' *Harvard Public Law Working Paper* No. 8-3 https://papers.ssrn.com/sol3/papers.cfm?abstract_id=1084585.

[156] For instance, Hannah Z. Sidney (2014) *Inventing Burke: Edmund Burke and the Conservative Party, 1790-1918* (doctoral thesis) New York: City University of New York.

[157] Michael J. Wood (2016) 'Some Dare Call It Conspiracy: Labeling Something a Conspiracy Theory Does Not Reduce Belief in It' *Political Psychology* 37(5): 695-705.

[158] For instance: 'The poor increase like fleas and lice, and these vermin will eat us up unless we enclose'. Quoted in Christopher Hill (1978 4th) *The World Turned Upside Down* London: Pelican, p.52.

[159] Richard Norton-Taylor (2014) 'MI5 spied on leading British historians for decades, secret files reveal' *Guardian* https://www.theguardian.com/world/2014/oct/24/mi5-spied-historians-eric-hobsbawm-christopher-hill-secret-files.

[160] Donnelly, op cit., p. 51.

[161] National Commission on Terrorist Attacks Upon the United States (2004) http://govinfo.library.unt.edu/911/hearings/index.htm. The pages on the hearings are hard to navigate. See the video of military personnel hearings: https://www.c-span.org/video/?182320-1/september-11-commission-hearing. Some examples of obfuscation: 'I don't recall'; 'I'm aware of one program which is classified'; 'We'll leave that to

the lawyers'; 'I apologize but I need to get to the next venue up in New York' (Gen. Richard Myers, Joint Chiefs of Staff). 'I didn't recall those facts' (Maj. Gen. Larry Arnold (Ret.) former Commander, NORAD). '...[A] tape that we were unaware of at the time...' (Gen. Ralph Eberhart, NORAD Commander). Members of the public who shouted, 'Tell us about the war games!' were silenced.

162 Some of the ample evidence includes a leaked memo from the Deputy Undersecretary of Defense to Secretary of State, Dean Rusk, which says:

> The Department of Defense has requested our approval to initiate the operational phase of Project Popeye in selected areas along the infiltration routes in North Vietnam and southern Laos. The objective of the program is to produce sufficient rainfall along these lines of communication to interdict or at least interfere with truck traffic between North and South Vietnam. Recently improved cloud seeding techniques would be applied on a sustained basis, in a non-publicized effort to induce continued rainfall through the months of the normal dry season ...
>
> In our view, the experiments were undeniably successful, indicating that, at least under weather and terrain conditions such as those involved, the U.S. Government has realized a capability of significant weather modification. If anything, the tests were "too successful"—neither the volume of induced rainfall nor the extent of area affected can be precisely predicted.

Memorandum From the Deputy Under Secretary of State for Political Affairs (Kohler) to Secretary of State Rusk (1967) *Foreign Relations of the United States, 1964–1968: Volume XXVIII, Laos* Department of State Office of the Historian, Washington, DC: Government Printing Office https://history.state.gov/historicaldocuments/frus1964-68v28/d274.

163 'Secretary of Defense Laird was questioned by both Senator Pell and Senator Fulbright about rainmaking in Vietnam. The Secretary said: "We have never engaged in that type of activity

over North Vietnam." ' Committee on Commerce, Science, and Transportation (1978) *Weather Modification: Programs, Problems, Policy, and Potential* United States Senate 95th, Congress 2nd Session Washington, DC: Government Printing Office, pp. 441-42n35.

 Defense Secretary Melvin Laird wrote to Senator Pell's Committee:

> I responded to your question concerning weather modification with the statement "we have never engaged in that type of activity over North Vietnam." That statement represented, first, my knowledge that I had never approved operations over North Vietnam and secondly, my understanding of activities authorized by preceding Secretaries of Defense. I have just been informed that such activities were conducted over North Vietnam in 1967 and again in 1968. I want to take this opportunity to both express my regret that this information was not available to me.

Subcommittee on Oceans and International Environment (1974) *Weather Modification* 93rd Congress, 2nd Session, Washington, DC: Government Printing Office, pp. 109-110.

[164] Philip Bump (2013) '12 Million Americans Believe Lizard People Run Our Country' *The Atlantic* https://web.archive.org/web/20160930144228/https://www.theatlantic.com/national/archive/2013/04/12-million-americans-believe-lizard-people-run-our-country/316706/.

[165] Predictably, Steven Seidman not only uses the terms liberalism and libertarianism interchangeably, but also traces their origins to the European Enlightenment. The names cited as the founders are not peasant names, but the usual suspects: Hume, Voltaire, and so on. Seidman (1983) *Liberalism and the Origins of European Social Theory* Berkeley: University of California Press.

[166] Like any 'ism' libertarianism is a broad spectrum. Jason Brennan cites the economist Milton Friedman as a libertarian, even though Friedman called for a strong state to rescue failing corporations (a point omitted by Brennan). The so-called hard-

libertarians appear, at least in Brennan's reading, to oppose state intervention. These include Eric Mack, Robert Nozick, Ayn Rand, and Murray Rothbard. No doubt Enlightenment liberals would cringe. Brennan (2012) *Libertarianism: What Everyone Needs to Know* Oxford: OUP, pp. 47, 11.

[167] For example, Walter Wilcox (1962) 'The Press of the Radical Right: An Exploratory Analysis' *Journalism and Mass Communication Quarterly* 39(2): 152-60.

[168] https://anarchapulco.com/.

[169] 'I grew up in Dallas, Texas, with my family doing things like helping take in East German defectors, OK? Whenever I go to a family reunion, half the people in the room are former, retired CIA'. Jones interview on The Opie & Anthony Show, 17 April 2013 https://www.youtube.com/watch?v=bBMXmjVr954.

[170] An academic book on Michigan's militia cites Alex Jones as an influence among that group, and by implication other groups. Jones's hyper-madness could trigger some kind of militia activity. The author writes that after 9/11:

> Militia groups in Michigan met at once to discuss their response ... Instead of seeing them as allies, government agencies regarded the Michigan Militia as part of the "homegrown" terrorists who posed an expanded threat to "homeland security" and one more justification for the Patriot Act[,]'

or at least that's how the Militia felt. 'Texas radio personality Alex Jones, well known in militia circles for revealing government "conspiracies," maintained the government was doing "exactly what I said they would do..." '. JoEllen McNergney Vinyard (2011) *Right in Michigan's Grassroots: From the KKK to the Michigan Militia* Ann Arbor: University of Michigan Press, p. 299.

[171] Jones said:

> [Putin] took away our first-strike capability ... That will mean virtual annihilation of our top-brass military ... They're threatening to nuke us every other week ... Military traffic is

everywhere, scrambled … If you haven't got potassium io-
dine, I've got several cases of it … They used to issue it … in
case of Russian attack … Yeltsin had been threatening to
nuke us until he resigned … We're sitting here calmly and
you're telling me it's on ABC News that five missiles were
launched and they won't tell us where they were launched
from?!

It can be heard here:
http://hourofthetime.com/bcmp3B/1777.mp3.

[172] For details and sources, see T.J. Coles (2017) *President Trump, Inc.* West Sussex: Clairview Books.

[173] Niels H. Harrit et al. (2009) 'Active thermitic material discovered in dust from the 9/11 World Trade Center catastrophe' *The Open Chemical Physics Journal* 2: 7-31. See also Kevin Ryan et al. (2009) 'Environmental anomalies at the World Trade Center: evidence for energetic materials' *The Environmentalist* 29: 56-63.

[174] This Week (2016) 'David Icke talks conspiracy theories' BBC News https://www.youtube.com/watch?v=GlAjeTunopo.

[175] 'The use of the Internet could channel public interest towards already appropriately declassified material and possibly lessen FOIA requests'. The 'diversion' part reads: 'A strategy could then be devised by DoD and the components, based upon this evaluation, to implement a coherent and complimentary plan to achieve the declassification goals'. But this doesn't necessary refer to distracting the public. It could equally refer to distracting people from filing more interesting FOIA requests. Booz Allen & Hamilton (1998) 'Operations Security Impact On Declassification Management Within The Department of Defense' MD: Booz Allen & Hamilton https://fas.org/sgp/othergov/dod_opsec.html.

[176] London: Penguin, 1990.

[177] *Late Victorian Holocausts* London: Verso, 2002.

[178] The classic study is Joseph Stiglitz (2002) *Globalisation and Its Discontents* London: Penguin. Stiglitz is the former chief economist at the World Bank and a Nobel Prize Laureate.

179 Michael Cox (2005) 'Empire by denial: The strange case of the United States' *International Affairs* 81(1): 15-30.

180 A book length-series of interviews notes:

> Dependency was never a "theory" and both its characterisation and critique can be quite clichéd. Its intellectual heritage stretched back to the 19th-century resistance against colonialism; its 20th-century proponents range from [scholars] Raúl Prebisch to Adebayo Adedeji.

Jimi Adesina (2017) 'Preface' in Ushehwedu Kufakurinani et al. (eds.) *Dialogues on Development Volume 1: On Dependency* Young Scholars Initiative New York: Institute for New Economic Thinking, p. iv http://eprints.kingston.ac.uk/38253/6/McKenzie-R-38253-VoR.pdf.

181 Tat notes: 'South Korea ... has experienced such a transition over the past 20 years. The financial crisis of 1997 represented a defining moment, marking the transition from gradual to accelerated liberalisation'. Tat Yan Kong (2012) 'Neoliberal Restructuring in South Korea before and after the Crisis' in C. Kyung-Sup et al. (eds.) *Developmental Politics in Transition* London: Macmillan, p. 235.

On Singapore, see Liow:

> Singapore has undergone much structural changes to its economy in the past decade. The economy has gradually been deregulated, liberalised and privatised to conform more to the neoliberal model. However, existing interests embedded within the developmental state prevents a transition to a full-fledged neoliberal regulatory one.

Eugene Dili Liow (2012) 'The Neoliberal-Developmental State: Singapore as Case Study' *Critical Sociology* 38(2): 241.

182 *The State of Africa* London: The Free Press, 2005. See the last chapter.

183 Ernest C. Madu (2010) '20 Years - The Convention on the Rights of the Child' UNICEF https://web.archive.org/web/20100417114709/https://www.unicef.org/rightsite/364_617.htm.

184 Royal College of Physicians and the Royal College of Paediatrics and Child Health cited in National Health Service (2016) 'Air pollution "kills 40,000 a year" in the UK, says report' https://www.nhs.uk/news/heart-and-lungs/air-pollution-kills-40000-a-year-in-the-uk-says-report/.

185 Jonathan Watkins et al. (2017) 'Effects of health and social care spending constraints on mortality in England: a time trend analysis' *BMJ* 7(11): e017722. 'Economic murder' found in Sara Sjolin (2017) ' "Economic murder": Study links U.K. austerity to 120,000 deaths' *MarketWatch* https://www.marketwatch.com/story/uk-austerity-linked-to-120000-deaths-in-economic-murder-landmark-study-finds-2017-11-16.

186 For example, Thorsten Hoffmann (2011) *The Muslim Brotherhood in Egypt: Pursuing Moderation within an Authoritarian Environment* (Master's thesis) Monterey: Naval Postgraduate School http://www.dtic.mil/dtic/tr/fulltext/u2/a547851.pdf.

187 Even the BBC acknowledges this, but asks plaintively what went wrong. BBC News Online (2017) 'Why is Libya so lawless' https://www.bbc.com/news/world-africa-24472322.

188 Shockingly: 'More than half of South Africans were poor in 2015, with the poverty headcount increasing to 55,5% from a series low of 53,2% in 2011'. Statistics South Africa (2018) 'Poverty on the rise in South Africa' Government http://www.statssa.gov.za/?p=10334.

189 Ministry of Defence (2007 3rd) *The DCDC Global Strategic Trends Programme: 2007-2036* Swindon: Developments, Concepts and Doctrine Centre, p. 79 https://ia800407.us.archive.org/18/items/20072036UK_201606/2007-2036%20UK.pdf.

190 Mark Roland Thomas and Dino Merotto (2012) 'African Debt since Debt Relief: How Clean is the Slate?' *World Bank* http://blogs.worldbank.org/africacan/african-debt-since-debt-relief-how-clean-is-the-slate.

191 The House of Commons Library says:

> NATO involvement in the Former Yugoslavia began in 1992 when the Alliance began to monitor UN sanctions imposed on Serbia and Montenegro in the Adriatic by both air and

sea. Called Operation Sharp Guard, the authority for this action was derived from UNSCR 787 ... NATO combat air patrols to enforce the Zone were authorized under UNSCR 820 and began on 10th June 1993. UNSCR 836 of June 1993 then authorized the use of NATO air power in and around the Safe Areas in support of UNPROFOR either in a strategic or close air support role.

This is a flat-out lie. Neither Resolution mentions NATO. Tom Dodd (1995) 'War and Peacekeeping in the Former Yugoslavia' House of Commons Library Research Paper 95/100. UNSCR 787 http://www.un.org/en/ga/search/view_doc.asp?symbol=S/RES/787(1992) and UNSCR 836 https://documents-dds-ny.un.org/doc/UNDOC/GEN/N93/330/21/IMG/N9333021.pdf?OpenElement.

[192] Sarah Helm (1995) *Independent* https://www.independent.co.uk/news/world/riddle-of-serb-exodus-from-krajina-1598339.html.

Human Rights Watch states:

The offensive, which lasted a mere thirty-six hours, resulted in the death of an estimated 526 Serbs, 116 of whom were reportedly civilians, and in the displacement of an estimated 200,000 who fled in the immediate aftermath. However, while the Croatian military committed violations of humanitarian law during the course of the offensive such as the bombardment of a column of retreating Serbian civilians and soldiers which caused deaths among the civilians, the vast majority of the abuses committed by Croatian forces occurred after the area had been captured.

HRW (1996) *Impunity for abuses committed during "Operation Storm"* New York: HRW https://www.hrw.org/legacy/reports/1996/Croatia.htm.

[193] Christian Parenti writes:

...fundamentalist warriors from Chechnya, Saudi Arabia, Egypt, and Pakistan fought alongside the same government forces that soon were to receive covert U.S. training. According to international observer troops, the mujahedeen in Bosnia grew from a few hundred to around 6,000 in 1995.

(2001) 'America's Jihad: A History of Origins' *Social Justice* 3(85): 34.

[194] *Newsnight* (2015) BBC https://www.bbc.co.uk/news/world-europe-33345618.

[195] Michel Collon (2007) *Media Lies and the Conquest of Kosovo: NATO's Prototype for the Next Wars of Globalization* New York: Unwritten History, Inc.

[196] Speculating, Honig and Yahel write on:

> the KLA's provocation strategy. The KLA succeeded in bringing about an international intervention that imposed independence of sorts on Kosovo by using terrorism to provoke Serbian ruler Slobodan Milosevic to repress too heavily the Kosovar Muslims (at least heavily enough for the KLA to claim in their propaganda that a genocide was taking place).

Or Honig and Ido Yahel (2019) 'Israel-PLO: from national liberation to deterrence stability' in Elli Lieberman (eds.) *Deterring Terrorism: A Model for Strategic Deterrence* London: Routledge. Chapter 3.

Timothy W. Crawford, for example, writes that in 1998,

> the KLA came down from the hills and resumed the campaign of provocations—ambushing Serb police patrols, even firing on diplomatic observers who accompanied them, and occupying and fortifying key positions vacated by Serb forces.

Crawford (2003) *Pivotal Deterrence: Third-party Statecraft and the Pursuit of Peace* Ithaca: Cornell University Press, 181-82.

[197] Tim Youngs (1998) 'Kosovo: The Diplomatic and Military Options' House of Commons Library, Research Paper 98/93 London: Stationary Office, p. 28.

[198] In April 1999, NATO admitted: 'During 1998, open conflict between Serbian military and police forces and Kosovar Albanian forces resulted in the deaths of over 1,500 Kosovar Albanians

and forced 400,000 people from their homes'. Conflict resulted in 1,500 Kosovar deaths, not the tens- or hundreds of thousands alleged by the media. NATO (1999) 'NATO's role in relation to the conflict in Kosovo'
https://www.nato.int/kosovo/history.htm.

[199] Youngs op cit., p. 7.

[200] Select Committee on Defence (2004) Third Report para. 465. https://publications.parliament.uk/pa/cm200304/cmselect/cm dfence/57/5718.htm.

[201] One of his books (also 1997) is called *The Grand Chessboard*.

[202] One military report says:

> Camp Bondsteel strategically lies close to the planned Albanian-Macedonian-Bulgarian Oil (AMBO) pipeline. Also known as the Trans-Balkan, the pipeline project will transport the Caspian oil from Bulgaria to Albania via Macedonia. The $1.5bn AMBO pipeline is sponsored by the US-based consortium Albanian Macedonian Bulgarian Oil Corporation.

Army Technology (2010) 'Camp Bondsteel, Kosovo' https://web.archive.org/web/20101102225459/https://www. army-technology.com/projects/campbondsteel/.

[203] De Hoop Scheffer also said: 'the present strategic concept of NATO, of dating back, as you know, to 1999, is already talking about the free flow of energy. So you cannot possibly state and argue that this is a subject alien to NATO'. (2009) 'Transatlantic Leadership For A New Era' Security and Defence Agenda Brussels: NATO
https://www.nato.int/docu/speech/2009/s090126a.html.

[204] University of Colorado (no date) 'The Trolley Problem' http://rintintin.colorado.edu/~vancecd/phil3160/trolley.pdf.

[205] International Committee of the Red Cross (2001) *Explosive Remnants of War* Geneva: ICRC https://www.icrc.org/eng/asse ts/files/other/icrc_002_0780.pdf.

[206] Edwin Black (2009) *The Transfer Agreement: The Dramatic Story of the Pact Between the Third Reich and Jewish Palestine* New York: Dialog Press and Avraham Barkai (1990) 'German In-

terests in the Haavara-Transfer Agreement 1933–1939' *The Leo Baeck Institute Year Book* 35(1): 245-66.

[207] Yosef Grodzinsky (1998) *Good Human Material* Tel Aviv: Hed Arzi Publishing.

[208] David A. Janicki (2014) 'The British Blockade During World War I: The Weapon of Deprivation' *Inquiries: Social Sciences, Arts &, Humanities* 6(6): 1-5.

[209] National Archive (no date) 'The blockade on Germany' http://www.nationalarchives.gov.uk/pathways/firstworldwar/spotlights/blockade.htm.

[210] Hew Strachan (2015) *The First World War: A New History* New York: Penguin Books, p. 215.

[211] See Antony C. Sutton (2010 [1976]) *Wall Street and the Rise of Hitler* West Sussex: Clairview Books.

[212] For extensive quotes and sources, see T.J. Coles (2018) *Manufacturing Terrorism* West Sussex: Clairview Books.

[213] Chris Hastings (2009) 'Lord Halifax tried to negotiate peace with the Nazis' *Telegraph* https://www.telegraph.co.uk/news/uknews/2650832/Lord-Halifax-tried-to-negotiate-peace-with-the-Nazis.html.

[214] Churchill:

> Up till the year 1933 or even 1935, Germany might have been saved from the awful fate which has overtaken her and we might all have been spared the miseries Hitler let loose upon mankind. There never was a war in all history easier to prevent by timely action than the one which has just desolated such great areas of the globe. It could have been prevented in my belief without the firing of a single shot, and Germany might be powerful, prosperous and honoured today; but no one would listen and one by one we were all sucked into the awful whirlpool. We surely must not let that happen again.

(1946) 'The Sinews of Peace' Fulton: Westminster College, https://winstonchurchill.org/resources/speeches/1946-1963-elder-statesman/the-sinews-of-peace/.

[215] Historian Gerald Kirwin writes: 'since May 1941 the air war had become a very one-sided affair and the Luftwaffe, tied up in Russia, was unable to launch more than the occasional light raid on British targets' (1981) 'Waiting for Retaliation - A Study in Nazi Propaganda Behaviour and German Civilian Morale' *Journal of Contemporary History* 16(3): 565-583.

[216] Winston Churchill (1948) *LIFE Magazine*, p. 29.

[217] Michael Peck writes:

> rearming ex-Nazis paled in comparison to an absolute foundation of Operation Unthinkable, which was that the United States would join Britain in attack on the Soviet Union. Roosevelt, and initially Truman until he knew better, were convinced that it was possible to work out a postwar accommodation with Stalin.

(2017) 'Operation Unthinkable: Britain's Secret Plan to Invade Russia in 1945' *National Interest* http://nationalinterest.org/blog/the-buzz/operation-unthinkable-britains-secret-plan-invade-russia-22521/page/2/1.

[218] In a pathetic effort to deflect responsibility onto Arabs, pro-imperialist historian Andrew Roberts writes:

> [I]n late 1946 the Labour government of Clement Attlee asked MI6 for "proposals for action to deter ships masters and crews from engaging in illegal Jewish immigration and traffic," adding, "Action of the nature contemplated is, in fact, a form of intimidation and intimidation is only likely to be effective if some members of the group of people to be intimidated actually suffer unpleasant consequences." Among the options contemplated were "the discovery of some sabotage device, which had 'failed' to function after the sailing of a ship," "tampering with a ship's fresh water supplies or the crew's food," and "fire on board ship in port." Sir Stewart Menzies, the chief of the SIS, suggested these could be blamed on an invented Arab terrorist group called The Defenders of Arab Palestine.

Andrew Roberts (2010) 'MI6 attacked Jewish refugee ships after WWII' *Daily Beast* https://web.archive.org/web/20170603010552/www.thedailybeast.com/mi6-attacked-jewish-refugee-ships-after-wwii. The article draws on Keith Jeffrey's book, *MI6: The History of the Secret Intelligence Service 1909-1949* London: Bloomsbury, 2010.

[219] For example, two Chatham House scholars note: 'The British do not have to flaunt their nuclear capability. Both friends and enemies know of its existence and behave accordingly'. Admiral Sir Raymond Lygo, former Chief of Naval Staff, said: 'Having a nuclear deterrent does give us the freedom to operate at lower levels of convention [i.e., non-nuclear] capability should we be required to do so politically'. Both quotes can be found in T.J. Coles (2016) *The Great Brexit Swindle* West Sussex: Clairview Books, pp. 62-63.

[220] See T.J. Coles (2018) *Manufacturing Terrorism* West Sussex: Clairview Books.

[221] BP (2016) 'Rumaila oilfield achieves 3 billion barrel production landmark' https://www.bp.com/en/global/corporate/media/press-releases/rumaila-oilfield-achieves-3-billion-barrel-production-landmark.html. Aref Mohammed (2018) 'Iraq, BP sign Kirkuk oilfield development contract, official says' Reuters https://uk.reuters.com/article/uk-iraq-oil-kirkuk/iraq-bp-sign-kirkuk-oilfield-development-contract-official-says-idUKKBN1I81SB.

[222] The UK Foreign and Security Policy Working Group says:

> Imports and exports of goods and services make up more than 60 per cent of the UK's GDP, twice the figure for the US, half again as much as Australia, and close to the figures for other large European economies such as France, Italy and Spain.

(2015) *Strengthening Britain's Voice in the World* London: Chatham House https://www.chathamhouse.org/sites/default/files/publications/research/20151103UKForeignSecurityWorkingGroupReport.pdf.

[223] Stanhope:

> ...the ability to influence is also dependent on maintaining a capable and credible military which can operate in support of a wider Government strategy. If non-kinetic activity to contain or deter others is to be effective, it must be underpinned by the existence and proven success of credible, conventional military forces, capable of wielding a big stick and a willingness, if necessary, for Government to compel others to act in a desired manner.

Admiral Sir Mark Stanhope (2009) 'The Royal Navy: Afghanistan and Beyond' London: Chatham House https://web.archive.org/web/20101229070315/http://www.chathamhouse.org.uk/files/15469_271109stanhope.pdf.

[224] For example: 'Six of Britain's 10 biggest multinationals, including Shell, British America Tobacco (BAT) and Lloyds Banking Group, paid no UK corporation tax in 2014, an investigation has claimed'. Chloe Farand (2016) 'Six British multinationals "did not pay any UK corporation tax in 2014" ' *Independent* https://www.independent.co.uk/news/uk/six-british-multinationals-including-shell-vodafone-lloyds-banking-group-did-not-paid-any-a6844676.html.

[225] Shell has left such devastation in Nigeria, particularly in Ogoniland—and has for decades—that to this day villagers in some areas literally wade knee-deep in oil spills. Some have burned to death and been injured in oil slick-related house fires (Johann Hari (2017) 'Our cry for cheap oil is crude and deadly' *Independent* www.independent.co.uk/voices/commentators/johann-hari/johann-hari-our-cry-for-cheap-oil-is-crude-and-deadly-866899.html.). Shell blames poor management and extraction practices on the part of locals who attempt to sell oil on the black market, as well as theft and organised gangs. (You can read the UN's report from 2011, which contains shocking visual evidence, to get an idea of the level of destruction. United Nations Environment Programme (2011) 'Environmental Assessment of Ogoniland' Nairobi: UNEP https://postconflict.unep.ch/publications/OEA/UNEP_OEA.pdf.) According to ActionAid, France's Total and Italy's Eni entered a consortium

with Shell. In 1990, when Nigeria was under military rule, the British-armed junta granted Shell a huge tax break, which came into force in 1999, meaning that the three companies paid no corporation tax in Nigeria until 2012, saving the firms £2.3bn, or twice the country's annual health budget. (Mark Leftly (2016) 'Shell attacked for its part in "extraordinary" £2.3bn Nigerian tax break' *Independent* www.independent.co .uk/news/business/news/shell-attacked-for-its-part-in-extraordinary-23bn-nigerian-tax-break-a6822061.html.

Due to losses resulting from theft (reportedly), Shell is turning to Nigerian gas, along with Eni and Total. Seemingly without irony, the *Daily Mail* reports that 'Shell entered Nigeria in 1936 [under British colonial rule] and the country's oil has helped the Anglo-Dutch firm become the £170billion mega-business it is today' (Rachel Millard (2017) 'Shell retreats from Nigerian oil business' *Daily Mail* http://www.thisismoney. co.uk/money/markets/article-4630018/Shell-retreats-Nigerian-oil-business.html). As well as helping many Nigerian villagers to live knee-deep in toxic waste, the NGO Platform alleges that Shell has helped fuel what is basically a civil war between rival gangs and the government by paying protection money to gangs. Shell denies the charges (David Smith (2011) 'Shell accused of fuelling violence in Nigeria by paying rival militant gangs' *Guardian* https://www.theguardian.com/world/2011/oct/03/shell-accused-of-fuelling-nigeria-conflict). In 2015, Shell agreed to pay £55m to the Bodo community due to what the *Telegraph* describes as '[b]arrels of bad publicity'. The report says that by 2017, clean-up work had still not been done (Emily Gosden (2017) 'Why Shell's Bodo oil spill still hasn't been cleaned up' *Telegraph* https://www.telegraph.co .uk/business/2017/01/08/yet-clean-nigerian-oil-spills-two-years-compensation-deal/). By 2016, the Ogoni king Emere told the media: 'Shell has been responsible for the damage in my community. The same people we loved are killing us now' (John Vidal (2016) 'Ogoni king: Shell oil is killing my people' *Guardian* https://www.theguardian.com/world/2016/dec/03/ogoni-king-shell-oil-is-killing-my-people). Some 45,000

Nigerians took Shell to court for damages over the oil catas-
trophes (or 'spills' as the media call them). But in 2018, the
Court of Appeal in London ruled that the two communities
(Ogale and Bille) cannot have be heard in UK courts, supposed-
ly due to a jurisdictional technicality in their case against
Shell's subsidiary, Shell Petroleum Development Company.
(*The Oil and Gas Year* (2018) 'Nigerians can't sue Shell in UK:
Court' https://www.theoilandgasyear.com/news/nigerians-
cant-sue-shell-in-uk-court/.)

[226] Ministry of Defence:

> Globalisation is about the spread of capital, trade, intellec-
> tual property, economic activity, wealth and resources. It al-
> so encompasses the guaranteed access to and exploitation
> of these resources in developing states.

(2010) *Strategic Trends Programme: The Future Character of
Conflict* Swindon: Development, Concepts and Doctrine Centre, p. A2 https://assets.publishing.service.gov.uk/government
/uploads/system/uploads/attachment_data/file/486301/2015
1210-Archived_DCDC_FCOC.pdf.

[227] Alice Hancock (2017) 'Younger consumers drive shift to ethical
products' *Financial Times* https://www.ft.com/content/
8b08bf4c-e5a0-11e7-8b99-0191e45377ec.

[228] Oxfam (2016) '3.6 billion clothes left unworn in the nation's
wardrobes, survey finds' https://www.oxfam.org.uk/media-
centre/press-releases/2016/06/over-three-billion-clothes-left-
unworn-in-the-nations-wardrobes-survey-finds.

[229] Laurence Martin and John Garnett (1997) *British Foreign Policy:
Challenges and Choices for the 21st Century* London: Pinter
(Chatham House), pp. 77-78.

[230] On Lawson, see T.J. Coles (2018) *Human Wrongs* London: Iff
Books, pp. 118-119.

[231] DFID (2004) *Victoria Project: Sri Lanka* EvSum 392
https://assets.publishing.service.gov.uk/government/uploads/
system/uploads/attachment_data/file/67900/ev392s.pdf.

[232] DFID (2018) 'Where we work'
https://www.gov.uk/guidance/where-we-work.

233 Tony Blair's adviser Robert Cooper wrote in 2004:

> Hard power and soft power are two sides of the same coin
> ... Behind every law there stands a policeman, willing in the
> end to use force. And behind every constitutions there
> stands an army willing to defend the state ... Soft power is
> the velvet glove, but behind it there is always the iron fist.

Robert Cooper (2004) 'Goals of Diplomacy, Hard Power, Soft
Power' in David Held and Mathias Koenig-Archibugi *American
Power in the 21st Century* Cambridge: Polity, p. 179.

234 Madeleine Moon MP to DFID head, Andrew Mitchell:

> You have tied the Department for International Develop-
> ment in with defence and security ... Are we, in fact, risking
> DFID's independence and neutrality? Is it not interested in
> need and good causes, rather than being an arm of Gov-
> ernment? In fact, I think DFID was recently described by the
> Prime Minister [Cameron] as a modern equivalent of a bat-
> tleship.

(2011) *Strategic Defence and Security Review and the National
Security Strategy* House of Commons Defence Committee Correct Oral Evidence HC 761-ii https://publications.parliament.uk
/pa/cm201012/cmselect/cmdfence/c761-ii/c76101.htm.

235 British Council (2018) 'Our global locations' https://www.briti
shcouncil.org/active-citizens/global-locations.

236 One report says, for instance:

> Elections are still new and youth remain reluctant because
> they feel they are ill equipped with information. Youth's
> route to politics seems to be through involvement in the
> work of some of the CSOs [civil society organisations] that
> engage in politics, and the most successful CSOs are man-
> aged by youth. Some participants conclude that youth have
> not yet earned society's trust and therefore recommend
> that they make an effort to earn trust in order to prove that
> they are capable of handling responsibility

British Council (2013) *The Revolutionary Promise: Youth Perceptions in Egypt, Libya and Tunisia* Cairo: The American University in Cairo, p. 10 https://www.britishcouncil.org/sites/default/files/revolutionary-promise-summary_0.pdf.

[237] Westminster Foundation for Democracy (2018) 'Georgia' http://www.wfd.org/where-we-work/europe-and-central-asia/georgia/.

[238] College of Policing (2017) Ref FOIA-2017-004.

[239] *Britain's Secret Wars* (2016, Clairview).

[240] Winnie was referring to the Mau Mau in 1950s' Kenya. Quoted in Richard Toye (2015) *Churchill's Empire: The World that Made Him and the World He Made* London: Pan Macmillan, p. ix.

[241] British Embassy Rangoon (2013) 'Head of the UK armed forces visits Burma' https://www.gov.uk/government/news/head-of-the-uk-armed-forces-visits-burma.

Yadana Htun (2013) 'UK military chief discusses Burma training link' *The Irrawaddy* https://www.irrawaddy.com/news/burma/uk-military-chief-discusses-burma-training-link.html. Jonah Fisher (2014) 'Burmese army trained by UK military' http://www.bbc.co.uk/news/av/world-asia-25855168/burmese-army-trained-by-uk-military. Ben Riley-Smith (2015) 'Burmese Army gets £130,000 of taxpayer-funded training despite using child soldiers' *Telegraph* http://www.telegraph.co.uk/news/politics/11413577/Burmese-Army-gets-130000-of-taxpayer-funded-training-despite-allegedly-using-child-soldiers.html. Simon Lewis (2014) 'British minister defends Burma army training' *The Irrawaddy* https://www.irrawaddy.com/news/burma/british-minister-defends-burma-army-training.html. Claire Ellicott (2017) 'Britain gave £200,000 of foreign aid last year to Burmese forces accused of war crimes against Rohingya Muslims' *Daily Mail* http://www.dailymail.co.uk/news/article-4852106/Britain-gave-200-000-foreign-aid-Burmese-forces.html.

[242] For example, an arms export document from 2009:

Arms sanctions against DPRK [Democratic People's Republic of Korea, or North Korea] are currently in place under UN Security Council resolution 1718 (amended by UNSCR 1874). The arms embargo prohibits the supply, sale or transfer of arms (and a ban on related financial transactions, technical training or services), with the exception of the provision by States to the DPRK of small arms and light weapons and their related materiel, on which States are required to notify the Committee in advance.

In the same year, £20m-worth of 'equipment' was sold to Iran, including 'chemicals' (which could be used in a weapons programme), 'civil aero-engines' (which could be used for military plans), and 'imaging cameras', which could be used by the military. Department for International Trade (2009) *Strategic Export Controls: Country Pivot Report: 1st January 2009 - 31st December 2009* London: Stationary Office, pp. 326-27, 213-14 https://assets.publishing.service.gov.uk/government/uploads/ system/uploads/attachment_data/file/559487/strategic-export-controls-country-pivot-report-2009.pdf.

For more recent exports to Iran, consider 2015: 'chemicals', 'marine engines', and 'components for civil aero-engines' were exported – £9m-worth. Department for International Trade (2015) *Strategic Export Controls: Country Pivot Report 1st January 2015 - 31st December 2015* London: Stationary Office, pp. 281-82 https://assets.publishing.service.gov.uk/government/ uploads/system/uploads/attachment_data/file/699263/2017 Q4-strategic-export-controls-country-pivot-report-2015.pdf. [243] Hague said:

> a review of our own files suggests that there were a number of exports of chemicals to Syria by UK companies between 1983 and 1986 which were likely to have been diverted for use in the Syrian programme ...
>
> [These included] several hundred tonnes of the chemical dimethyl phosphite (DMP) in 1983 and a further export of several hundred tonnes in 1985; several hundred tonnes of

trimethyl phosphite (TMP) in 1986; a smaller quantity of hydrogen fluoride (HF) in 1986 through a third country ...

The review of our records also confirmed an export of ventilation fans by a UK company to Syria in 2003. The fans were not controlled goods.

Even in 2015 while Britain was attacking Syria, we sold it £69m-worth of military equipment, 'body armour', 'components for military equipment for initiating explosives', and 'military helmets'. Department for International Trade (2015) *Strategic Export Controls: Country Pivot Report 1st January 2015 - 31st December 2015* London: Stationary Office, p. 604 https://assets.publishing.service.gov.uk/government/uploads/system/uploads/attachment_data/file/699263/2017Q4-strategic-export-controls-country-pivot-report-2015.pdf.

[244] Quoted in Sally Bedell Smith (1996) *Reflected Glory: The Life of Pamela Churchill Harriman* NY: Simon and Schuster, eBook.

[245] BBC News Online (2013) 'Conservative membership has nearly halved under Cameron' https://www.bbc.co.uk/news/uk-politics-24143443.

[246] For example:

> ...only a minority [of Tory Party members] feels the leadership pays them insufficient attention - although in the Conservative Party that minority, at 29%, is much bigger than it is in other parties. This might account for the fact that, when we asked members of all four parties whether they thought they were respected by the leadership, the proportion of Tory members agreeing (around six out of ten) was significantly lower than the nine out of ten members of the Labour Party, the Lib Dems and the SNP [Scottish National Party].

Tim Bale, Paul Webb and Monica Poletti (2018) *Grassroots Britain's party members: who they are, what they think, and what they do* London: Mile End Institute and Queen Mary University of London, p. 26.

[247] For example Bradshaw:

> We strongly condemn the return to violence by the Maoists in Nepal, and urge them to cease violence and return to dialogue. We understand the reasons behind the declaration of a state of emergency in Nepal, and hope that the Nepalese Government will quickly be able to bring peace to the country ...
>
> The MOD has supplied training and other support to the Royal Nepalese Army as well as significant infrastructure assistance to Nepal's UN peacekeeping training centre.

Bradshaw as Sec. of State for Foreign and Commonwealth Affairs, 'Nepal' (2001) HC vol. 376, cc214-5W http://hansard.millbanksystems.com/written_answers/2001/dec/04/nepal#S6CV0376P0_20011204_CWA_369

[248] Press Association (2009) 'London mayor Boris Johnson dismisses £250,000 second salary as "chicken feed" ' *Guardian* https://www.theguardian.com/politics/2009/jul/13/boris-johnson-second-salary-chickenfeed.

[249] In 2017, the percentage of eligible Britons who voted Labour was 40% compared to 42.3% who voted Tory. *Financial Times* (2017) 'Election results 2017: full list and map' https://ig.ft.com/election-results-2017/.

[250] BBC News Online (2015) 'More than 2,300 died after fit for work assessment - DWP figures' https://www.bbc.co.uk/news/uk-34074557 and Patrick Butler (2015) 'Thousands have died after being found fit for work, DWP figures show' *Guardian* https://www.theguardian.com/society/2015/aug/27/thousands-died-after-fit-for-work-assessment-dwp-figures.

[251] BBC News Online (2016) 'Ian Hislop meets Iain Duncan Smith - Workers or Shirkers? Ian Hislop's Victorian Benefits - BBC Two' https://www.youtube.com/watch?v=tc5-tWfmSb4.

[252] The DWP says:

> The percentage overpaid due to official error in the preliminary 2013/14 estimate is 0.4% which is a decrease when compared to the 2012/13 and 2011/12 estimates, 0.5%. The monetary value of official error overpayments in the prelim-

inary 2013/14 estimate is £0.7bn, which has decreased from those in the 2012/13 and 2011/12 estimates, £0.8bn.

Department for Work and Pensions and Office for National Statistics (2014) *Fraud and Error in the Benefit System: Preliminary 2013/14 Estimates* Newcastle: DWP, p. 4 https://assets.publishing.service.gov.uk/government/uploads/system/uploads/attachment_data/file/311237/FEM_1314P.pdf.

[253] Joint Chiefs of Staff (1962) 'Justification for US military intervention in Cuba (TS)' Memorandum for the Secretary of Defense Washington, DC: Department of Defense http://documents.theblackvault.com/documents/jfk/northwoods.pdf.

[254] Ferguson: 'But few, if any, of the graduates of Harvard, Stanford, Yale or Princeton aspire to spend their lives trying to turn a sun-scorched sandpit like Iraq into the prosperous capitalist democracy of Paul Wolfowitz's imaginings'. And: 'bin Laden is the offspring of the Middle East's distinctive civilization of clashes, a retarded political culture in which terrorism has long been a substitute for both peaceful politics and conventional warfare'. Niall Ferguson (2004) *Colossus: The Rise and Fall of the American Empire* London: Penguin, eBook.

[255] Re Pinochet:

> But was it worth it? Was it worth the huge moral compromise ... when they [the US administration and its intellectuals] got into bed with a torturing, murderous dictatorship? Well, the answer to that question very much depends on whether or not you think their reforms helped pave a peaceful way back to sustainable democracy in Chile. I think they did.

Ferguson (2009) *The Ascent of Money: A Financial History of the World* Channel 4, available at: https://www.youtube.com/watch?v=WmOaU52Qo1s. At 2.57.51.

[256] It says on page 24: 'This project has been made possible by the generous support of BAE Systems, Barclays Capital and BP'. Alex Evans and David Steven (2010) 'Organizing for Influence: UK Foreign Policy in an Age of Uncertainty' Chatham House

London: Royal Institute for International Affairs https://www.
chathamhouse.org/sites/default/files/public/Research/Eur
ope/r0610_stevens_evans.pdf.

[257] Jamie Gaskarth (2013) *British Foreign Policy: Crises, Conflicts and Future Challenges* London: Polity, eBook.

[258] The CIA said of the French:

> There is a new climate of intellectual opinion in France—a spirit of anti-Marxism and anti-Sovietism that will make it difficult for anyone to mobilize significant intellectual opposition to US policies. Nor will French intellectuals be likely to lend their weight, as they did before, to other West European colleagues who have become hostile to the United States on broad issues like disarmament. Although American policies are never immune to criticism in France, it is clearly the Soviet Union that is now on the defensive with New Left intellectuals—and is likely to remain there at least in the medium term ...
>
> [President] Mitterand's failure to garner needed support among France's historically powerful leftist intellectuals, moreover, reflects a historic shift that may presage a new role for the intelligentsia. No longer can his Social Party rely on intellectuals to provide a rationale for his policies and actions and to sell that rationale to a French public that has customarily placed great store in the explanations of its intellectual elites.

Central Intelligence Agency (1985) *France: Defection of the Leftist Intellectuals* [Redacted] Office of European Analysis EUR 85-10199 https://www.cia.gov/library/readingroom/docs/CIA-RDP86S00588R000300380001-5.PDF.

[259] Historian, Lawrence S. Wittner, writes:

> the government conducted an attack on peace studies courses. As early as 1981, the British Secretary of State had publicly attacked peace studies as "appeasement" education and, thereafter, public officials issued dire warnings about peace and antinuclear bias in the nation's schools.

Wittner writes that Thatcher 'repeatedly' attempted to close Bradford University's peace studies programme, asking if it 'been dealt with yet?' (2003) *The Struggle Against the Bomb Volume III: Toward Nuclear Abolition: A History of the World Nuclear Disarmament Movement, 1971 to the Present*, Stanford University Press, pp. 276-9.

[260] Paul Bignell (2011) 'Secret memos expose link between oil firms and invasion of Iraq' *Independent* https://www.independent.co.uk/news/uk/politics/secret-memos-expose-link-between-oil-firms-and-invasion-of-iraq-2269610.html.

[261] Williams:

> ...unravelling how and when UK foreign policy is "responsible for X" or "to blame for Y" or, indeed, "successful in achieving Z" is difficult, if it is possible at all. Generalisations and the attribution of blame, responsibility and success must be made cautiously and remain sensitive to the contingencies of specific issues under examination.

Like Gaskarth, Williams thanks 'the politicians and government officials from the UK and abroad who have shared with me their thoughts on various aspects of British foreign policy'. Paul. D. Williams (2005) *British Foreign Policy Under New Labour, 1997-2005* London: Palgrave, pp. xii, 6.

[262] B.H. Bourdillon said 1924:

> the British public, even the more intelligent sections of it, regard Iraq in the light of a rather unattractive war baby of highly suspicious parentage ... Consequently, they take very little interest in the child and, are constantly expecting it to be naughty. When it fulfils these expectations they take a rather unseeming delight in spanking it. We have had a good many spankings in the last five or six years, and we have honestly felt that some of them have been rather undeserved.

(1924) 'The Political Situation in Iraq' *Journal of the British Institute of International Affairs* 3(6): 273-287.

[263] Raffael Scheck (1999) 'Swiss Funding for the Early Nazi Movement: Motivation, Context, and Continuities' *The Journal of Modern History* 71(4): 793-813.

[264] In 1841, a colonial administrator called Australia 'an extraordinary nation owning no chief, literally a pure democracy', referring to its Aboriginal peoples. (Quoted in John Pilger (1988) *The Last Dream: Secrets* ITV.)

In 1881, two years into Britain's second occupation of Afghanistan, Captain T.H. Holdich pointed out that, 'not in free England has the private individual so strong a voice in the government of his country as he has in Afghanistan'. Holdich discovered that 'even the most apparently unimportant provincial chief must have his opinion consulted before any great political move can be made'. Holdich concluded that:

> Every Afghan is a diplomat by nature and education, and he has accordingly a perception of the political interests of his country which, for clearness and keenness, has no counterpart whatever among the lower orders of England.

Captain T.H. Holdich (1881) 'Geographical Results of the Afghan Campaign' *Proceedings of the Royal Geographical Society and Monthly Record of Geography* 3(2): 65-84.

In 1892, British colonial administrator A.F. Mockler-Ferryman remarked of peoples living in what is now Nigeria: 'the Mitshi ... are a difficult people to deal with, since they acknowledge no one as head of the whole tribe, and live in independent families' (Quoted in Alvin Magid (1976) *Men in the Middle: Leadership and Role Conflict in Nigerian Society* Manchester: Manchester University Press, p. 41).

[265] For example:

> Some 80% of people in England support having more powers devolved to local areas, a poll on devolution commissioned by the BBC has suggested ...
>
> 67% of people living in the South East support only English MPs deciding English issues

> 74% of people in the East Midlands backed the plan –
> the highest number in England
>
> 61% of people in London supported the idea - the lowest
> number in England.

BBC News Online (2014) ' "Support" for English devolution - BBC poll' https://www.bbc.co.uk/news/uk-england-29880995.

[266] Laura Sharman (2014) 'Councillors trusted more than MPs, reveals poll' LocalGov https://www.localgov.co.uk/Councillors-trusted-more-than-MPs-reveals-poll/36279.

[267] Eleanor M.L. Scerri et al. (2018) 'Did Our Species Evolve in Sub-divided Populations across Africa, and Why Does It Matter?' *Trends in Ecology and Evolution* (in press) https://doi.org/10.1016/j.tree.2018.05.005.

[268] Eli Sagan (1985) *At the Dawn of Tyranny: The Origins of Individualism, Political Oppression, and the State* London: Faber and Faber.

[269] The Imperial War Museum writes of the Christmas Truce 1914:

> The following day, British and German soldiers met in no man's land and exchanged gifts, took photographs and some played impromptu games of football. They also buried casualties and repaired trenches and dugouts. After Boxing Day, meetings in no man's land dwindled out.
>
> The truce was not observed everywhere along the Western Front. Elsewhere the fighting continued and casualties did occur on Christmas Day. Some officers were unhappy at the truce and worried that it would undermine fighting spirit.

Amanda Mason (2017) 'The real story of the Christmas truce' Imperial War Museum https://www.iwm.org.uk/history/the-real-story-of-the-christmas-truce.

[270] BBC News Online (circa 2010) 'Councils' cash with Iceland banks' http://news.bbc.co.uk/1/hi/uk_politics/7659783.stm

[271] Bureau of Investigative Journalism figures cited in BBC News Online (2011) 'More than half of Conservative donors "from the City" ' https://www.bbc.co.uk/news/uk-politics-12401049.

Nicolas Watt and Jill Treanor (2011) 'Revealed: 50% of Tory funds come from City' *Guardian* https://www.theguardian.com/politics/2011/feb/08/tory-funds-half-city-banks-financial-sector. Andrew Porter (2011) 'City financiers "provided half of Tory funding" ' *Telegraph* https://www.telegraph.co.uk/news/politics/8312588/City-financiers-provided-half-of-Tory-funding.html.

[272] Worker Participation (2013) 'Trade Unions' https://www.worker-participation.eu/National-Industrial-Relations/Across-Europe/Trade-Unions2.

[273] Guy Standing (2011) *Precariat: The New Dangerous Class* London: Bloomsbury.

[274] Office for National Statistics (2018) 'Contracts that do not guarantee a minimum number of hours: April 2018' https://www.ons.gov.uk/employmentandlabourmarket/peopleinwork/earningsandworkinghours/articles/contractsthatdonotguaranteeaminimumnumberofhours/april2018.

[275] In Bracknell Forest Council, there were 50,000 'bids' for just 400 properties. Becky Barnes (2012) '50,000 bid for just 400 council homes' *Get Reading* (local paper) https://www.getreading.co.uk/news/local-news/50000-bid-just-400-council-4200614.

[276] Martin and Garnett op cit., p. 84.

[277] Polls cited in Michael Clarke (1992) *British external policy-making in the 1990s* London: Macmillan, p. 332.

[278] David Blagden (Cambridge) (2014) 'Written Evidence to the Parliamentary Joint Committee on the National Security Strategy: Priorities for the 2015 NSS' in *The next National Security Strategy: Written evidence* Joint Committee on the National Security Strategy London: Stationary Office, p. 4 https://www.parliament.uk/documents/joint-committees/national-security-strategy/The%20next%20security%20strategy%20(forth%20review)/ThenextNationalSecurityStrategyEvidence18122014.pdf.

[279] *Bulletin of the Atomic Scientists* (2018) 'Timeline' https://thebulletin.org/doomsday-clock/past-announcements/.

[280] The three women were Jo Blackman, Lotta Kronlid, and Andrea Needham. There were seven others who supported the action.

Andrea Needham (2016) *The Hammer Blow: How 10 Women Disarmed a War Plane* London: Peace News Press.

[281] Asa Winstanley (2015) 'Case dropped against protesters who cost Elbit drone parts factory $280,000' *Electronic Intifada* https://electronicintifada.net/blogs/asa-winstanley/case-dropped-against-protesters-who-cost-elbit-drone-parts-factory-280000.

[282] *The Intercept* reports that in March 2018:

> ...as many as 500 antifascists converged on the campus of Michigan State University [MSU] in East Lansing to protest a speech by white supremacist golden boy Richard Spencer. The protesters — including MSU students, campus workers, antifa organizers, and people from surrounding towns — outnumbered those who had come to hear Spencer speak by an order of magnitude.
>
> White nationalists were also vastly outnumbered by cops. According to a police document obtained by The Intercept, there were more than 200 cops on hand for the event, from eight different jurisdictions. In addition, there were nine "undercover" officers dispersed throughout the crowd, including two from the MSU Police Department.

Sam Adler-Bell (2018) 'Michigan State University sent nine "undercover" cops to Richard Spencer protest -- but it says that's not surveillance' *The Intercept* https://theintercept.com/2018/03/30/msu-richard-spencer-antifa/.

[283] *Strategic Trends...* (2007), op cit., p. 18.

[284] Maxwell said:

> I have a dear friend that worked in Hollywood for many years. Worked with all the big names, George Lucas, Spielberg, all of them. And he was telling me about an event that happened one time in Los Angeles where Steven Spielberg was making some kind of a movie or a documentary or something. And my friend was working on the piece with him. And he said that at lunchtime, that first of all the location where they were shooting this was way down south in

Los Angeles in a very deserted area. Nothing around. It was a very deserted area. And they set up their cameras there to shoot these scenes. And he said that at lunchtime … 'cause everybody working on there had to have scooters, because it was such a large area … And so, he says, one day at noon he was getting ready to go out on the scooter and just drive around for a few minutes. And he says, 'As I pulled out, Spielberg happened to pass me and he's in a golf cart. So I saw Spielberg in the golf cart and I wanted to go say 'Hello' to him. I was trying to catch up with him and as I get close to his cart, and I'm following him, trying to catch up to him, Spielberg heard my scooter and he turned around, but he didn't turn all the way around, to see who it was. He just turned around a little bit, showing me that he heard that I was back, behind him. Then he turned around straight and looked up in the heavens and shook his head saying, 'Yes!'. He nodded his head as if he's saying, 'Yes!'. And all of a sudden popped two men. They materialized right in front of me'. And he said, 'I almost hit them. I hit my brakes and I almost hit these two guys. They're in black coats. Black suits. Black ties. And they said, 'What are you doing? Who are you?''. And he said, 'I'm just out… I'm working here with Steven and I just wanted to say, 'Hello'. And they said, 'Turn around and get out of here. Go back to work! Leave him alone''. And so he says, 'I turned around and when I looked back they were gone!' … They just popped in and popped out.

Now what does that tell you about Steven Spielberg? Hmm? What does that tell you? Something's going on here that all he has to do is nod his head and extra-terrestrial, other-world entities materialize instantly to protect him. What does that tell you?

The Richie Allen Show (2018) 'Jordan Non Human Entities Control Banks & Politicians & Cont' [sic] YouTube https://www.youtube.com/watch?v=szA87H-QKmM. At circa 106 minutes.
[285] For example:

Throughout the centuries, some Jewish bankers have gathered the reputation of backers and financers of wars and even one communist revolution. Though some rich Jews have been happily financing wars using their own assets, Alan Greenspan, the Chairman of the Federal Reserve of the United States, found a far more sophisticated way to facilitate or at least divert attention from the wars perpetrated by [Scooter] Libby, [Paul] Wolfowitz and PNAC [the Project for the New American Century].

... Greenspan ... knew very well that as long as Americans were doing well, buying and selling homes, his President would be able to continue implementing the 'Wolfowitz doctrine' and PNAC philosophy ...

Atzmon (2011) *The Wandering Who? A Study of Jewish Identity Politics* London: Zero Books, p. 27.